PLANT RESPONSE TO ENVIRONMENTAL STRESS

ENV BOOKS SERIES

PLANT RESPONSE TO ENVIRONMENTAL STRESS

Editors

Dr. Alka Chauhan
Society for Environment, Health
Awareness of Nutrition & Toxicology (SEHAT)
B-225/5D, Top Floor, Subhash Gali, Road No. 7, Block B
Ashok Nagar, Shahdara, Delhi - 110 093
(India)

Dr. Pawan Kumar 'Bharti'
Society for Environment, Health
Awareness of Nutrition & Toxicology (SEHAT)
B-225/5D, Top Floor, Subhash Gali, Road No. 7, Block B
Ashok Nagar, Shahdara, Delhi - 110 093
(India)

&

Dr. Avnish Chauhan
Department of Applied Science
Phonics Group of Institutions
Roorkee, Haridwar - 247 667
(India)

Associate Editor

Dr. Prasann Kumar
Assistant Professor
Department of Agronomy, School of Agriculture
Lovely Professional University, Jalandhar - 144 411
Punjab (India)

DPH

DISCOVERY PUBLISHING HOUSE PVT. LTD.
INDIA

Published by:

Namit Wasan

DISCOVERY PUBLISHING HOUSE PVT. LTD.

4383/4B, Ansari Road, Darya Ganj
New Delhi-110 002 (India)
Phone : +91-11-23279245, 43596064 65
Fax : +91-11-23253475
E-mail : discoverypublishinghouse@gmail.com
namitwasan9@gmail.com
sales@discoverypublishinggroup.com

web : www.discoverypublishinggroup.com

First Edition: **2018**

ISBN: 978-93-86841-58-2

Plant Response to Environmental Stress

Printed at:
Infinity Imaging Systems
Delhi

ENV Books Series, India

Calls descriptive and error free chapters for upcoming volumes of books on various environmental issues. Send your manuscripts to envbooks@gmail.com

Founding Editor (Editor-in-Chief)

Dr. Pawan Kumar 'Bharti'
Society for Environment, Health, Awareness of Nutrition & Toxicology (SEHAT-India)
1775, Sohanganj, Near Clock Tower, Delhi-7, (India)
E-mail:*gurupawanbharti@rediffmail.com*

Other Important Titles by Editor-in-Chief:

1. **Advances in Biotechnology and Ecological Sciences**
   Bharti, P.K., Chauhan, A. and Ray, J. (eds.)
   (ISBN: 978-93-5056-358-8).
2. **Advances in Agriculture and Ecology**
   Bharti, P.K.; Chauhan, A. and Ezeaku Peter Ikemefuna (eds.)
   (ISBN: 978-93-5056-362-5).
3. **Agriculture and Environmental Biotechnology**
   Bharti, P.K. and Chauhan, A. (eds.)
   (ISBN: 978-93-5056-479-0).
4. **Agriculture Crops and Food Security**
   Bharti, P.K., and Chauhan, A. (eds.)
   (ISBN: 978-93-5056-881-1)
5. **Agriculture Development and Sustainable Environment**
   Ray, J. and Bharti, P.K. (eds.)
   (ISBN: 978-93-5056-759-3).
6. **Agriculture Ecology and Environment**
   Bharti, P.K. and Olubukola O. Babalola (eds.)
   (ISBN: 978-93-5056-480-6).
7. **Agriculture Ecology, Sustainable Development and Agribusiness Management**
   Mehta Piyush; Sharma Pankaj; and 'Bharti' P.K. (eds.)
   (ISBN: 978-93-5056-851-4).
8. **Agriculture, Environment and Nano-science**
   Bharti, Pawan K. (ed.)
   (ISBN: 978-93-5056-760-5).
9. **Agriculture Production and Climate Change**
   Khalid, Monowar Alam; Bharti, P.K. and Chauhan, Alka (eds.)
   (ISBN: 978-93-86841-54-4).

10. **Agricultural Practices and Crop Disease Control**
Chauhan Alka and Sharma Anubhuti (eds.)
(ISBN: 978-93-5056-859-0).

11. **Agro-biodiversity:** ***Conservation and Sustainable Development***
Sharma, Pankaj; Singh, Narayan; and Bharti, P.K. (eds.)
(ISBN: 978-93-505-782-1).

12. **Agro-forestry and Climate Change**
Bharti, Pawan K. and Singh, Narayan (eds.)
(ISBN: 978-93-5056-514-8).

13. **Agro-forestry and Sustainable Agriculture**
Sharma, Pankaj; Bharti, P.K. (eds.)
(ISBN: 978-93-5056-786-9)

14. **Air Pollution and Ecosystem Health**
Swami Abhishek and Bharti, P.K. (eds.)
(ISBN: 978-93-5056-877-4).

15. **Analytical Techniques in Chemical and Biological Sciences**
Mala, Deep & 'Bharti', P.K. (eds.)
(ISBN: 978-93-86841-59-9).

16. **Aquaculture and Fisheries Environment**
Gupta, S.K. and Pawan K. Bharti (eds.)
(ISBN: 978-93-5056-408-0).

17. **Aquatic Biodiversity and Pollution**
Bharti, P.K.; Chauhan, A. and Kaoud, H.A.H. (eds.)
(ISBN: 978-93-5056-359-5).

18. **Aquatic Ecology and Biotechnology**
Bharti, P.K. and Zaki, M.S.A. (eds.)
(ISBN: 978-93-5056-451-6).

19. **Aquatic Environment and Toxicology**
Bharti, Pawan K. (ed.)
(ISBN: 978-93-5056-236-9).

20. **Biodiversity, Biotechnology and Environmental Conservation**
Bharti, P.K. and Bhandari, G. (eds.)
(ISBN: 978-93-5056-750-0).

21. **Biodiversity, Biotechnology & Pollution Control**
Bharti, P.K., and Chauhan, A. (eds.)
(ISBN: 978-93-5056-887-3)

22. **Biodiversity of Aquatic Ecosystem:** ***Significance, Threat and Conservation***
Bharti, P.K. and Kaoud, H.A.H. (eds.)
(ISBN: 978-93-5056-297-0).

23. **Biological Diversity and Ecology**
Arya, M.K.; Bharti, P.K. and Ritesh Joshi (eds.)
(ISBN: 978-93-5056-785-2).

24. **Bioremediation and Microbial Biotechnology**
Gupta, Sandeep; and Bharti, P.K. (eds.)
(ISBN: 978-93-5056-783-8).

25. **Biotechnological Approaches and Water Ecosystem**
Zaki, M.S.A.; and Bharti, P.K. (eds.)
(ISBN: 978-93-5056-779-1).

26. **Biotechnology, Agro-ecology and Environment**
Chauhan, Avnish and Bharti, P.K. (eds.)
(ISBN: 978-93-5056-757-9).

27. **Biotechnology and Environmental Management**
Arya Arun; Maheswari Raaz K., & Bharti, P.K (eds.)
(ISBN: 978-93-5056-862-0).

28. **Clean Technologies and Environmental Protection**
Chauhan, A.; Sharma, S. and Bharti, P.K. (eds.)
(ISBN: 978-93-5056-731-9).

29. **Climate Change and Agriculture**
Bharti, P.K. and Chauhan, Avnish (eds.)
(ISBN: 978-93-5056-148-5).

30. **Climate Change and Biodiversity**
Bharti, P.K. and Chauhan, Avnish (eds.)
(ISBN: 978-93-5056-360-1).

31. **Climate Change, Disaster Management and Environment**
Chauhan, Alka; Bharti, P.K. (eds.)
(ISBN: 978-93-5056-784-5).

32. **Conservation and Cultivation of Medicinal Plants**
Bharti, P.K. and Singh Narayan (eds.)
(ISBN: 978-93-5056-740-1).

33. **Crop Irrigation and Farming System**
Chauhan, Alka and P.K. Bharti (eds.)
(ISBN: 978-93-86841-40-7).

34. **Crop Productivity and Plant Disease Management**
Chauhan, Alka; Bharti, P.K. and Sadana, Deepti (eds.)
(ISBN: 978-93-5056-791-3).

35. **Eco-tourism, Environmental Problems and Sustainable Development**
Singh, Soubam Premchandra; Rathoure, Ashok Kr. and Bharti, P.K. (eds.)
(ISBN: 978-93-86841-57-5)

36. **Eco-toxicology and Eco-technology**
'Bharti', P.K. and Zaki, M. (eds.)
(ISBN: 978-93-5056-313-7).

37. **Energy Technologies for Clean Environment**
Bharti, Chhavi Kumar and 'Bharti', P.K. (Eds.)
(ISBN: 978-93-86841-22-3).

38. **Environmental Biotechnology and Application**
Bharti, P.K. and Chauhan, Avnish (eds.)
(ISBN: 978-93-5056-262-8).

39. **Environmental Conservation and Biotechnology**
Chauhan, A. and P.K. Bharti (eds.)
(ISBN: 978-93-5056-512-4).

40. **Environmental Economics and Sustainability**
José G. Vargas-Hernández; Khalid Alam Monowar and Bharti, P.K. (eds.)
(ISBN: 978-93-86841-37-7).

41. **Environmental Health and Problems**
Bharti, P.K. and Gajananda, Kh. (eds.)
(ISBN: 978-93-5056-263-5).

42. **Environmental Pollution and Biodiversity**
Bharti, P.K.; Chauhan, Avnish and Kumar, P. (eds.)
(ISBN: 978-93-5056-149-2).

43. **E-waste and Environmental Issues**
Bhalla, R., and Bharti, P.K. (eds.)
(ISBN: 978-93-5056-886-6)

44. **Experiments on Enhancement of Agricultural Yield**
Chauhan, Alka and P.K. Bharti (eds.)
(ISBN: 978-93-86841-50-6).

45. **Farming Techniques and Crop Production**
Chauhan Alka; Sharma Anubhuti; Ray Jaswant and 'Bharti' P.K. (eds.)
(ISBN: 978-93-5056-855-2).

46. **Faunal Biodiversity and Biotechnology**
Sethi, V. Kumar; Bharti, P.K. (eds.)
(ISBN: 978-93-86841-44-5).

47. **Fisheries and Toxicology**
Zaki, M.S.A.; Bharti, P.K. and Chauhan, A. (eds.)
(ISBN: 978-93-5056-452-3).

48. **Fish Habitat and Aquaculture**
Bharti, P.K.; Gupta Kr. Sanjay (eds.)
(ISBN: 978-93-5056-744-9).

49. **Forest and Biodiversity Conservation**
Chauhan Alka; Bharti, P.K. (eds.)
(ISBN: 978-93-5056-873-6).

50. **Food Processing, Management and Nanotechnology**
Chauhan, Avnish; Bharti, P.K. (eds.)
(ISBN: 978-93-5056-796-8).

51. **Food Technology and Research Advancement**
Chauhan, Avnish; Bharti, P.K. (eds.)
(ISBN: 978-93-86841-49-0).

52. **Freshwater Ecosystem and Xenobiotics**
Bharti, P.K.; Zaki, M. and Chauhan, A. (eds.)
(ISBN: 978-93-5056-299-4).

53. **Geospatial Technology and Ecosystem Assessment**
'Bharti' Chhavi Kumar; Chauhan, Alka & Bharti, P.K. (eds.)
(ISBN: 978-93-86841-36-0).

54. **Geospatial Technology and Water Management**
Chauhan, Alka; Bharti, P.K. (eds.)
(ISBN: 978-93-5056-885-9).

55. **Heavy Metals and Metalloids in Biosphere:** ***Impacts & Assessment***
Chauhan, Avnish, Gupta, Sandeep; and Bharti, P.K. (eds.)
(ISBN: 978-93-5056-860-6).

56. **Heavy Metals and Pesticides in Environment**
'Bharti', P.K.; Bhalla, Resham; Chauhan, Abhishek & Mala, Deep (eds.)
(ISBN: 978-93-86841-60-5).

57. **Land Reclamation, Soil Quality and Agriculture**
Bharti, P.K., and Chauhan, A. (ed.)
(ISBN: 978-93-5056-882-8).

58. **Limnology and Aquatic Science**
Sharma, S., and Bharti, P.K. (eds.)
(ISBN: 978-93-5056-735-7).

59. **Medicinal and Nutritional Values of Plants**
Chauhan, Alka; Bharti, P.K. (eds.)
(ISBN: 978-93-5056-883-5).

60. **Medicinal Plants:** ***Distribution, Utilization and Significance***
Sharma, P.; Bharti, P.K. and Narayan Singh (eds.)
(ISBN: 978-93-5056-734-0).

61. **Microbial Applications and Environment**
Bharti, Pawan K. (ed.)
(ISBN: 978-93-5056-515-5).

62. **Microbial Ecology and Habitat**
'Bharti', Pawan K. (ed.)
(ISBN: 978-93-5056-514-8).

63. **Microbial Environment and Bioremediation**
Chauhan Alka; K. Ashok Rathoure; and K Maheshwari Raaz (eds.)
(ISBN: 978-93-5056-856-9).

64. **Microbiological and Pharmacological Aspects of Biodiversity**
Sharma, P., Sharma, N.G.; Sharma, P., and Bharti, P.K. (ed.)
(ISBN: 978-93-5056-878-1).

65. **Natural Ecosystem and Climate Change**
Bharti, P.K., and Kh. Gajananda (ed.)
(ISBN: 978-93-5056-745-6).

66. **Nutraceuticals and Pharmaceuticals from Medicinal Plants**
Bharti, P.K., Khan, M.M. Abid Ali and Rathoure, Ashok Kumar (ed.)
(ISBN: 978-93-86841-55-1).

67. **Organic Farming and Bio-fertilizers**
Sethi, Vinaya Kumar; and Bharti, P.K. (eds.)
(ISBN: 978-93-86841-23-0).

68. **Pest Management and Agro-Techniques**
Biswas, Asim; Bharti, P.K., Chauhan, Avnish (eds.)
(ISBN: 978-93-5056-794-4).

69. **Physical and Chemical Analysis of Environment**
Mala, Deep; Bharti', P.K. & Bhalla, Resham (eds.)
(ISBN: 978-93-86841-61-2).

70. **Plant Biomass and Energy Solutions**
'Bharti', P.K.; 'Bharti' Chhavi Kumar; Rastogi, Amit and Chauhan, Alka (eds.)
(ISBN: 978-93-86841-62-9)

71. **Plant Biotechnology and Industrial Applications**
Chauhan, A., and Bharti, P.K. (ed.)
(ISBN: 978-93-5056-884-2).

72. **Plant Disease Management:** ***Control & Elimination Strategies***
Chauhan, A., and Bharti, P.K. (ed.)
(ISBN: 978-93-86841-41-4).

73. **Pollution, Plant Health and Biotechnology**
'Bharti', P.K.; Rathoure, Ashok Kumar; Tripathi, Rashmi (eds.)
(ISBN: 978-93-86841-63-6).

74. **Prakriti me Aushadhi (*in Hindi*)**
Singh, J.R.; Bharti, P.K. and Bharti, B.
(ISBN: 978-93-5056-200-0).

75. **Production of Fruits and Vegetables:** ***Technologies and Challenges***
Chauhan, Avnish; Bharti, P.K. and Chauhan, Alka (ed.)
(ISBN: 978-93-86841-25-4).

76. **Seed Technology, Plant Growth and Cropping System**
Tyagi, P.K. and Bharti, P.K. (eds.)
(ISBN: 978-93-5056-738-8).

77. **Seed Treatment, Plant Health and Agro-technology**
Chauhan, A. and Bharti, P.K. (eds.)
(ISBN: 978-93-5056-810-1).

78. **Soil Characteristics and Agro-ecology**
Avnish Chauhan and Bharti, P.K. (eds.)
(ISBN: 978-93-5056-758-6).

79. **Soil Contamination and Conservation**
Ezeaku, P.I. and Bharti, P.K. (eds.)
(ISBN: 978-93-5056-737-1).

80. **Soil Quality and Contamination**
Bharti, P.K. and Chauhan, Avnish (eds.)
(ISBN: 978-93-5056-361-8).

81. **Stress Tolerance and Plant Productivity**
Kumar, Prasann; 'Bharti', P.K (eds.)
(ISBN: 978-93-86841-56-8).

82. **Sustainable Aquaculture Management**
Gupta, S.K.; Bharti, P.K (eds.)
(ISBN: 978-93-5056-797-5).

83. **Waste Disposal and Management**
Bharti, P.K.; Tabassum, B. and Bajaj, P. (eds.)
(ISBN: 978-93-5056-729-6).

84. **Waste Generation and Utilization**
Bajaj Priya; Tabassum, B., and Bharti, P.K. (eds.)
(ISBN: 978-93-5056-792-0).

85. **Waste Management and Environmental Health**
Tabassum, B., Bajaj Priya, and Bharti, P.K. (eds.)
(ISBN: 978-93-5056-777-7).

86. **Water Resources:** ***Mapping Monitoring and Management***
Tyagi, P.K., Chauhan, Avnish and Bharti, P.K. (eds.)
(ISBN: 978-93-5056-861-3).

87. **Water Resources and Agriculture**
Bharti, P.K. and Ezeaku Peter Ikemefuna (eds.)
(ISBN: 978-93-5056-481-3).

88. **Waste Resources Management:** ***Monitoring and Assessment***
Gupta, Sandeep and Bharti, P.K. (eds.)
(ISBN: 978-93-5056-799-9).

Preface

Abiotic stresses including drought, temperature extremes, flooding, salinity, and toxic metals limit crop productivity, particularly in developing countries where people are resource-poor and have limited options. Anticipated global climate changes are expected to exacerbate the impact of stresses even further. Therefore, knowledge of stress response mechanisms is urgently needed for developing novel molecular breeding and genomics approaches for generating plants and management systems that will improve performance in hostile environmental conditions. This course explores the molecular, physiological, developmental and morphological characteristics that plants use to adapt to environmental stresses. Emphases are placed on stresses associated with global climate change including drought, flooding, extreme temperatures, salt, and environmental pollution. The book will also discuss strategies for improving stress tolerance in crops.

The aim of the book is to understand mechanisms of plant responses to their environment. The book will be a literature review of plant responses to different types of environmental stresses. A focus is put on molecular mechanisms as they have allowed tremendous progress in our understanding of plant responses to stress.

Responses of plants to drought, temperature stress, toxic concentrations of heavy metals, biotic stress, etc. are presented. The book also includes advances in the improvement of plant resistance to stress by genetic engineering. Scientific strategies and experimental design to study plant response to environmental pollutants and other stresses are discussed through analysis of case studies.

Editors
(envbooks@gmail.com)

Contents

Plant Response to Environmental Stress
Edited by: Dr. Alka Chauhan; Dr. Pawan Kumar 'Bharti' and Dr. Avnish Chauhan
ISBN: 978-93-86841-58-2
Edition: 2018
Published by: Discovery Publishing House Pvt. Ltd., New Delhi (India)

1 Introduction

Plants are frequently exposed to a plethora of unfavorable, or even adverse, environmental conditions, termed abiotic stresses, such as salinity, drought, heat, cold, flooding, heavy metals, ozone, ultraviolet radiation, nutrient deficiencies, etc., and these stresses pose serious threats to the sustainability of crop yield. Abiotic stresses are the greatest constraints for crop production worldwide. All plants possess adaptations to cope with the stresses imposed by the environments in which they exist. Most of the crops grown under field conditions are frequently exposed to various abiotic stresses. The complex nature of the environment, along with its unpredictable conditions and global climate change, are increasing gradually, which are creating more adverse situations. Abiotic stresses modify plant metabolism, leading to harmful effects on growth, development, and productivity. If the stress becomes very high and/or continues for an extended period, it may lead to an intolerable metabolic load on cells, reducing growth, and, in severe cases, result in plant death. A key sign of such stresses at the molecular level is the accelerated production of reactive oxygen species (ROS), which cause oxidative stress. However, plant stress may vary depending on the types of stressor and on the prevailing period. In nature, plants may not be completely free from abiotic stresses. All plants possess adaptations to cope with the stresses imposed by the environments in which they exist. Plants also employ different tolerance mechanisms to cope with these adverse conditions. The new knowledge acquired through research of abiotic and biotic stress tolerance mechanisms in plants will help in the application of stress-responsive determinants and in engineering plants with enhanced tolerance to stress.

Increasing global population, urbanization and industrialization are increasing the rate of conversion of arable land into wasteland. Supplying food to an ever-increasing population is one of the biggest challenges that agriculturalists and plant scientists are currently confronting. Environmental stresses make this situation even graver. Despite the induction of several tolerance mechanisms, sensitive plants often fail to survive under environmental extremes. New technological approaches are imperative. Conventional breeding methods have a limited potential to improve plant genomes against environmental stress. Recently, genetic engineering has contributed enormously to the development of genetically modified varieties of different crops such as cotton, maize, rice, canola and soybean. The identification of stress-responsive genes and their subsequent introgression or overexpression within sensitive crop species are now being widely carried out by plant scientists. Engineering of important tolerance pathways, like antioxidant enzymes, osmolyte accumulation, membrane-localized transporters for efficient compartmentation of deleterious ions and accumulation of essential elements and resistance against pests or pathogens is also an area that has been intensively researched.

In plant biology, the transgenic approach has emerged as an important tool to adapt crops to rapidly changing environmental conditions. The use of transgenic crops has increased considerably over the past decade. The primary step before proceeding with transgenics is the identification of genes serving as key regulators of different metabolic pathways, including osmolyte synthesis, ion homeostasis through selective ion uptake, antioxidant defence system and other frontline defence pathways (Ahmad *et al.* 2012).

Abiotic stress is defined as the negative impact of non-living factors on the living organisms in a specific environment. The non-living variable must influence the environment beyond its normal range of variation to adversely affect the population performance or individual physiology of the organism in a significant way. Whereas a biotic stress would include such living disturbances as fungi or harmful insects, abiotic stress factors, or stressors, are naturally occurring, often intangible, factors such as intense sunlight or wind that may cause harm to the plants and animals in the area affected. Abiotic stress is essentially unavoidable. Abiotic stress affects animals, but plants are especially dependent on environmental factors, so it is particularly constraining. Abiotic stress is the most harmful factor concerning the growth and productivity of crops worldwide. Research has also shown that abiotic stressors are at their most harmful when they occur together, in combinations of abiotic stress factors.

Abiotic stress, as a natural part of every ecosystem, will affect organisms in a variety of ways. Although these effects may be either beneficial or detrimental, the location of the area is crucial in determining the extent of the impact that abiotic stress will have. The higher the latitude of the area affected, the greater the impact of abiotic stress will be on that area. So, a taiga or boreal forest is at the mercy of whatever abiotic stress factors may come along, while tropical zones are much less susceptible to such stressors.

Plants are very sensitive to environmental stimuli and can undergo changes in physiology and development that acclimate them to their particular surroundings. For example, in response to gravistimulation, plant roots will turn to grow towards the gravity vector, while shoots will turn away. A more overall growth response occurs following mechanical stimuli such as touch and wind.

Plants generally grow shorter and stockier and often become stronger or more exible. These developmental changes, called thigmomorphogenesis, enable plants to withstand further environmental challenges, such as wind gusts.

Considerable progress is being made in identifying genes that are important for tolerance to abiotic stress and in defining stress-responsive gene promoters and signal-transduction pathways. Although genetically engineered crop plants with greater resistance to environmental stress have not yet been produced, research is at a turning point where correlative changes can now be tested for effectiveness in conferring stress tolerance.

Major stresses are:

- Drought stress
- Salinity stress
- Water stress
- Cold stress
- Heat/temperature stress
- Heavy metals stress
- Fungicide & Herbicides stress
- Nutrient stress
- Oxidative stress
- Antioxidant defense
- Phytohormones
- Pollutants
- UV radiation
- Deficiencies

Several intrinsic protective mechanisms are triggered in plants when they are exposed to various environmental stresses (Sadiq *et al.* 2017). Deciphering the regulatory mechanisms involved in initiating these tolerance pathways has remained under intensive research for decades. Testing of the validity of these assumptions has provided new insights towards the better understanding and elucidation of stress-induced changes in plants. Plant physiologists and biochemists have remained the key players in elucidating the basics of these mechanisms, which are now being extensively explored at the genetic and molecular levels using various molecular, genomic and biotechnological approaches.

The identification and selection of key stress responsive genes and their subsequent introgression for developing resistant crop cultivars through conventional breeding protocols are time-consuming. Plant biotechnology, despite being costly in comparison with conventional breeding, is very efficient. Several stress responsive genes have been identified and successfully introduced into other crops to create transgenic crops with enhanced stress tolerance. However, it is important to point out here that during the development of a transgenic crop variety, care is taken to introduce genes that result in enhanced tolerance to multiple stresses, specifically at the whole plant level. This requires the development of sets of markers designed to enhance stress tolerance.

The advantages of biotechnology in the development of transgenic plants for efficient crop varieties are undoubtedly enormous, but their commercialization after proper field testing is still an unavoidable reality. In addition, risk assessment of transgenic plants/crops is one of the preliminary steps required before the release or use of transgenic plants. The set standard all over the world explains the risk and official registration of plants and plant products has to be under taken. In addition, the risks to the environment from the transgenic crop plants must be examined with many field tests prior to commercialization, with institutional assessments, decisions on plants or varieties and adequate management practices in place to tackle inherent risks. For decision making, risk assessment must be followed in a scientific, sound and transparent manner. There are many operational governmental regulations in many countries for the safety assessment of GM crops. Furthermore, there are some international agreements that regulate the cultivation and commercialization of transgenic plants and their derivatives. All over the world, the major objective of these regulations and risk assessment strategies is focused on protecting the environment and human/animal health. The adoption of transgenic plants entirely depends on the assessments of the risks or benefits, regulatory approval, cost and time period, commercialization as well as the economic status, requirements and values of different countries.

The major relevant points to be discussed are:

- Have an in-depth understanding of the impact of various abiotic stresses on plant metabolism, growth, development and yield.
- Describe adaptation/resistance mechanisms of plants to different abiotic factors.
- Compare common and unique effects of various abiotic stress and crosstalk between pathways that lead to plants adaptation/resistance.
- Understand approaches and scientific basis behind approaches for improving plant stress tolerance.
- Improve ability to analyze and critique the primary scientific literature, scientific writing and communication skills.
- Explain, evaluate and interpret original experimental data of the response of plants to environmental conditions, and design and interpret results of one's own experiments.

REFERENCE

https://www.ncbi.nlm.nih.gov/pubmed/1368289

http://www.vub.ac.be/en/study/fiches/56594/plant-responses-to-environmental-stress

http://www.sciencedirect.com/science/article/pii/095816699290147B

https://academic.oup.com/aobpla/article/doi/10.1093/aobpla/plx025/3894178/Plant-responses-to-environmental-stresses-from

http://courses.cornell.edu/preview_course_nopop.php?catoid=26&coid=417280

http://www.mdpi.com/journal/plants/special_issues/abiotic_environmental

https://en.wikipedia.org/wiki/Abiotic_stress

http://onlinelibrary.wiley.com/doi/10.1111/pce.12274/pdf

http://study.com/academy/lesson/environmental-stimuli-stress-plant-adaptations-responses.html

http://citeseerx.ist.psu.edu/viewdoc/download?doi=10.1.1.420.1276&rep=rep1&type=pdf

Plant Response to Environmental Stress **Page: 6-27**
Edited by: Dr. Alka Chauhan; Dr. Pawan Kumar 'Bharti' and Dr. Avnish Chauhan
ISBN: 978-93-86841-58-2
Edition: 2018
Published by: Discovery Publishing House Pvt. Ltd., New Delhi (India)

2

Plant Response to Abiotic Stresses

A Focus on Heavy Metal Toxicity

Prasann Kumar[1] and Shweta Pathak[2]

ABSTRACT

During their life span, plants can be subjected to a number of abiotic stresses, like drought, temperature (both high and low), radiation, salinity, soil pH, heavy metals, lack of essential nutrients, air pollutants, etc. When affected by one, or a combination of abiotic stresses, a response is induced by changes in the plant metabolism, growth and general development. Reactive Oxygen Species (ROS) are a natural consequence of the aerobic metabolism, and plants have mechanisms to deal with them in normal conditions, controlling the formation and removal rates.

Keywords: Agriculture, Biotic, Cadmium, Density, Ecosystem, Forage, Sorghum.

INTRODUCTION

Metals are a natural part of terrestrial ecosystems. Also out of the 10 most abundant elements in earth's crust, seven are metals (Mason, 1953). Heavy metal refers to all metals having a specific gravity greater than four (Anonymous, 1964). Only those lower (metal) members of the periodic table which are (1) relatively abundant in earth's crust, (2) extracted and used in reasonable amounts, (3) used in places where the public may come into contact with them, and (4) toxic to human beings are generally referred to as heavy metals (Sahu *et al.*, 2004). Based on their solubility under physiological conditions, 17 heavy metals may be available for living cells and are of importance to organisms and ecosystem. Among these metals, Fe, Mo, Zn and Mn are important as micronutrients and Ni, Co, Cu, V etc. possess importance as traces elements. Hg, As, Cd and Pb have no known function and seem to be more or less toxic to plants and microbial population (Godbold and Huttermann, 1985). Heavy metals

[1] Assistant Professor, Department of Agronomy, School of Agriculture, Lovely Professional University, Jalandhar, Punjab-144411, India

[2] Research Trainee, Department of Plant Physiology, Institute of Agricultural Sciences, Banaras Hindu University, Varanasi, 221005, U.P., India

enter the food chain from industrial sources, natural sources and geochemical cycle. Heavy metals are important environmental pollutants and their toxicity is a problem of increasing significance for ecological, evolutionary, nutritional, and environmental reasons. Of all non-essential heavy metals, cadmium (Cd) are perhaps the metal that has attracted the most attention in soil science and plant nutrition due to its potential toxicity to humans, and also its relative mobility in the soil–plant system. Friedrich Stromeyer and Karl Hermann discovered cadmium (Cd) almost simultaneously in 1817 in samples of zinc oxide obtained by roasting zinc carbonate from Salzgitter (Germany). Cadmium, a group II B transition element was discovered by a German chemist Freidrich Strohmeyer in 1817. It is considered a non-nutrient element, since it has no known function in plant development and life, with the exception of Cd-carnomis anhydrase of marine diatoms (Lane and morel, 2000).

The average natural abundance of Cd in the earth's crust has most often been reported from 0.1 to 0.5 ppm. According to Wagner (1993), non-polluted soil solutions contain Cd concentrations ranging from 0.04 to 0.32 mM. Because Cd is a naturally occurring component of all soils, all food stuffs will contain some Cd and therefore all humans are exposed to natural levels of Cd. It has been reported that leafy vegetables and potato tubers naturally accumulate higher levels of Cd than do fruits and cereals.Maize (*Zea mays* L.) is a suitable crop for tropical and subtropical regions of the world. Maize can be an excellent model plant to study the physiological changes responsible for reduced productivity under stressful conditions. Being a rich source of nutrition (72% starch, 10% protein, 8.5% fiber, and 4.8% edible oil), maize is a major source of food, sugar, cooking oil, and animal feed all over the globe. Maize is preferred in poultry feed because of its easy availability; maize constitutes about 60 per cent of the feed in the poultry feed industry and therefore is a critical raw material. With its wide applications, maize is also referred to as the Queen of Cereals. Maize also finds application in food containers, plastic food packaging, baby powder, diapers, medicine, vitamin tablets, textile products, candies and so on. Maize rich breakfast cereals, cooking oils, snacks and popcorn have also become popular. Internationally, maize has been processed to produce bio-ethanol in a big way of blending with auto fuels. In fact, maize is the only cereal that has such diverse uses. Keeping the value of maize crop in mind, cadmium stress being the harmful menace to its crop growing, the experiment was performed to assess the effect of various cadmium concentrations on different agronomical, physiochemical attributes of maize seedlings after different time intervals. Gisbert *et al.* (2003) examined that the heavy metal stress is one of the major abiotic stresses that causes environmental pollution in recent decades. These metals unlike other organic pollutants are not degraded and converted into harmless compounds via biological processes.Liu *et al.* (2003) reported that the cadmium (Cd) pollution in agricultural farmland has become a serious problem in many parts of the world, due to industrial development and the heavy use of chemical fertilizers, pesticides and herbicides, which produce serious threats to human health through the food chain.Arduini *et al.* (2004) found that changes in root morphology did not affect Cd translocation to the above ground parts of the plant. The distribution of Cd in leaves, bulbs and roots of M. *plumbea* differed with increasing Cd concentrations. Cadmium accumulation in the leaves increased with increasing Cd. Bavi *et al.* (2006) studied that isolated chloroplast of 21 days old bean plants grown in nutrient solution containing different concentrations of cadmium did not show a significant change in the rate of Hill reaction. This indicates that during the 7 days of treatment any cadmium ions taken up by plants may have been localized in root cell vacuoles thus have been kept away from photosynthesis sites, protecting photosynthesis from the harmful effects of cadmium.Wu *et al.* (2006) elucidated that Zn^{2+} concentration of rice genotypes increased to Cd levels up to 0.1mM for the shoot and 0.5mM for roots, while at Cd levels exceeding these levels, Zn^{2+} concentrations were reduced; Fe concentrations increased up to 0.1mM Cd in both shoot and roots, while higher Cd levels resulted in a sharp decrease of Fe.Krupper and Kroneck (2007) studied that the increasing industrial production leads to elevated release of heavy metals into the environment, thus increasing risk for human health if accumulated in crop plants. Among others, nickel **(Ni)** and cadmium (Cd) are potentially dangerous because of their toxic effects and their accumulation in the food chain. Ni abundance in soils worldwide is >5 kg ha^{-1} and in terms of plant metabolism, Ni is an essential ultra micronutrient found to be the active centre of urease and the cofactor of one superoxide dismutase isoforms. Krantev *et al.* (2008) noticed that cadmium (Cd) is a highly toxic trace element that enters the environment mainly from industrial processes and phosphate fertilizers. It can reach high levels in agricultural soils and is easily assimilated by plants. When taken up by plants, it induces various visible symptoms of phytotoxicity e.g. leaf roll, chlorosis, growth reduction in root and shoot, browning of root tips and eventually death.Khan *et al.* (2008) elucidated that the concentration of heavy metals determined in selected plants are well below the critical limit. Maximum concentration of Mn (52.94 ppm), Ni (4.35 ppm) and Cu (9.65 ppm) were found in A.*vulgaris*, Zn (47.18 ppm) in S.*rebaudiana*, Fe (206.69 ppm) in W.*somnifera* and Cr (5.89 ppm) in G. aparine. Lead and cadmium were below the detection limits. The implication of the findings may be taken into consideration whilst using the herbs for human consumption.Bharadwaj *et al.* (2009) studies that the higher concentration of Cd is responsible for the complete inhibition of germination and growth was also decreased as concentration of heavy metals was increased as compared to control plants; minimum morphological growth occurred in the plants in which Pb concentration was 8 g/kg soil and for Cd, it was 2.5g/kg soil when compared with control plants.Monteiro *et al.* (2009) reported that Cd in the nutrient solution produced growth inhibition in lettuce plants, the growth of lettuce shoots was significantly reduced after 14 days when compared to the control. Root growth was also lower in Cd exposed plants, but the difference was not significant and there were macro and micronutrient imbalances in leaves and roots of lettuce. Wang *et al.* (2009) reported that accumulation of metals in crops including medicinalplants such as chamomile is a global problem owing to health risk to human. Therefore, selection of cultivars with reduced root to shoot metal translocation is of great importance. Auda *et al.* (2011) concluded that Cd toxicity was more obvious than Pb toxicity, and these symptoms were more severe in foliar treated than in root treated plants. Cd application decreased the dry weight of whole plants, shoot and roots, when compared with untreated control plants (Figure 2.1).

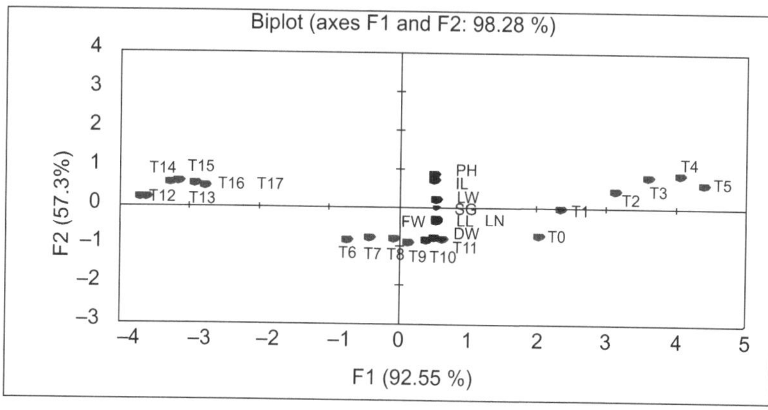

Fig. 2.1: PCA analysis of plant morphological parameters

(**Source:** Based on an authors research work, 2017, unpublished)

Effects of Cadmium

It has been reported that uptake, transport, and subsequent distribution of nutrient elements by the plants can be affected by the presence of Cd ions. Cd has been shown to interfere with the uptake, transport, and use of several elements (Ca, Mg, P, and K) and water by plants (Das *et al.*, 1997). Chang *et al.* (2003) reported Cd induced iron deficiency in sugar beet. In pea plants, the uptake of P, K, S, Ca, Zn, Mn, and B was inhibited strongly after Cd exposure (Metwally*et al.*, 2005). Treatment of barley plants with 1.0 μM Cd decreased the concentrations of P, K, Ca, Mg, Cu, Fe, Mn, Zn, Mo, and B in roots, whereas the concentrations of these elements in shoots were not decreased in comparison with the control (Guo*et al.*, 2007). Cd also reduced the absorption of nitrate and its transport from roots to shoots, by inhibiting nitrate reductase activity in the shoots (Hernandez *et al.*, 1996). Appreciable inhibition of the nitrate reductase activity was also found in plants of *Silenecucubalus*(Mathys, 1975). Nitrogen fixation and primary ammonia assimilation decreased in nodules of soybean plants during Cd treatments (Karina *et al.*, 2003).

Effect of Cadmium on Plants and Its Symptoms

Cd does not have any beneficial physiological role in plants, but when accumulated, it affects all aspects of growth and development. In plants, Cd is one of the most readily absorbed and most rapidly translocated heavy metals, and can cause numerous morphological and physiological changes even at low concentrations (Seregin and Ivanov, 1998). At the morphological level, an excessive amount of Cd causes inhibition of plant growth, photosynthesis, enzyme function and cell metabolism in addition to disturbances in plant-water relationships (Mobin and Khan, 2007; Shi and Cai, 2008; Shi *et al.*, 2010). These effects are strongly dependent upon the plant species and the level of Cd applied. Plants exposed to Cd can show many symptoms such as chlorosis, leaf roll, and necrosis (Benavides *et al.*, 2005). Chlorosis, leaf roll and stunting are the main and most easily observed toxic symptoms in the presence of excessive amounts of heavy metals. Toxicity may result from the binding of metals to sulphydryl groups in proteins leading to disruption of structure, inhibition of activity and deficiency of essential elements (Van Assche and Clijsters, 1990). The excess amount of heavy metal may stimulate free radical production and reactive oxygen species resulting in oxidative stress (Dietz *et al.*, 1999). Some research has indicated that the effect of cadmium toxicity depends on the applied concentration, the age of the leaves, phenological development, plant species and cultivars (Baszynski *et al.*, 1980; Becerril *et al.*, 1989; Costa and Morel, 1994; Lang *et al.*, 1995; Vassilev *et al.*, 1995). As reported by Singh *et al.*, (2003) cadmium induced changes inwater status of plants viz., total water content, specific water content, water saturation deficit (WSD) and transpiration when subjected to 250 ppm concentration of Cd.

Effect of Cadmium Physiology of Plants

Chen and Kao (1995) showed that proline accumulation can be induced in rice roots by treating seedlings with Cd. Proline has been reported to play important role in osmo-regulation, protecting enzyme denaturation, acting such as a source of carbon and nitrogen, stabilizing the machinery of protein synthesis, regulating the cytosolic acidity and/or scavenging hydroxyl radicals. Galli *et al.* (1996) reported a strong reduction in root dry weight for a root Cadmium concentration of 562 mg kg^{-1} DM. Being highly mobile in phloem, Cadmium can accumulate in any part of the plant causing stunted growth, chlorosis (Chaffei *et al.*, 2004) and leaf epinasty (Zhao *et al.* 2006). It also induces biochemical change in roots and leaves, such as lignification of cell walls in root tissues and leaf main vein. Larsson *et al.* (1998) performed an experiment in *Brassica napus* plants and showed that cadmium lowered total chlorophyll content, carotenoid content, and increased the non-photochemical quenching. Furthermore, cadmium inhibited the oxidative mitochondrial phosphorylation, probably increasing the passive permeability to H^+ of the mitochondrial inner membrane.

Measured as CO_2 uptake, the photosynthetic rate in spruce (*Piceaabies*) was significantly decreased by cadmium. With the enhanced Cadmium accumulation, as a characteristic visual symptom, the reduction of the chlorophyll content of leaves could be observed. This fact is supported by the experiment done by Hegedus *et al.*(2001). Sandalio *et al.* (2001) reported that the chloroplasts, the major component of photosynthetic organ, are highly sensitive to damage exposed Cd toxicity. Oncel *et al.* (2000) observed that the two wheat varieties to which Cd and Pb were applied, total chlorophyll decreased. Cho and Kim (2003) noticed that cadmium has a greater mobility in soil as compared with other metals, and easily taken up by the roots and is translocated to different plant parts. Singh *et al.* (2003) showed that both growth and photosynthetic pigments affected by the presence of heavy metals. The stronger effect, after Hg was that of Cd and the smaller inhibitor effect wastomato leaf. In the case of $Cd(NO_3)_2$ the inhibitory effect of Cd was smaller than $CdCl_2$, probably due NO_3^- anion, which is used as chemical nutrient. The excess level of Cd decreased the concentrations of chlorophylls increased the ratio of chorophyll a/b.Claussen (2005) reported an increase in the level of proline in plants, such as heavy metals, temperature and drought. Hayat *et al.* (2007) also determined that proline level increased the physiological drought stress generated by cadmium (Figure 2.2).

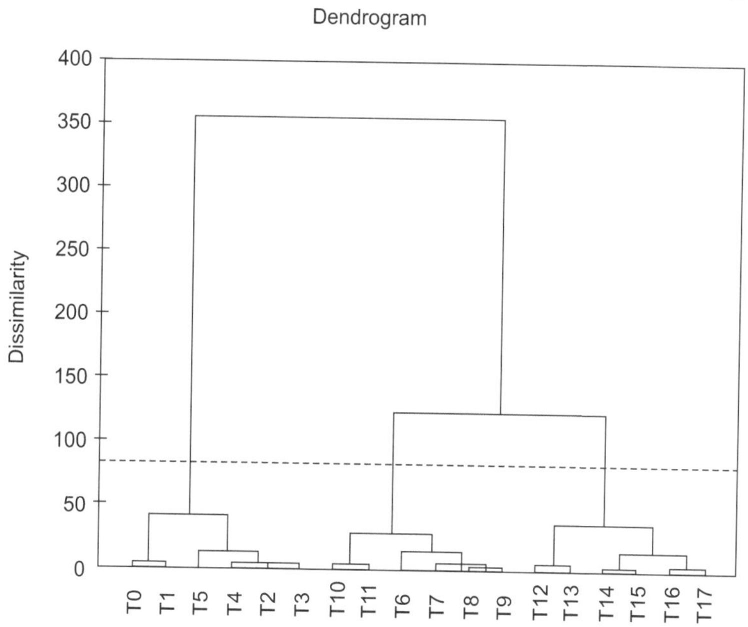

Fig. 2.2: AHC analysis of cadmium treated plants

(**Source:** Based on author's research work, unpublished, 2017)

Zengin and munzuroglu (2005) reported that the heavy metals inhibit metabolic processes by inhibiting the action of enzymes, and this may be the most important cause of inhibition. Decreased chlorophyll content associated with heavy metal stress may be the result of inhibition of the enzymes responsible for chlorophyll biosynthesis. Cadmium was reported to affect chlorophyll biosynthesis and inhibit protochlorophyll reductase and aminolevulinic acid (ALA) synthesis (Stobart *et al.* 1985). The chlorophyll content declined progressively with increasing concentration of heavy metals. A significant increase of proline, and ascorbic acid content was detected in primary leaves after 10 days exposure to heavy metals.Jain and srivastava (2006) studies that the effect of different level of Cd (0, 10, 100, 200 ppm) as cadmium chloride, on growth, cell division, chlorophyll content, activity of catalase, peroxidase enzymes, foliar anatomical characters and essential nutrient content in sugarcane and found that Cd effect being less pronounced in variety CO 64 in terms of lower decrease in growth attributes (Figure 2.3).

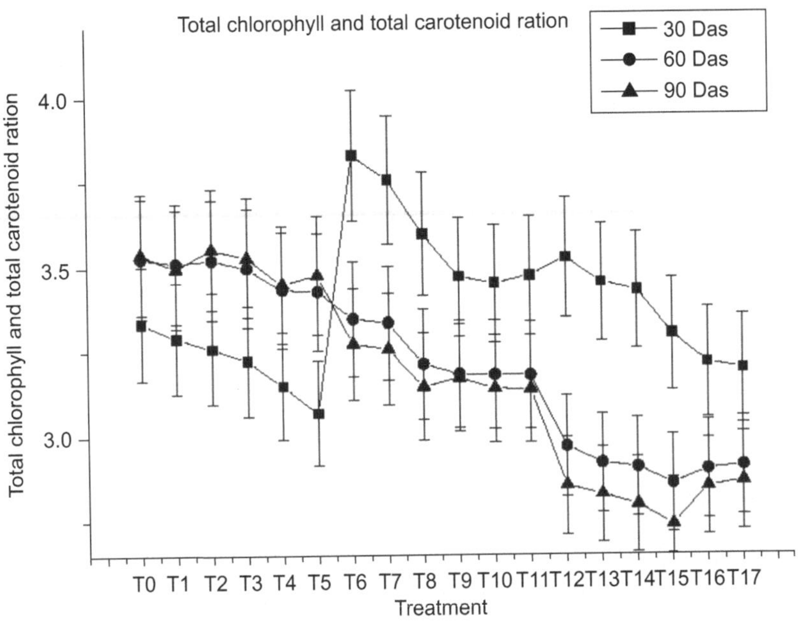

Fig. 2.3: Effects of cadmium on pigmentation system of plants with special reference to carotenoids

(**Source:** Based on an author's research work)

Bavi *et al.* (2006) noticed that the cadmium has a greater mobility in soil as compared with other heavy metals and is easily taken up by the roots and is translocated to different plant parts, the uptake of heavy metals by plants is controlled by both soil and plant factors cadmium causes perturbations in various plant processes such as photosynthesis, sulfate assimilation and respiration. Plant growth inhibition and alteration in metabolism are mainly due to direct effects of cadmium on various enzyme activities and on growth processes. The selective accumulation of intracellular amino acids often occurs in response to environmental stresses such as drought, flooding, low temperature, or salinity (Figure 2.4).

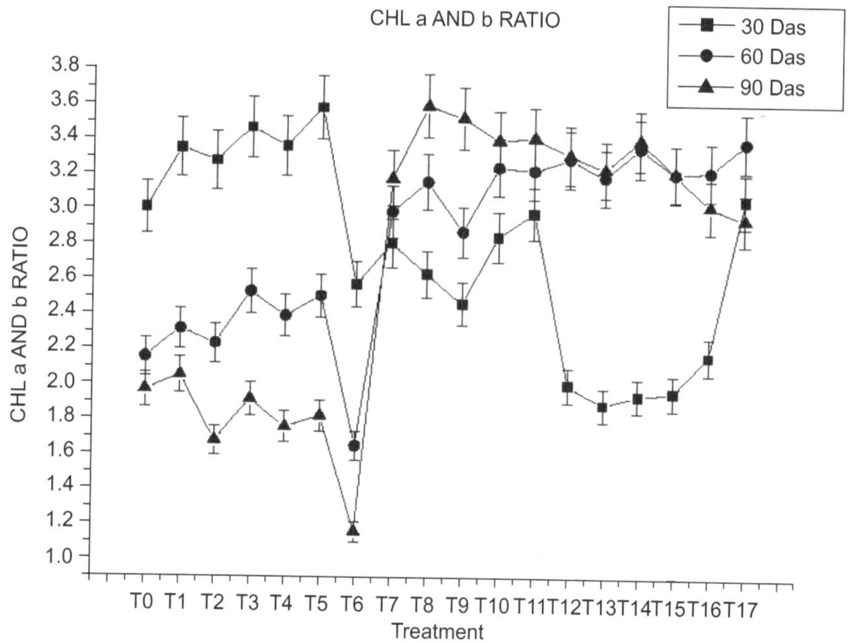

Fig. 2.4: Effects of heavy metal on pigmentation system with special reference to chlorophyll

(**Source:** Based on author's research work, unpublished, 2017)

Jhon R. *et al.* (2008) also demonstrated the vivid results of cadmium stress on chlorophyll quantity that eventually affect photosynthesis. It was observed that 1 mg/l of each Cadmium and Pb used individually marginally increased the chlorophyll (chl a, chl b, and total chlorophyll).The prolonged exposure to high concentration of Cadmium (40 mg/l) reduced chl a significantly to about 82% of the control, and Pb showed the decline of 77% of the control after 30 days. Similarly, chl b decreased from 0.36 to 0.01 and 0.04 mg/g fw after 24 days of exposure to 40 mg/l of Cadmium and 40 mg/l of Pb, respectively. Thus, heavy metal alters chloroplast ultrastructure and reduces the net photosynthetic rate, stomatal conductance and leaf transpiration (Souza *et al.*, 2011).Krantev *et al.* (2008) examined that net photosynthesis is also sensitive to Cd because it directly affects chlorophyll biosynthesis (Stobort *et al.* 1985; Padmaja *et al.* 1990; Gadallah 1995) and the proper development of the chloroplast ultrastucture (Stoyanova and Merakchiiska-Nikolo 1992, Stoyanaova and Tchakalova 1997). The negative effect of Cd can also be observed in the carboxylating phase of photosynthesis. The main targets of the influence of Cd are two key enzymes of CO_2 fixation, ribulose 1,5-bisphosphate carboxylase

(Rubpc) and phosphoenol pyruate carboxylase (PEPC). It has been shown that Cd_2^+ ions lower the activity of RuBPC and damage its structure by substituting for Mg^{2+} ions, which are important cofactors of carboxylation reactions, and may also shift RuBPC activity towards oxygenation reactions (Siedlecka *et al.* 1998). Bharadwaj *et al.* (2009) reported that along with the growth of plants under increasing concentration of heavy metals, the entire metabolic activity of the plants under metal stress was affected resulting in reduced metabolic activities. Under the metal stress, the levels of photosynthetic pigments, namely chlorophyll 'a' and chlorophyll 'b' and carotenoids decrease as the concentration of Pb and Cd in soil increases. Chlorophyll 'a' was more affected in comparison to carotenoids. Daud *et al.* (2009) studied the toxic effect of cadmium at increasing concentrations with special attention being given to the root morphological and ultrastructural changes in two transgenic cotton cultivars *viz.* BR001 and GK30 and their wild relative *viz.* Coker 312. In comparison to their respective controls, low concentration (10 and 100 μM) of Cadmium greatly stimulated seed germination, while it was inhibited by the highest concentration of Cadmium (1000 μM) in case of two transgenic cultivars. It was observed that different Cadmium concentrations posed inhibitory effects on all the studied parameters of cultivar BR001 and were significantly different ($P < 0.05$) as compared to their respective controls. It revealed that inhibition in all these parameters of BR001 was started at 10 μM of Cadmium level. The same inhibitory effects of Cadmium treatments were also recorded for cultivar GK30. However, its roots fresh weight, root length's tolerance index and root tip percentage at 10 μM of Cadmium were not significantly different ($P > 0.05$) with respect to their controls, while others showed significant differences at the 5% level of probability. Hasan *et al.* (2009) reported that all the non-essential heavy metals, cadmium (Cd) is perhaps the metal which has attracted the most attention in soil science and plant nutrition due to its potential toxicity to humans, and also its relative mobility in the soil-plant system. This review summarizes the toxic symptoms of Cd in plants (i.e. growth retardation, alterations of photosynthesis, stomatal movement, enzymatic activities, water relations, interferences with mineral uptake, protein metabolism, membrane functioning, etc.) but also includes the mechanisms of cadmium uptake, translocation and deposition. Moreover, it also throws light on chelation, including identification of Cd ligands present in cytosol and vascular tissue. Cadmium-induced oxidative stress is also considered as one of the most widely studied topics in this review. Kakoniova *et al.* (2009) reported that toxic metals in high concentrations inhibit growth and development of plants and disturb or change their biochemical and physiological processes. Other studies the higher concentrations of Cd are responsible for the photosynthetic pigments, total soluble sugar, starch content as well as soluble protein content decreased as the concentration of metals was increased in comparison of control plants (Bharadwaj *et al.* 2009). Mei Li Na *et al.* (2010) did a pot trial with 4 lucerne varieties (Xinjiang Daye, Longdong Muxu, Manasi Muxi and Shihezi Muxu) in Lanzhou, Gansu, China, to study the effects of different degrees of cadmium stress (heavy, moderate and heavy stress with the Cadmium levels of 0 as the control, 1, 5, 10, 25 and 50 mg Cadmium/kg soil) on their seedling growth, and to explore differences in Cadmium tolerance among them. The morphological and the physiological characteristics of lucerne in the treatment with the low level of Cadmium (1 mg Cadmium/kg) were superior to those in the control, indicating that the low level of Cadmium could promote plant growth. The height and weight of lucerne seedlings and the ability of chlorophyll synthesis, decreased, the contents of proline and malondialdehyde (MDA) increased, and the catalase activity reduced at the high level of cadmium (50 mg/kg). Rodriguez *et al.* (2010) the induction of proline accumulation in response to stresses commonly found in natural environments (e.g. heavy metal toxicity, nutrient deficiency, photo-oxidative stress) suggests that genetic engineering of proline overproduction in agriculturally important crops might increase their overall environmental tolerance and thereby enhancing productivity (Eraslan *et al.* 2007).Shafi Md. *et al.* (2010) conducted a hydroponics experiment at the University of Zhejiang Hangzhou, China to investigate the effect of salinity (NaCl) and cadmium (Cadmium) on root morphology of different wheat cultivars differing in salt tolerance. Cadmium and NaCl stress inhibited shoot and root dry weight, number of root tips (lateral roots), total root length, root average diameter and total root volume. Increasing concentration of Cadmium and NaCl had negatively affected root morphology of all cultivars under study. The combined effect of Cadmium and NaCl on these parameters was more than both Cadmium and NaCl alone. There was an obvious difference in response to both stresses among the three cultivars with Bakhtawar-92 being less affected.Sharma *et al.* (2010) observed that the significantly increments in proline and total phenolic contents were also observed at increasing Cd treated plants as compared to the control, Cd applied @100 mg L^{-1} increased proline and total phenolic contents has been suggested to be an early indicator of heavy metal stress in the plants.Sharma *et al.* (2010) reported that the higher magnitude of reduction in photosynthesis rate in increasing concentration of Cd is caused by inhibition of PS 2 activities as shown by the reduction in Fv/Fm ratio as well as reduction in photosynthetic pigments, the highest concentration of Cd reductions in chlorophyll a, b, total and carotenoids content, respectively as compared to the control. The result suggests that chlorophyll b is more sensitive than chlorophyll a to Cd stress. Auda *et al.* (2011) observed that reduction of growth charecters and plant pigments, with increasing cadmium soil addition either alone of combined with zinc soil addition might be partially due to the increase in cadmium concentration and consequently its negative effects on net photosynthesis, transpiration, chlorophyll a as well as nutrient contents, The concentration of all of the plant pigment (chlorophyll a, chlorophyll b and total carotenoids) significantly decreased with increasing Cd soil addition, either alone or combined with Zn at all levels, the inhibition of chlorophyll synthesis by Cd is achieved both by reaction with constituent biosynthesis enzymes as well as peroxidase degradation. Jazi *et al.* (2011) studied that lead toxicity effects in plants usually appear in concentrations higher than 30 micrograms per gram of leaf and leads to reduction in growth and decrease of chlorophyll synthesis (Ruley *et al.* 2004). It causes such problem as reduction in growth and production levels, yellowing of young leaves, reduction in absorption of essential elements such as iron and reduction in the rate of photosynthesis (Pallavi and Rama, 2005).Ozdener and Kutbay (2011) reported that the chlorophyll a and b contents were decreased under Cd treatments, chlorophyll a and b contents decreased due to increased Cd concentrations. Although low Cd concentrations have no significant effects on chlorophyll content, it was remarkably decreased at high concentrations of Cd.Singh Gill and Tuteja (2011)reported that Among heavy metals, cadmium (Cd) is a non-essential and toxic metal, rapidly taken up by the roots and accumulated in various plant tissues which hamper the crop growth and productivity worldwide. Plants employ various strategies to counteract the inhibitory effect of Cd, among which nutrient management is one of a possible way to overcome Cd toxicity. Sulfur (S) uptake and assimilation are crucial for determining crop yield and resistance to Cd stress. Cd affects S the assimilation pathway which leads to the activation of pathway responsible for the synthesis of cysteine (Cys), a precursor of glutathione (GSH) biosynthesis. GSH, a non-protein thiol acts as an important antioxidant in mitigating Cd-induced oxidative stress. It also plays an important role in phytochelatins (PCs) synthesis, which has a proven role in Cd detoxification. Therefore, S assimilation is considered a crucial step for plant survival under Cd stress. The aim of this review is to discuss the regulatory mechanism of S uptake and assimilation, GSH and PC synthesis for Cd stress tolerance in crop plants. Yusuf *et al.* (2011) studied that content of chlorophyll, inhibition of photosynthesis, deposition of lignin and suberin (Ghanati *et al.* 2002), reduced proton extrusion from roots (Roldan *et al.* 1992), increased membrane leakage, peroxidation of lipids and altered activities of antioxidant pathways.Aghaz *et al.* (2013) performed an experiment with 10 dill (*Anethum graveolens*) ecotypes to cadmium stress (0, 100 and 200 micro M Cadmium) in hydroponic culture system. Plant growth parameters, electrolyte leakage, relative water content and proline were measured 30 days after stress induced by cadmium (Cadmium). Results showed that Cadmium caused to decrease morphological traits such as root dry weight, shoot dry weight, total dry weight, root length, height and leaf area. Among the ecotypes, Ardabil showed higher amounts in shoot dry weight, total dry weight and height compared with the rest of the ecotypes, indicating that the former ecotypes were more cadmium tolerant than the others. All growth parameters decreased in cadmium stress. Proline increased and electrolyte leakage and relative water content decreased under cadmium stress. Lu Zi Wei Zhang *et al.* (2013) investigated that root morphology may play a crucial role in the variation in Cadmium accumulation among peanut (*Arachis hypogaea* L.) cultivars. The biomass, Cadmium accumulation and root morphology of five peanut cultivars were determined under 2 and 20 micro M $CdCl_2$ in a hydroponic experiment. Excess Cadmium considerably decreased the root lengths (RL), surface area (SA), specific root length (SRL) and number of root tips, but increased the root diameters (RD). Cadmium-induced decreases in RL and SA were significant in the 0-0.2 and 0.2-0.4 mm diameter classes. A positive correlation was observed between RL and cadmium amount in shoots. RD negatively correlated with cadmium concentrations in roots and shoots. Positive correlations were also found between RL vs. shoot Cadmium concentration, SA vs. Cadmium amount in shoots, SRL vs. root cadmium concentration, SRL vs. shoot Cadmium concentration, and SRL vs. cadmium amount in shoots. The fine roots play a crucial role in determining Cadmium accumulation in peanut plants. Cultivars with more fine roots in their root system (i.e. Haihua 1 and Zhenghong 3) have high capability of Cadmium accumulation.

Effect of Cadmium Toxicity on Maize Plant

Keltjens *et al.* (1998) reported that Heavy metal contaminated soils often show increased levels of more than one metal, e.g. copper (Cu), cadmium (Cd), zinc (Zn), lead (Pb) and nickel (Ni). In case such soils are used for crop production, prediction of yield reduction or quality decline due to heavy metals in the soil is inadequate when based only on chemical soil analysis. The use of biomarkers such as phytochelatins (PC), non-protein thiols specifically induced in plants upon exposure to heavy metals, may be an additional indicator. Copper and Cd uptake and induction of PC synthesis were studied with hydroponically grown maize and wheat plants exposed to mixtures of the two metals. A close positive relationship was observed between the concentrations of Cd and PC in the plant shoot material. A decreased shoot concentration of Cd after addition of Cu, due to metal competition at common root absorption sites, coincided with lower shoot PC levels. The observed direct relationship between shoot PC concentration and the degree of metal-induced growth inhibition makes the use of PC promising. Magda pal *et al.* (2006) reported that Heavy metals such as cadmium (Cd) enter the ecosystem chiefly as the result of human activities. So the changes induced by one of the most toxic heavy metals, Cd, in maize plants are a cause of some concern. This review discusses not only the toxic symptoms caused by Cd stress, but also the tolerance mechanisms activated in the plants. Cadmium induces a number of physiological changes, such as growth inhibition, changes in the water and ion metabolism, the inhibition of photosynthesis, changes in enzyme activities, and the formation of free radicals.

The synthesis and compartmentalization of phytochelatins are induced shortly after the initiation of Cd stress, while other defense mechanisms also play an important role.Abdul Ghani (2010) conducted a pot experiment to determine the toxic effects of some heavy metals on the plant growth and seed yield of maize (*Zea mays* L.). Heavy metals Mn, Pb, Cd, Cr and Co individually and in combinations were added as chloride salts in solutions to the pots before sowing. Heavy metals caused significant decreases in growth and protein content. Cd was the most toxic metal followed by Co, Hg, Mn, Pb, and Cr. Protein content decreased from 16.0–68.4% in metal exposed plants. Metal accumulation by seeds was directly related to the applied heavymetal with greater concentrations of metals found in cases where metals were added individually rather than in combinations. The toxic effects on the plant growth, nitrogen content in different plant parts, and protein content in seeds, exerted by two metals in combination were only as harsh as for the most toxic metal individually probably due to their antagonistic effects.Tian Yong *et al.* (2012) investigated the phytoremediation potential of the bioenergy crop maize (*Zea mays*) in Cadmium-contaminated soil. Pot experiments with Cadmium concentration gradients of 0, 5, 10, 30, 50 and 100 mg/kg were performed, and the growth parameters, photosynthetic activity and Cadmium accumulation characteristics were evaluated during the entire growth period. The experimental results indicated that the maize germination was not sensitive to elevated Cadmium stress, and that the photosynthetic activity only declined due to Cadmium stress during the early growth stage. Cadmium concentrations greater than 30 mg/kg inhibited maize growth and reduced biomass production. The experiments demonstrated that maize has a great potential for phytoremediation in Cadmium-contaminated soil, where 1025.03 or 117.67 μg cadmium per plant was accumulated when the Cadmium concentration in the substrate was 47.17 or 3.80 mg/kg. The bioconcentration factors of the roots (BCF > 2.7) were greater than that of the aerial organs, and the translocation factors (TF) were all less than 1, which indicated that Cadmium readily accumulated in the root but was not readily transported to the aerial part. Due to its high biomass production and Cadmium accumulation capacity, maize is a good candidate for use in bioenergy production on Cadmium-contaminated soil.Abbasi *et al.* (2015)conducted ahydroponic experiment to investigate single and combined effects of 5 micro mol/L Cadmium and 100 mM NaCl on growth, root morphology, photosynthetic parameters, leaf and root ultra-structure of two maize hybrids (26204 and 8441) differing in salt tolerance. indicated that 8441 was more sensitive than 26204 to both Cadmium and NaCl stresses. The reduction in growth and photosynthetic parameters were associated with severe disorganization of nucleus, chloroplast, mitochondrial damage, vacuolation, and increased number and size of pastoglobuli. Interestingly, the combined stress of both NaCl and Cadmium had an obvious beneficial effect on the plant growth, photosynthetic parameters and cell ultra-structure relative to Cadmium or Na stress alone in the two maize hybrids. The study suggested that there is involvement of same genetic and physiological mechanisms in response to both Cadmium and NaCl stresses.

A. Wahid & S. Khaliq (2015) they investigated that the influence of cadmium ($CdCl_2.2.5H_2O$) on some germination, morphological, biochemical and histological characteristics of developing embryonic tissue of maize. Cd stress reduced cortical cell size and vascular tissues, and deformed xylem and phloem parenchyma in all plant parts. In conclusion, the main reason for reduced germination was the influence of Cd on architecture of the coleorhiza and coleoptile, which was the result of oxidative stress and other physiological changes taking place in these tissues. Deng *et al.* (2016) reported that the effects of heavy metals (Cu^{2+}, Cd^{2+} and Hg^{2+}) on maize seed germination were investigated at 20 °C and 40 °C. Compared with 20 °C, heat stress induced thermodormancy. However, this thermodormancy could be significantly alleviated by the addition of a low concentration of heavy metals. Heavy metals, as well as heat stress induced H_2O_2 accumulation in germinating seeds. Accordingly, H_2O_2 addition, reinforced this promoting effect on seed germination, which was induced by a low concentration of heavy metal. However, this alleviation or aggravation could be partly attenuated by a low concentration of heavy metals. In addition, germination that was inhibited by high concentrations of heavy metals was also partly reversed by fluridone. The obtained results support the idea that heavy metal-mediated ROS and hormone interaction can finally affect the thermodormancy release or not. Zhang *et al.* (2016) reported that in order to evaluate the growth and physiological characteristics of maize plants under multiple heavy metal stress in rocky desertification soil, the pot experiment was conducted on 9 kinds of heavy metal contaminated soils from Yangshuo country in Guangxi. The results showed that low concentration of available heavy metal promoted the maize plant height and biomass of maize, while available heavy metal with high concentrations suppressed the growth and plant biomass of maize. Multiple heavy metal pollution could significantly affect the enzyme activity of maize plants ($P<0.05$). The results also showed that available heavy metal with low concentrations could decrease malondialdehyde (MDA) activity.

Efficacy of Mycorrhiza on Heavy Metal Toxicity in Zea Maize

Griffioen *et al.* (1994) investigate the possible natural development of heavy metal tolerance in VA-mycorrhizal fungi, plants of *Agrostis capillaris* from an uncontaminated, a copper-contaminated and a zinc/cadmium contaminated area was examined for VA-mycorrhizal infection. A detailed analysis of the surroundings of the copper-enriched site revealed the presence of VA-mycorrhizal fungi and a negative correlation between the infection rate of *A. capillaris* and the copper content of the soil. In contrast to the copper-contaminated soil, the abundant presence of VA-mycorrhizal fungi in the area contaminated by zinc and cadmium indicates that these fungi have evolved a zinc and cadmium tolerance and that they may play a role in the zinc and cadmium tolerance of *A. capillaris*. Weissenhorn *et al.* (1995) conducted an two pot-culture experiments with maize in a silty loam contaminated by atmospheric deposition from a metal smelter, root colonization by indigenous or introduced arbuscular mycorrhizal (AM) fungi and their influence on plant metal uptake (Cd, Zn, Cu, Pb, Mn) were investigated. suggesting a protection against metal toxicity. The results show that the influence of AM on plant metal uptake depends on plant growth conditions.It is suggested that metal-tolerant mycorrhizal inoculants might be considered for soil reclamation, since under adverse conditions AM may be more important for plant metal resistance.

Abdul Khaliq Muhammad Arshad Zahir, (1997) Observed that In a pot experiment conducted in a growth cabinet, maize cv. LG-11 plants were grown for two weeks in sterilized sand with and without VAM (*Glomuscaledonium*) inoculation at 3 phosphorus application levels (3, 10 and 30 mg kg-1). Inoculation significantly suppressed seedling growth, particularly in roots. Phosphorus inhibition of mycorrhizal infection increased with increasing rates of P application. Plant weight increased with increasing P rate.Mikael *et al.* (2004) examined that the Molecular and cellular mechanisms underlying the sustained metal tolerance of ectomycorrhizal fungi are largely unknown. Some of the main mechanisms involved in metal detoxification appear to involve the chelation of metal ions in the cytosol with thiol-containing compounds, such as glutathione, phytochelatins, or metallothioneins. We used an improved high-performance liquid chromatography method. We found that glutathione and γ-glutamylcysteine contents increased when the ectomycorrhizal fungus Paxillus involutus was exposed to cadmium. An additional compound with a 3-kDa molecular mass, most probably related to a metallothionein, increased drastically in mycelia exposed to cadmium. The relative lack of phytochelatins and the presence of a putative metallothionein suggest that ectomycorrhizal fungi may use a different means to tolerate heavy metals, such as Cd, than do their plant hosts (Figure 2.5).

Sathiyanathan, M. Kiran, M.V (2014) conducted to know the efficacy of mycorrihizaeon heavy metal toxicity in *Zea mays*. Heavy metal toxicity is an increasing problem in agriculture due to industrialization and urbanization. The application of mycorrhizal for crops was found to be promising and useful in reducing heavy metal toxicity and enhancing nutrient uptake. The efficacy of VAM in reducing the heavy metal toxicity is scantly studied and seldom exploited in heavy metal polluted soil. The present study aims at understanding the role of VAM in the reduction of heavy metal toxicity using the nitrate reductase system and the role of VAM in the alleviation, absorption and translocation of heavy metal.

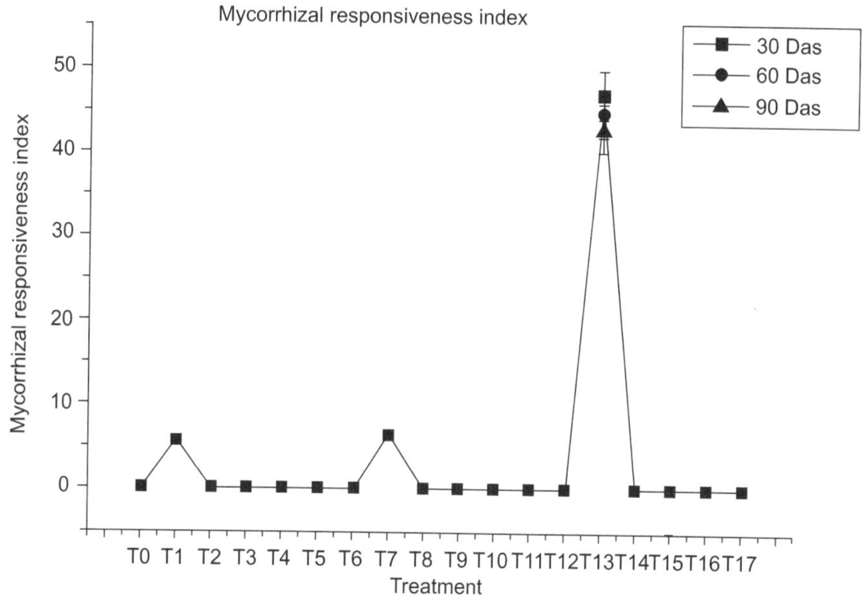

Fig. 2.5: Mycorrhizal responsiveness index of treated plants

(**Source:** Based on the author's research work, unpublished, 2017)

Physiological Function of Polyamines (Putrescine)

Raina A, Janne J (1975) reported the biochemistry and biological function of the naturally occurring polyamines, putrescine, spermidine, and spermine, have been reviewed with special reference to animal organisms. These compounds are universally distributed in all living material. Their biosynthesis from ornithine and methionine is accurately controlled and may fluctuate according to the metabolic needs of the cell. Polyamines strongly and specifically interact with nucleic acids in vitro. It appears that under physiological conditions a substantial portion of cellular polyamines is noncovalently bound to nucleic acids and nucleic acid-containing structures such as ribosomes. Polyamines are able to stimulate protein and ribonucleic acid synthesis in vitro. In several systems characterized by rapid growth polyamines and ribonucleic acid accumulate in parrallel. Evidence that polyamines may have an essential role in protein and/or nucleic acid synthesis is substantiated by recent observations on polyamine-deficient bacterial mutants, although no specific function has been established with certainty as yet. Some clinical applications of polyamine research related to cancer are also discussed briefly.Heby (1981) reported that the aliphatic polyamines, putrescine (1,4 diaminobutane), spermidine, and spermine, are normal cell constituents that play an important role in cell proliferation and differentiation. Pegg *et al.* (1982) Polyamines are ubiquitous organic cations of low molecular weight. The content of these amines is closely regulated by the cell according to the state of growth. The reactions responsible for the biosynthesis and interconversion of the polyamines and their precursor putrescine are described and the means by which polyamine content can be varied in response to exogenous stimuli are discussed. The role of polyamines in the cell cycle, cell division, tissue growth, and differentiation is considered. Recent studies using highly specific inhibitors of polyamine biosynthesis, such as alpha-difluoromethylornithine to prevent accumulation of polyamines have indicated that the synthesis of polyamines is intimately associated with these processes. Such inhibitors have great potential for investigation of the cellular role of polyamines. Galston *et. al.* (1990) The diamine putrescine, the triamine spermidine, and the tetramine spermine are ubiquitous in plant cells, while other polyamines are of more limited occurrence. Their chemistry and pathways of biosynthesis and metabolism are well characterized. In cereals, the activity of one of the major polyamine biosynthetic enzymes, arginine decarboxylase, is rapidly and dramatically increased by almost every studied external stress, leading to 50-fold or greater increases in putrescine titer within a few hours. Polyamines produced through the action of ornithine decarboxylase, by contrast, seem essential for DNA replication and cell division. The application of exogenous polyamines produces effects on patterns of senescence and morphogenesis, suggesting but not proving a regulatory role for polyamines in these processes. The evidence for such a regulatory roleis growing. Groppa *et al.* (2001) reported that role of Polyamines antioxidant properties in sunflower leaf discs under cadmium and copper induced oxidative stress. Both metals induced oxidative damage in the studied tissue, as evidenced by an increment in lipid peroxidation and a decrease in antioxidant enzymes ascorbate peroxidase (APOX), glutathione reductase (GR) and superoxide dismutase (SOD) activities. Polyamines concentrations were differently affected, according to the metal used. Putrescine (Put) was reduced 52% by Cd^{2+} and 39% by Cu^{2+}, spermidine (Spd) was decreased to 21 and 59% of the control by Cd^{2+} and Cu^{2+}, respectively and spermine (Spm) content was not modified by any of the metals. Pretreatment with exogenously added polyamines (1 mM) showed that Spm reverted the effect of Cd^{2+} and Cu^{2+} on lipid peroxidation almost to control values. This work suggests that polyamines are undoubtedly related to the protection against metal-induced oxidative stress.

CONCLUSION

Cd does not have any beneficial physiological role in plants, but when accumulated, it affects all aspects of growth and development. In plants, Cd is one of the most readily absorbed and most rapidly translocated heavy metals, and can cause numerous morphological and physiological changes even at low concentrations.

REFERENCES

Anonymous (2014-15). India Stat. Retrived from, https://www.indiastat.com/table/agriculture/2/totalcereals/963997/401525/data.aspx

https://www.indiastat.com/table/agriculture/2/maize/17199/454876/data.aspx

Abdul, G. (2010). Effect of Cadmium Toxicity on the Growth and Yield Components of Mungbean [*Vignaradiata* (L.) Wilczek]. World Applied Sciences Journal, 8(Special Issue), 26-29.

Adriano, D. C. (1986). Cadmium. In *Trace elements in the terrestrial environment* (pp. 106-155). Springer New York.

Andresen, E., & Küpper, H. (2013). Cadmium Toxicity in Plants. In *Cadmium: From Toxicity to Essentiality* (pp. 395-413). Springer Netherlands.

Auda, M. A., Zinada, I. A., & Ali, E. E. S. (2011). Accumulation of Heavy Metals in Crop Plants from Gaza Strip, Palestine and Study of the Physiological Parameters of Spinach Plants. *Journal of the Association of Arab Universities for Basic and Applied Sciences*, 10(1), 21-27.

Arduini, I., Masoni, A., Mariotti, M., Ercoli, L. (2004). Low Cadmium Application Increase Miscanthus Growth and Cadmium Translocation. Environmental and Experimental Botany, 52,89-100.

Azizian, A., Amin, S., Maftoun, M., Emam, Y. and Noshadi, M. (2013). Response of Corn to Cadmium and Drought Stress and Itsý Potential Use for Phytoremediation. *Journal of Agricultural Science and Technology*, 15(2), 303-310.

Bavi Khadijeh, Bahma Kholdebarin and AliMoradshashi (2006). Effect of Cadmium on Some of the Biochemical and Physiological Processes in Bean Plant. American Journal of Plant Physiology. 1(2),177-184.

Benavides, M. P., Gallego, S. M. and Tomaro, M. L. (2005). Cadmium Toxicity in Plants. *Brazilian Journal of Plant Physiology*, 17 (1), 21-34.

Bhardwaj, Priti, Ashish K. Chaturvedi, and P. Prasad. "Effect of Enhanced Lead and Cadmium in Soil on Physiological and Biochemical Attributes of Phaseolus Vulgaris." *L. Nat Sci* 7.8 (2009): 63-75.

Bhat, T. M., Choudhary, S., Ansari, M. Y. K. and Aslam, R. (2012). Genotoxicity and Molecular Screening of Proteins in Root Tip Cells of Trigonella Foenum-graecum (Fenugreek var-Azad) Under Cadmium Stress Condition. *International Journal of Plant Physiology and Biochemistry*, 4(3), 46-51.

Chen, X., Wang, J., Shi, Y., Zhao, M. Q. and Chi, G. Y. (2011). Effects of Cadmium on Growth and Photosynthetic Activities in Pakchoi and Mustard. *Bot Stud*, 52(1), 41-46.

Courbot, M., Diez, L., Ruotolo, R., Chalot, M. and Leroy, P. (2004). Cadmium-responsive Thiols in the Ectomycorrhizal Fungus Paxillus Involutus. *Applied and Environmental Microbiology*, **70**(12), 7413-7417.

Das, P., Samantaray, S. and Rout, G. R. (1997). Studies on Cadmium Toxicity in Plants: A Review. *Environmental Pollution*, **98**(1), 29-36.

Da-lin, L., Kai-qi, H., Jing-jing, M., Wei-wei, Q., Xiu-ping, W. and Shu-pan, Z. (2011). Effects of Cadmium on the Growth and Physiological Characteristics of Sorghum Plants. *African Journal of Biotechnology*, 10(70), 15770-15776.

de Andrade, S. A. and da Silveira, A. P. (2008). Mycorrhiza Influence on Maize Development Under Cd Stress and P Supply.

Deng, B., Yang, K., Zhang, Y. and Li, Z. (2016). Can Heavy Metal Pollution Defend Seed Germination Against Heat Stress? Effect of Heavy Metals ($Cu^{2+,}$ Cd^{2+} and $Hg^{2+)}$ on Maize Seed Germination Under High Temperature. *Environmental Pollution*, 216, 46-52.

Food and Agriculture Organization. (2014). Online Available at: http://faostat.fao.org. FAO, Rome.

Galli U, Schüepp H, Brunold C (1995). Thiols of Cu-treated Maize Plants Inoculated with the Arbuscular Mycorrhizal Fungus Glomus Intraradices. Physiol. Plant. 94,247-253.

Galston, A. W. and Sawhney, R. K. (1990). Polyamines in Plant Physiology. *Plant Physiology*, 94(2), 406-410.

Gaur, A. and Adholeya, A. (2004). Prospects of Arbuscular Mycorrhizal Fungi in Phytoremediation of Heavy Metal Contaminated Soils. *Curr Sci*, 86(4), 528-534.

Gill, S. S., and Tuteja, N. (2010). Polyamines and Abiotic Stress Tolerance in Plants. *Plant Signaling & Behavior*, 5(1), 26-33.

Ghani, A. (2010). Toxic Effects of Heavy Metals on Plant Growth and Metal Accumulation in Maize (Zea mays L.). Iranian Journal of Toxicology, 4(3), 325-334.

Godbold, D.L. and Huttermann, A. (1985). Effect of Zinc, Cadmium and Mercury on Root Elongation of *Picea abies* (Karst.) Seedlings, and the Significane of these Metals to Forest Die-back. *Environ. Pollution* (series A). 38, 375-381.

Groppa, M. D., Zawoznik, M. S., Tomaro, M. L. and Benavides, M. P. (2008). Inhibition of root Growth and Polyamine Metabolism in Sunflower (Helianthus annuus) Seedlings Under Cadmium and Copper Stress. *Biological Trace Element Research*, 126(1-3), 246.

Groppa, M. D., Tomaro, M. L. and Benavides, M. P. (2001). Polyamines as Protectors Against Cadmium or Copper-induced Oxidative Damage in Sunflower Leaf Discs. *Plant Science*, 161(3), 481-488.

Guo TR, Zhang GP, Zhou MX, Wu FB & Chen JX. 2007. Influence of Aluminum and Cadmium Stresses on Mineral Nutrition and Root Exudates in Two Barley Cultivars, *Pedosphere* 17, 505–512.

Hassan, M. J., Shao, G. and Zhang, G. (2005). Influence of Cadmium Toxicity on Growth and Antioxidant Enzyme Activity in Rice Cultivars with Different Grain Cadmium Accumulation. *Journal of Plant Nutrition*, 28(7), 1259-1270.

Hassen, A., Saidi, N., Cherif, M. and Boudabous, A. (1998). Resistance of Environmental Bacteria to Heavy Metals. *Bioresource Technology*, 64(1), 7-15.

Hasan, S. A., Fariduddin, Q., Ali, B., Hayat, S. and Ahmad, A. (2009). Cadmium: Toxicity and Tolerance in Plants.

Hayat, S. H. A. M. S. U. L., Hayat, Q., Alyemeni, M. N. and Ahmad, A. (2013). Nitrogen Metabolicsm and Activity of Antioxidative Enzymes in Chickpea Plants Grown in Cadmium Amended Soils. *Pak J Bot*, 45(3), 835-841.

Heby, O. (1981). Role of Polyamines in the Control of Cell Proliferation and Differentiation. *Differentiation*, 19(1-3), 1-20.

Hernandez LE, Carpena-Ruiza R & Garatea A., 1996. Alterations in the Mineral Nutrition of Pea Seedlings Exposed to Cadmium, *Journal of Plant Nutrition* 19, 1581–1598.

Hildebrandt, U., Regvar, M., & Bothe, H. (2007). Arbuscular Mycorrhiza and Heavy Metal Tolerance. *Phytochemistry*, 68(1), 139-146.

Hussain, I., Akhtar, S., Ashraf, M. A., Rasheed, R., Siddiqi, E. H. and Ibrahim, M. (2013). Response of Maize Seedlings to Cadmium Application After Different Time Intervals. *Isrn Agronomy*, 2013.

Jain, M., Pal, M., Gupta, P. and Gadre, R. (2007). Effect of Cadmium on Chlorophyll Biosynthesis and Enzymes of Nitrogen Assimilation in Greening Maize Leaf Segments: Role of 2-oxoglutarate.

Jing, D. O. N. G., Fei-bo, W. U. and Guo-ping, Z. (2005). Effect of Cadmium on Growth and Photosynthesis of Tomato Seedlings. *Journal of Zhejiang University-Science B*, 6(10), 974-980.

Karina BB, Benavides MP, Gallego SM & Tomaro ML. 2003. Effect of Cadmium Stress on Nitrogen Metabolism in Nodules and Roots of Soybean Plants, *Function Plant Biology* 30, 57– 64.

Keltjens, W.G. and van Beusichem, M. L. (1998), Phytochelatins as Biomarkers for Heavy Metal Toxicity in Maize: Single Metal Effects of Copper and Cadmium. Journal of Plant Nutrition. 21(4), 635-648.

Khaliq, A., Arshad, M., Zahir, Z. A. and Khalid, M. (1997). Effect of Vesicular-arbuscular Mycorrhizal (VAM) Inoculation and Phosphorus Application on Maize (*Zea mays* L.) Seedlings. *Sarhad Journal of Agriculture (Pakistan).*

Khan, W., Prithiviraj, B. and Smith, D. L. (2003). Photosynthetic Responses of Corn and Soybean to Foliar Application of Salicylates. *Journal of Plant Physiology*, 160(5), 485-492.

Khan, A. G., Kuek, C., Chaudhry, T. M., Khoo, C. S. and Hayes, W. J. (2000). Role of Plants, Mycorrhizae and Phytochelators in Heavy Metal Contaminated land Remediation. *Chemosphere*, 41(1), 197-207.

Khan, A., Ahmed, I., Lang, I., Ahmed, F., Ghani, A., Shah, A. and Tufail, S. (2012). Physiological and Biochemical Changes Produced in Maize (Zea mays L.) by the Application of Nickel. *Journal of Medicinal Plants Research*, 6(7),1340-1343.

Kurtyka, R., Ma³kowski, E., Kita, A. and Karcz, W. (2008). Effect of Calcium and Cadmium on Growth and Accumulation of Cadmium, Calcium, Potassium and Sodium in Maize Seedlings. *Polish Journal of Environmental Studies*, 17(1).

Lachman, J., Kotíková, Z., Zámeèníková, B., Miholová, D., Száková, J., & Vodièková, H. (2015). Effect of Cadmium Stress on Barley Tissue Damage and Essential Metal Transport into Plant. *Open Life Sciences*, 10(1), 30-39.

Liang, Y., Wong, J. W. C. and Wei, L. (2005). Silicon-mediated Enhancement of Cadmium Tolerance in Maize (*Zeamays* L.) Grown in Cadmium Contaminated Soil. *Chemosphere*, 58(4), 475-483.

Liu, J. G., Liang, J. S., Li, K. Q., Zhang, Z. J., Yu, B. Y., Lu, X. L. and Zhu, Q. S. (2003). Correlations Between Cadmium and Mineral Nutrients in Absorption and Accumulation in Various Genotypes of Rice Under Cadmium Stress. Chemosphere, 52(9), 1467-1473.

Mazen, A. M. A. (1995). Assessment of Heavy Metal Accumulation and Performance of Some Physiological Parameters in Zea Mays l. And Vic1a faba l. Grown on Soil Amended by Sewage Sludge Resulting from Sewage Water Treatment in the State of Qatar.

Mathur, A., Sharma, Y.C., Rupainwar, D.C., Murthy, R.C. and Chandra, S. (1987). A Study of River Ganga at Varanasi with Special Emphasis on Heavy Metal Pollution. Pollution Research, 6,37-44.

Metwally, A., Safronova, V. I., Belimov, A. A. and Dietz, K. J., 2005. Genotypic Variation of the Response to Cadmium Toxicity in Pisum Sativum L. *Journal of Experimental Botany*, 56(409), 167-178.

Mihailovic, N. (2010). Growth and Ion Uptake in Maize Plants Exposed to Pb, Cd and Ni Depend on NO_3/NH_4^+ ratio. Botanica Serbica, 34(1),15-20. Retrieved from http://ovidsp.ovid.com/ovidweb.cgi?T=JS&PAGE=reference&D=caba6&NEWS=N&AN=20103384457.

Mitchell, G. A., Bingham, F. T. and Page, A. L. (1978). Yield and Metal Composition of Lettuce and Wheat Grown on Soils Amended with Sewage Sludge Enriched with Cadmium, Copper, Nickel and Zinc. *Journal of Environmental Quality*, 7(2), 165-171.

Miri, M. R., Moghadam, H. R. T., Ghooshchi, F. and Zahedi, H. (2013). Effect of Azotobacter and Arbuscular Mycorrhizal Colonization Enhance Wheat Growth and Physiological traits Under Well-Watered and Drought Conditions. Advances in Environmental Biology, 4630-4637.

Mondal, N. K., Das, C., Roy, S., Datta, J. K. and Banerjee, A. (2013). Effect of Varying Cadmium Stress on Chickpea (*Cicer arietinum* l) seedlings: An Ultrastructural Study. *Annals of Environmental Science*, 7.

Monteiro, M. S., Santos, C., Soares, A. M. V. M. and Mann, R. M. (2009). Assessment of Biomarkers of Cadmium Stress in Lettuce. *Ecotoxicology and Environmental Safety*, 72(3), 811-818.

Muddathir, A. M. (2015). *Effect of Vesicular Arbuscular Mycorrhizal (Vam) Inoculation and Phosphorus Treatments on Growth and Yield of Three Onions (Allium Cepa L.) Cultivars* (Doctoral dissertation, UOFK).

Muneer, S., Hakeem, K. R., Mohamed, R. and Lee, J. H. (2014). Cadmium Toxicity Induced Alterations in the Root Proteome of Green Gram in Contrasting Response Towards Iron Supplement. *International Journal of Molecular Sciences*, 15(4), 6343-6355.

Nalini, P. and Chandra, P.S. (2002). Effect of Heavy Metals CO^{2+}, Ni^{2+} on Growth and Metabolism of Cabbage. Plant Science, 163, 753-758.

Nazar, R., Iqbal, N., Masood, A., Khan, M. I. R., Syeed, S., & Khan, N. A. (2012). Cadmium Toxicity in Plants and Role of Mineral Nutrients in Its Alleviation.

Pál, M., Horváth, E., Janda, T., Páldi, E. and Szalai, G. (2006). Physiological Changes and Defense Mechanisms Induced by Cadmium Stress in Maize. *Journal of Plant Nutrition and Soil Science*, 169(2), 239-246.

Pandey, N. and Sharma, C. P. (2002). Effect of Heavy Metals Co^{2+}, Ni^{2+} and Cd^{2+} on Growth and Metabolism of Cabbage. *Plant Science*, 163(4), 753-758.

Parmar, P., Kumari, N. and Sharma, V. (2013). Structural and Functional Alterations in Photosynthetic Apparatus of Plants Under Cadmium Stress. *Botanical Studies*, 54(1), 45.

Pegg, A. E. and McCann, P. P. (1982). Polyamine Metabolism and Function. *American Journal of Physiology-Cell Physiology*, 243(5), C212-C221.

Raina, A. and Jänne, J. (1975). Physiology of the Natural Polyamines Putrescine, Spermidine and Spermine. *Medical biology*, 53(3), 121-147.

Rodríguez-Serrano, M., Romero-Puertas, M. C., Pazmino, D. M., Testillano, P. S., Risueño, M. C., Luis, A. and Sandalio, L. M. (2009). Cellular Response of Pea Plants to Cadmium Toxicity: Cross Talk Between Reactive Oxygen Species, Nitric Oxide, and Calcium. *Plant Physiology*, 150(1), 229-243.

Sandalio, L. M., Dalurzo, H. C., Gomez, M., RomeroPuertas, M. C. and Del Rio, L. A. (2001). Cadmiuminduced Changes in the Growth and Oxidative Metabolism of Pea Plants. *Journal of Experimental Botany*, 52(364), 2115-2126.

Sathiyanathan, M. and Kiran, M. V. (2014). In vitro Efficacy of Mycorrhizae on Heavy Metal Toxicity in Zea Mays. *Int. J. Curr. Microbiol. App. Sci*, 3(4), 942-949.

Singh PK. And Tewari RK. (2003). Effects of Heavy Metals on Plant Growth and Photosynthetic Activity. Journal of Environmental Biology. **24** (1), 107-112.

Singh, S. and Aggarwal, P.K. (2006). Efect of Heavy Metals on Biomass and Yield of Different Crop Species. *Indian J. Agril. Sci.***76**(11): 688-691.

Široká, B., Huttová, J., Tamás, L., Šimonovièová, M. and Mistrík, I. (2004). Effect of Cadmium on Hydrolytic Enzymes in Maize Root and Coleoptile. Biologia, **59**, 513-517.

Sharma, R. K., Agrawal, M., & Agrawal, S. B. (201). Physiological, Biochemical and Growth Responses of Lady's Finger (*Abelmoschusesculentus* L.) Plants as Affected by Cd Contaminated Soil. *Bulletin of Environmental Contamination and Toxicology*, **84**(6), 765-770.

Sharma, S. S. and Dietz, K. J. (2006). The Significance of Amino Acids and Amino Acid-derived Molecules in Plant Responses and Adaptation to Heavy Metal Stress. *Journal of Experimental Botany*, **57**(4), 711-726.

Stingu, A., Stanescu, I., Volf, I. and Popa, V. I. (2011). Hyperaccumulation of Cadmium in Maize Plant (Zea mays). *Cellulose Chemistry and Technology*, **45**(3-4), 287-290.

Subramanian, K. S. and Charest, C. (1997). Nutritional, Growth and Reproductive Responses of Maize (Zea mays L.) to Arbuscular Mycorrhizal Inoculation during and After Drought Stress at Tasselling. *Mycorrhiza*, **7**(1), 25-32.

Subramanian, K. S. and Charest, C. (1999). Acquisition of N by External Hyphae of an Arbuscular Mycorrhizal Fungus and Its Impact on Physiological Responses in Maize Under Drought-stressed and Well-watered Conditions. *Mycorrhiza*, **9**(2), 69-75.

Vassilev, A., Iordanov, I., Chakalova, E. and Kerin, V. (1995). Effect of Cadmium Stress on Growth and Photo-synthesis of Young Barley (H. vulgare L.) Plants. 2. Structural and Functional Changes in the Photosynthetic Apparatus.

Wahid, A. and Khaliq, S. (2015). Architectural and Biochemical Changes in Embryonic Tissues of Maize Under Cadmium Toxicity. *Plant Biology*, **17**(5), 1005-1012.

Wang, B., Li, Z., Eneji, E., Tian, X., Zhai, Z., Li, J. and Duan, L. (2008). Effects of Coronatine on Growth, Gas Exchange Traits, Chlorophyll Content, Antioxidant Enzymes and Lipid Peroxidation in Maize (Zea mays L.) Seedlings Under Simulated Drought Stress. *Plant Production Science*, **11**(3), 67-75.

Weissenhorn I, Leyval C, Berthelin J (1993) Cd-tolerant Arbuscular Mycorrhizal (AM) Fungi from Heavy-metal Polluted Soils. Plant Soil 157, 247-256.

Weissenhorn, I., Leyval, C., Belgy, G. and Berthelin, J. (1995). Arbuscular Mycorrhizal Contribution to Heavy Metal Uptake by Maize (*Zea mays* L.) in Pot Culture with Contaminated Soil. *Mycorrhiza*, **5**(4), 245-251.

Yusuf, M., Fariduddin, Q. and Ahmad, A. (2011). 28-Homobrassinolide Mitigates Boron Induced Toxicity Through Enhanced Antioxidant System in Vigna Radiata Plants. *Chemosphere*, **85**(10), 1574-1584.

Zhang, Y., Li, S., Xiong, L., Ye, L. and Jiang, J. (2016). Effects of Multiple Heavy Metal Stress on Growth and Physiological Characteristics of Maize in Rocky Desertification Region in Guangxi. *Southwest China Journal of Agricultural Sciences*, **29**(9), 2079-2085.

Plant Response to Environmental Stress **Page: 28-41**
Edited by: Dr. Alka Chauhan; Dr. Pawan Kumar 'Bharti' and Dr. Avnish Chauhan
ISBN: 978-93-86841-58-2
Edition: 2018
Published by: Discovery Publishing House Pvt. Ltd., New Delhi (India)

3

The Effect of Air Pollution on Pigments, Growth and Yield of Wheat Plant in Urban Area of Haridwar, Uttarakhand, India

Avnish Chauhan[1]

ABSTRACT

The present study was carried out to determine the effect of ambient gaseous and dust pollutants on wheat plants. The wheat plants at polluted site showed significant reduction in pigments (viz. chlorophyll "a", Chlorophyll "b", Total Chlorophyll, Carotenoids, Ascorbic Acid and Air Pollution Tolerance Index), plant height, shoot length, root length, shoot dry weight, root fresh weight, Root dry weight and number of grains per plant.

Key words: Photosynthetic pigments, chlorophyll, carotenoids, ascorbic acid, wheat plants, dust pollution.

INTRODUCTION

Air pollution is a broad term which can be defined as the presence of a substance, which has harmful or poisonous effects in the air (Anoob *et al.*, 2017). Air pollution has become a serious environmental stress to crop plants due to increasing industrialization during las few decades (Chauhan, 2013). Traffic emissions are the main source of air pollution in cities around the globe (Kumar *et al.*, 2013, 2015, 2016). Due to sharp increase in the vehicular population in recent years, the automobile emissions now constitute major sources of environmental pollution all over the world. In developing countries like India the problem is much more aggravated due to factors such as narrow and congested highways and old and poorly maintained vehicles (Pal *et al.*, 2000). Air pollution now becomes threat for our environment, health, plants and crops. In developing country like India, this problem is very considerable because in India about 70-75% Indians are involve in agriculture by directly and indirectly. Sixty to seventy percent of the pollution in urban environments is due to motors vehicles. With the increase in urbanization and industrialization and commercial activities in the urban areas, the demand for transport has also increased considerably. Normal air contains about 78% nitrogen and 21% oxygen, the remaining 1%

[1] Department of Applied Science, Phonics Group of Institutions, Roorkee, Haridwar-247667, India

is made up of carbon dioxide and several other trace gases. The average adult human exchanges about 16 kg of gases per day, about six times the weight of food and water consumed. Any alteration in the atmosphere effects the growth of plants and their yield which are of utmost concern to the man's perspectives (Mandloi and Dubey 2000). The important air pollutants which affect the well being of mankind, animals, and vegetation are sulphur dioxide (SO_2), oxides of nitrogen (NO_x), ozone (O_3), suspended particulate matters (SPM), hydrocarbons (HCs) and different heavy metals in the form of aerosols (Rao *et. al.* 1977). Air pollution of major concern in India is particulate and gaseous pollutants. Air pollution has become a serious environmental stress to crop plants due to increasing industrialization and urbanization during last few decades. The gaseous air pollutants known to cause adverse impact on crop production are sulphur dioxide (SO_2), nitrogen oxides (NO_x) and ozone (O_3) (Agrawal 2000). Emissions of these pollutants are increasing in India due to massive increase in urbanization and consequent increase in number of vehicles and small scale industries in cities (Rajput and Agrawal, 2004). Plants are invariably exposed to the mixture of air pollutants in the atmosphere. Many workers have described the effects of mixture of pollutants on plants field and laboratory conditions (Grosso *et al.*, 1971; Singh and Rao, 1981; Applegate and Durant, 1969; Chaphekar *et al.*, 1979). Crop plants have the ability to take up atmospheric gases without active metabolism and therefore, vegetation serve as a natural sink for air pollutants by providing expanded leaves for the absorption and setting of gases and particulate matter. The SO_2 and NO_2 gases reduced growth and yield of crops (Gupta and Sabaratnam, 1988; Anbazhagan and Bhagwat, 1991). Sulphur dioxide is one of the most prevalent phytotoxic air-pollutants and causes substantial damage to green plants (Khan and Khan, 1993). SO_2 and NO_x are known as a strongly damaging air pollutant (Cheng *et. al.* 2007).There is growing concern that air pollution may have adverse impacts on crops in developing countries, yet this has been little studied (Agrawal *et al.*, 2006). Sulphur dioxide is the most common air pollutant which causes damage to plants growing in vicinity of the sources which produces SO_2. It is known that SO_2 alters the metabolic processes of plants (Wellburn, 1982; Ziegler 1972), decreases their photosynthetic activity (White *et al.*, 1974; Black and Unsworth 1979) and yield (Thomas 1961; Godzik and Krupa 1982). Some workers reported that, even in the absence of visible injury, growth and yield have been reduced as a result of long-term to low concentrations of pollutants (Bell *et al.*, 1979; Bleasdale, 1973; Davies, 1980).Sulphur dioxide SO_2 is a primary air pollutant (Wilson and Murray, 1990). It is now well established that SO_2 can affect productivity of agricultural crops and forests (Last, 1982; Roberts, 1984; Treshow, 1984). Long-term, low-concentration exposures of plants to air pollutants often do not produce visible injury to the plant leaves. Even if injury occurs, degrees of chlorosis or necrosis are difficult to asses and quantify. Early assessment of crop yield losses using bioindicators may also be of a great value to agriculturists (Bytnerowicz *et al.*, 1987). Sulphur dioxide is one of the major gaseous air pollutants that cause damage to agricultural crops and natural vegetation. Reduced plant growth in the absence of visible injury has also been observed at relatively low ambient SO_2 concentrations (Lockyer *et al.*, 1976; Ashenden and Mansfield, 1977; Sprugel *et al.*, 1980).

MATERIALS AND METHODS

Study Area

Study was carried out to conduct the impact of air pollutants on wheat plants urban area of Hardwar. Hardwar is extended from latitude 29° 58′ in the north to longitude 78°13′ in the east. Hardwar is one of the holy cities in India and receives millions of tourist every month, sometimes in a day. After declaration of industrial zone in Hardwar city, there are almost more than 100% increase in population of Hardwar city, resulted very rapidly increase in number of vehicles and transportation facilities.

Study Sites

The present study was conducted in the urban area of shivalik nagar (referred as polluted site) and agriculture land about 2 km far from polluted site (referred to as control site). Shivalik nagar, which is 8 km far from Gurukul Kangri University, Hardwar. Shivalik nagar connect Industrial area to National Highway no. 58. There are very heavy traffic load, including large trucks, load trucks, mini trucks, private buses, very high number of three wheeler, cars, scooter, bikes etc., on the other hand the agricultural land take as control site no pollution source found.

Air Pollution Monotoring

Concentration of air pollutants viz. NO_x, SO_2, SPM and RSPM was measured with the help of RDS APM 460 by sucking air into appropriate reagent for 24 hours at every 30 days and after air monitoring it procured into lab and analysis for the concentration level. The concentration of NO_x was measured with standard method of Modified Jacobs- Hochheiser method (1958), SO_2 was measured by Modified West and Geake method (1956), SPM and RSPM using filter paper methods. The apparatus was kept at a height of 2 m from the surface of the ground.

Plalnt Sampling and Analysis

The studies were conducted on wheat plant (*Triticum aestivum*, var., PBW 343) growing under field condition. Crop samples were analyzed at every 30 days of intervals from 30th day of sowing to of crop maturity. The samples (in five replicates of wheat plants) were collected arbitrarily from both the site, polluted and control and washed carefully under tap water. The chlorophyll 'a', 'b' and total chlorophyll and carotenoids in the leaves of selected plant species were determined as per Arnon (1949) method. Ascorbic acid was determined by the method of Sadasivam and Manikam (1991). Air pollution tolerance index (APTI) was estimated using the method of by Singh and Rao (1983). The shoot length, root length and plant height were measure with the help of measuring tape. Shoot length was measured from the ground surface to the tip of the highest up stretched leaf with the help of measuring tape. Stem fresh and dry weight, root fresh and dry weight with the help of single PAN balance at a period of 30 days intervals. Stem (including petiole) was taken without leaves. Number of grains plant^{-1} by direct count method, dry grains plant^{-1} and 100 dry grains weight plant^{-1} were analysed with the help of single PAN balance.

Statistical Analysis

For the plant materials two-way-analysis of variance was performed. Least Significance Difference was calculated at 0.05%, 0.01% and 0.001% level as per standard method of Gomez and Gomez 1984.

RESULTS AND DISCUSSION

Air Pollution Monotoring

The 24 hr means concentration of primary pollutants during wheat seasons shown in Table 3.1.

Table 3.1: Concentration of Some Air Pollutants at Polluted Site During Wheat Crop.

Year-2006	**SO_2 µg m^{-3}**	**NO_x µg m^{-3}**	**SPM µg m^{-3}**	**RSPM µg m^{-3}**
January	10.12	13.42	379.21	125.21
February	12.40	16.30	388.95	139.42
March	9.80	18.44	402.29	111.23
April	11.40	15.80	407.12	122.43
Year-2007	**SO_2 µg m^{-3}**	**NO_x µg m^{-3}**	**SPM µg m^{-3}**	**RSPM µg m^{-3}**
January	9.82	16.28	423.19	123.20
February	10.80	17.32	412.18	128.20
March	13.36	19.18	404.24	135.80
April	10.12	16.70	401.34	125.44
CPCB standard (24 hr)	80.00 µg m^{-3}	80.00 µg m^{-3}	200.00 µg m^{-3}	

Concentration of SO_2, NOx, SPM and RSPM were reported as 10.12 µg m^{-3}, 13.42 µg m^{-3}, 379.21µg m^{-3} and 125.21 µg m^{-3} respectively in January 2006. In February 2006, the concentration of SO_2, NOx, SPM and RSPM were reported as 12.40 µg m^{-3}, 16.30 µg m^{-3}, 388.95 µg m^{-3} and 139.42 µg m^{-3} respectively.

Concentration of SO_2, NOx, SPM and RSPM were reported as 9.80 μg m^{-3}, 18.44 μg m^{-3}, 402.29 μg m^{-3} and 111.23 μg m^{-3} respectively in March 2006, While in April 2006 the concentration of Concentration of SO_2, NOx, SPM and RSPM were reported as 11.40 μg m^{-3}, 15.80 μg m^{-3}, 407.12 μg m^{-3} and 122.43 μg m^{-3} respectively.

In January 2007, the concentration of SO_2, NOx, SPM and RSPM were reported as 9.82 μg m^{-3}, 16.28 μg m^{-3}, 423.19 μg m^{-3} and 123.20 μg m^{-3} respectively, While in February 2007 , the concentration of SO_2, NOx, SPM and RSPM were reported as 10.80 μg m^{-3}, 17.32 μg m^{-3}, 412.18 μg m^{-3} and 128.20 μg m^{-3} respectively. In March 2007, the concentration of SO_2, NOx, SPM and RSPM were reported as 10.06 μg m^{-3}, 19.18 μg m^{-3}, 401.21 μg m^{-3} and 135.80 μg m^{-3} respectively, Whereas in April 2007, the concentration of SO_2, NOx, SPM and RSPM were reported as 10.12 μg m^{-3}, 16.70 μg m^{-3}, 401.34 μg m^{-3} and 125.44 μg m^{-3} respectively.

The concentration of SO_2, NOx, SPM and RSPM were found higher than as described by Joshi *et al.* (2006). The results shows the concentration of gaseous pollutants remained under the limit prescribed by Central Pollution Control Board (CPCB), however, particulate matter (SPM and RSPM) were higher than the prescribed limits of CPCB, New Delhi, India.

Pigments, Growth and Yield

The amounts chlorophyll 'a', chlorophyll 'b', Total chlorophyll, carotenoids, ascorbic acid, relative moisture content, pH and air pollution tolerance index are shown in Table 3.2.

Table 3.2: Concentration of Different Photosynthetic Pigments in the Leaves of Wheat Crops Collected from Polluted and Control Area in March 2006 and 2007 (Mean of 10 replicates ± SE)

Years	Wheat plants in 2006			Wheat plants in 2007		
Pigments	Control	Polluted	%R	Control	Polluted	%R
Chlorophyll "a" (mg/g)	2.79	2.57**	7.89	2.78	2.54**	8.63
Chlorophyll "b" (mg/g)	1.81	1.53***	15.47	1.82	1.43***	17.93
Total Chlorophyll (mg/g)	4.60	4.09**	11.09	4.59	4.03**	4.58
Carotenoids (mg/g)	1.36	1.21**	11.03	1.31	1.23*	6.11
Ascorbic Acid (mg/100gm)	1.85	1.25***	32.43	1.82	1.25***	31.31
Relative moisture content%	67.15	63.08^{ns}	6.06	68.71	62.57^{ns}	8.94
pH	6.15	5.81^{ns}	5.53	6.17	5.86^{ns}	5.02
Air Pollution Tolerance Index	8.71	7.54***	13.43	8.84	7.49***	s15.27

Significant at: *$p < 0.05$, **$p<0.01$, ***$p<0.001$, ns = non significant, N.A. = not analysed, C = control site, P = polluted site and%R reduction percentage.

Wheat Plant Pigments 2006

Chlorophyll 'a' and chlorophyll 'b' contents of *Triticum aestivum* were reported as 2.79 and 2.57 mg per gm in control and polluted site respectively. Thus a decrease of 7.89% was recorded at polluted site in chlorophyll 'a' as comparison to control site, showed significant reduction. While in case of chlorophyll 'b' a decrease of 15.47 was recorded and also showed significant reduction. Total chlorophyll in showed significant reduction at polluted site as compared control site. Carotenoid recorded in polluted site was 1.36, but at polluted site it was 1.21 mg/g, thus a significant reduction of 11.03% at polluted site as compared to control site. Ascorbic acid content recorded was 1.85 mg per 100 gm and 1.25 mg per 100 gm at control and polluted site respectively. Thus a reduction of 32.43% was recorded. Relative moisture content recorded at control site was 67.15 whereas it was 63.08 at polluted site. Thus there was a reduction of 6.06% in relative moisture content of samples collected from polluted site as compared to control. pH of leaves collected from polluted site was recorded as 6.15, where as at polluted site it was recorded as 5.81. Thus a change of 5.53% was recorded in the samples collected from polluted site. Air pollution tolerance index at control and polluted site were 8.71 and 7.54 respectively, showed significant reduction.

Wheat Plant Pigments 2007

Chlorophyll 'a' and chlorophyll 'b' contents of wheat in 2007 were reported as 2.78 and 1.82 mg per gm in control and 2.54 and 1.43 mg per gm at polluted site respectively. Thus a decrease of 8.63% and 17.93% reported in chlorophyll 'a' and chlorophyll 'b' at polluted sites as compared to control sites, showed significant reductions at both sites. Total chlorophyll recorded at polluted 4.03 mg per gm which was 4.59 mg per gm at control site, thus there was a 4.58% reduction at polluted site as compared to control site. Carotenoids recorded at control and polluted site were 1.31 mg per gm and 1.23 mg per gm respectively, thus in this case there was a significant reduction of 6.11% in polluted site as compared to polluted site. Ascorbic acid showed significant reduction of 31.31% at polluted site as compared to control site. Relative moisture content of leaves was slightly higher (68.71) in the plants samples collected from polluted site as compared to samples collected from control (62.57) site, did not show any significant reduction. pH of leaves of polluted site was recorded as 5.86, whereas pH of leaves samples collected from control site was recorded as 6.17. Thus a change of 5.02% towards the acidic side was recorded in the samples collected from polluted site, did not show significant reduction. Air pollution tolerance index at control and polluted site were 8.84 and 7.49 respectively, showed significant reduction.

Singh & Rao (1980) studied that dust pollution originated from cement factory, adversely affected the chlorophyll content and 100 grains weight of wheat plants. Agrawal et al (1982) reported that exposure of rice plants to low concentration of SO_2 adversely affected chlorophyll a , chlorophyll b , total chlorophyll and carotenoids content. Varshney and Varshney (1984) found that SO_2 exposed to *Brassica nigra* L. and *Phaseolus radiatus* L., reduced the ascorbic acid. Shukla *et al.* (1990) revealed that cement dust adversely affected the chlorophyll content of *Brassica campestris* L. Dusted or encrusted leaf surface is responsible for reduced photosynthesis and thereby causing reduction in chlorophyll content. Saquib & Khan (1999) reported that mustard plant growing at polluted site showed reduction in chlorophyll a, chlorophyll b and total chlorophyll in comparison to reference site. Rajput and Agrawal (2005) reported that wheat plant growing at polluted site showed reduction in total chlorophyll, carotenoids and ascorbic acid. Sabaratnam and Gupta (1988) reported that different concentration of NO_2 adversely affected soybean plants chlorophyll a, chlorophyll b and total chlorophyll. Mandloi & Dubey (2000) reported the effect of different concentration of SO_2 and cement dust reduced the total chlorophyll of wheat plants. Agrawal and Deepak 2003 reported that SO2 reduced the total chlorophyll and ascorbic acid of wheat plants (*Triticum aestivum* L. cv. Malviya 234 and HP 1209). Singh *et al.* (2005) studied the impact of air pollution reduced the total chlorophyll, carotenoids and ascorbic acid of palak (*Beta vulgaris*) leaves.

Table-3.3 for Wheat Plants Growth Parameters in 2006

Shoot length of wheat plants 24.98 cm and 23.68 cm in control and polluted site respectively in January whereas these were 87.61 cm and 83.52 at control site and polluted site respectively. Shoot length did not show any significant reduction from January to April. Root length reported as 7.0 cm and 6.44 cm at control and polluted site in January 07, the significant decrease in root length in Jan, compared to control site and showed very highly significant reduction in Feb., march and April 2006. Plant height reported as 31.98 cm, 72.38, 86.60 and 102.10 cm in Jan, Feb., March and April at control site however it was 30.12 cm.69 cm, 82.34 cm and 94.54 cm in Jan, Feb., March and April at polluted site, respectively. Plant height at polluted showed very highly significant reduction as compared to control site. Stem fresh weight showed non significant reduction in Jan, Feb and March, but in April it was not analysed because it became dry at maturity (April). Stem fresh weight reported as 0.30 gm, 6.91 gm, 7.92 gm and 9.26 gm in Jan, Feb, March and April at control site, respectively but at polluted site it was 0.22 gm, 5.72 gm, 6.13 gm and 7.78 gm in Jan, Feb, March and April, respectively, thus showed significant reduction in all four months (Jan-April). Root fresh weight as 0.21 gm and 0.12 gm at control and pollutes site, respectively in Jan. In March it was 28.34 gm and 25.75 gm at control and polluted site, thus showed significant reduction. Root dry weight reported as 0.04 gm and 0.02 gm at control and polluted site, respectively, showed non significant reduction. Root dry weight in Feb reported as 3.77 gm and 2.88 gm at control and polluted site respectively, showed significant reduction.

Table 3.3: Showing the Value of Plants Growth Parameters for Year of 2006.

Months	January 2006			February 2006			March 2006			April 2007		
Para-meters	C	P	% R	C	P	% R	C	P	% R	C	P	% R
Shoot length (cm)	24.98	23.68 ns	5.20	63.36	61.60 ns	2.78	75.30	73.14 ns	2.87	87.61	83.52 ns	4.67
Root length (cm)	7.00	6.44 *	8.00	9.02	7.40 ***	17.96	11.30	9.20 ***	18.58	14.50	11.02 ***	24.00
Plant height (cm)	31.98	30.12 ***	5.82	72.38	69.00 ***	4.67	86.60	82.34 ***	4.92	102.10	94.54 ***	7.40
Stem fresh weight (gm)	1.21	0.94 ns	22.31	56.90	50.41 ns	11.41	68.52	62.86 ns	8.26	N.A.	N.A.	N.A.
Stem dry weight (gm)	0.30	0.22 ***	26.67	6.91	5.72 ***	17.22	7.92	6.13 ***	22.60	9.26	7.78***	15.98
Root fresh weight (gm)	0.21	0.12 ns	42.86	26.00	21.13 ***	18.73	28.34	25.75 ***	9.14	N.A.	N.A.	N.A.
Root dry weight (gm)	0.04	0.02 ns	50.00	3.77	2.84 ***	24.67	23.14	17.92 ***	22.56	28.51	23.67 ***	16.98

Significant at: $^{*}p < 0.05$, $^{**}p<0.01$, $^{***}p<0.001$, ns = non significant, N.A. = not analysed, C = control site, P = polluted site and%R reduction percentage.

Table-3.4 for Growth Parameters in 2007

Shoot length reported as 28.24 cm, 64.84 cm, 75.74 cm and 85.36 cm in Jan, Feb, March and April at control site, respectively whereas at polluted site it was 26.04cm, 63.76 cm, 73.84 cm and 81.04 cm in Jan, Feb, March and April at polluted site, respectively. Root length reported as 9.40 cm and 8.10 cm at control and polluted site, respectively in January however in April it was reported as 85.36 cm and 81.04 cm at control and polluted site, respectively, thus showed significant reduction as compared to control site. Plant height reported as 37.64 cm and 34.14cm at control and polluted site, respectively in Jan whereas in April it was reported as 100.2 cm and 92.58 cm at control and pollutes site, respectively, showed significant reduction. Stem fresh weight reported as 1.23 gm and 1.04 gm at control site and polluted site, respectively, thus a decrease of 15.45% was recorded at polluted site as compared to control site, showed significant reduction. Stem dry weight did not show any significant reduction at control site as compared to polluted site January but in Feb, March and April show significant reduction. Root fresh weight was reported as 0.41 gm and 0.29 gm at control and pollutes site, respectively in Jan thus showed a reduction of 29.27% whereas in March it was 25.49 gm and 21.03 gm at control and polluted site, thus showed significant reduction. Root dry weight was reported as 0.06 gm and 0.03 gm in January at control and polluted site, respectively, showed non significant reduction, whereas in April it was reported as 5.65 gm and 4.81 gm at control and polluted site respectively, showed a significant reduction.

Table 3.4: Showing the Value of Plants Growth Parameters for Year of 2007.

Months	January 2007			February 2007			March 2007			April 2007		
Parameters	C	P	%R	C	P	%R	C	P	%R	C	P	%R
Shoot length (cm)	28.24	26.04 *	7.79	64.84	63.76 ns	1.67	75.74	73.84*	2.50	85.36	81.04 ***	5.06
Root length (cm)	9.40	8.10 **	13.83	11.82	9.66 ***	18.27	12.70	10.88 *** 9.37	14.84	11.54 ***	22.24	
Plant height (cm)	37.64	34.14 *	9.29	76.66	73.42 *	4.22	88.44	85.00 *	3.89	100.20	92.58 ***	7.60
Stem fresh weight (gm)	1.23	1.04 ***	15.45	56.94	50.07 ***	10.31	68.21	62.34 ***	8.61	N.A.	N.A.	N.A.
Stem dry weight (gm)	0.39	0.28^{ns}	28.20	6.93	5.78 ***	16.59	8.02	7.03 ***	12.34	9.21	7.51 ***	18.46
Root fresh weight (gm)	0.41	0.29 ns	29.27	25.49	21.03 ***	17.49	28.40	26.15 ***	7.92	N.A.	N.A.	N.A.
Root dry weight (gm)	0.06	0.03 ns	50.00	3.53	2.92 ***	17.28	4.51	3.66 ***	18.85	5.65	4.81 ***	14.87

Significant at: *$p < 0.05$, **$p<0.01$, ***$p<0.001$, ns = non significant, N.A. = not analysed, C= control site, P= polluted site and%R reduction percentage.

Table 3.5 for Comparative Study for Yield in 2006 and 2007

Difference in number of grain per plants, grain weight per plant (gm) and 100 grain weight per plant showed in Table 3.5. Number of grains per plant in 2006 at control and polluted site was reported as 157.00 and 148.80, respectively, showed significant reduction whereas in 2007 it was reported as 156.40 and 147.00 at control and polluted site respectively, also showed significant reduction. Grain weight per plant in 2006 was reported as 11.10 gm and 9.06 gm at control and polluted site, respectively, showed significant reduction at polluted site as compared to polluted site whereas in 2007 it was reported as 10.61 and 9.13 gm, also showed significant reduction. 100 grain weight in 2006 was reported as 7.07 gm and 6.37 gkm at control and polluted site, respectively, showed significant reduction at polluted site as compared to polluted site whereas in 2007 it was reported as 6.83 gm and 6.24 gm, respectively, also showed significant reduction.

Table 3.5

Years	Wheat plants in 2006			Wheat plants in 2007		
Yield	Control	Polluted	% R	Control	Polluted	% R
Number of grains per plant	157.00	148.80 ***	5.52	156.40	147.00***	6.01
Grains weight per plant (gm)	11.10	9.06*	18.38	10.61	9.13*	13.95
100 grains per plant (gm)	7.07	6.37***	9.90	6.83	6.24**	8.64

Significant at: $*p < 0.05$, $**p<0.01$, $***p<0.001$, ns = non significant, N.A. = not analysed, C= control site, P= polluted site and%R reduction percentage.

Shukla *et al.* (1990) found that when plants of *Brassica campestris* L. treated with cement dust, did not showed any symptoms of foliar injury, but showed stunted growth in comparison with the controls site. A significant reduction in height of treated plants compared with their controls was observed. When wheat plants exposed to ambient air pollution, showed reduction in number of ears per plant, number of grain per ears and 1000 grain weight significantly Maggs *et al.* (1995). Agrawal *et al.* (2003) reported that NO_2 and SO_2 reduced, plant height in wheat and mustard plants and the yield about 25% and 20% respectively. Pandey and Agrawal (1994) have reported reduction in height of three woody perennial under varying level of air pollution stress in urban environment of Varansi. SO_2 and HF (Hydrogen Fluoride) have been found disturb metabolic activities in plant resulting reduction in reduced growth and yield Matsushima and Brewer (1972) SO_2 at 0.5 ppm concentration reduced number of spikes plant^{-1}, number of grain spike^{-1}, yield as gm plant^{-1} and 1000 grains of wheat plants as compared to control site. SO_2 adversely affected and reduced the total seed weight and 100 seed weight of winter wheat. The higher level of SO_2 reduced shoot weight, number of ears. Wilson and Murray (1990) found that SO_2 exposure to wheat plant, significantly reduced growth of wheat plants. Davieson *et al.* (1990) reported that exposure of SO_2 to wheat cv. Eradu to 0.05 μl litre^{-1} reduced the dry weight of shoots, ears and grain by approximately 25%. Bytnerowicz *et al.* (1987) yield reductions in wheat cv. Yecora Rojo after exposure to SO_2 for 118 days. Compared to the CF (charcoal filter) open-top chamber treatments, the NF (non filter) open-top chamber showed a significant reduction of the percentage dry matter of stem and leaves, 1000 grain weight was reduced significantly in the NF OTC and root growth was most adversely affected Vandermeiren *et al.* (1989). It is most likely that the reduction in root growth mainly attribute to NO_2 and SO_2 uptake by the leaves. Singh and Prakash (1995) studied and found that exposure of SO_2 to wheat plant reduced plant height of root and shoot, dry weight of shoot and root and whole plants, number of tillers per plants.

Decrease in shoot and root lengths have also been reported by Khan and Khan (1991) and Gupta *et al.* (1993).Wahid *et al.* (1995) carried study using open-top chambers ventilated with ambient or charcoal-filtered air in Pakistan and found that it reduced the tiller number, yield, total 1000 grain weight, number of ear per plant and number of grain per ear of wheat plants in ambient unfiltered air (UFA), compared to activated charcoal filtered (FA). Rajput and Agrawal (2005) showed that exposure of air pollution to wheat plants resulted reduced in plant height, number of seeds per plant and yield. Agrawal *et al.* (2003) also reported significant yield reductions in wheat, mungbean and mustard plants growing along a gradient of air pollution. Heggestad and Lesser (1990) have shown that O_3, SO_2 and NO_2 individually and in combination reduce yield of several crop plants.

CONCLUSION

The results show adverse impact of low level of gaseous pollutant viz. SO_2 and NO_2 and high level of particulate matter (SPM and RSPM) on wheat plants. The results from the two years showed significant reduction in wheat yield and photosynthetic pigments. Pigments are essential site for manufacture of food for plants and air pollutants adversely affected the pigment concentration of wheat crops, resulted overall reduction in performance of wheat plants because it well known that wheat plants are sensitive to air pollutants. The study emphasizes that urban air pollution is becoming a serious threat to urban agriculture crop.

REFERENCE

Agrawal, M.: 2000, 'Research on Air Pollution Effects on Vegetation in India: A Review', *The Botanica* **50**, 75-83.

Agrawal, M., Singh, B., Rajput, M. Marshall, F. and Bell, J.N.B.: 2003, 'Effects of Air Pollution on Peri-urban Agriculture: A Case Study', *Environ. Pollut.* **126**, 323-329.

Agrawal, M., Singh, B., Agrawal, S.B., Bell, J.N.B. and Marshall, F.: 2006, 'The Effects of Air Pollution on Yield and Quality of Mung Bean Grown in Peri-urban Areas of Varansi', *Water Air, Soil and Pollut.* **169**, 239-254.

Anbazhagan, M. and Bhagwat, K.A.: 1991, 'Study on the Progeny of Rice Plan Grown at An Unpolluted and Polluted Site', *Environ. Pollut.* **69**, 17-23.

Anoob, P., Santhoshkumar, A. V. and Paul C. Roby: 2017, Impact of Particulate Pollution on Photosynthesis, Transpiration and Plant Water Potential of Teak (Tectona grandis L.). Current Science, 112(6), 1272-1276.

Applegate, H.G. and Durant, L.C.: 1969 'Synergistic Action of Ozone-sulphurdioxide on Peanuts', *Envir. Sci. Technol.* **3**, 758-760.

Ashenden, T.W. and Mansfield, T.A.: 1977, 'Influence of Windspeed on the Sensitivity of Ryegrass to SO_2', *Journal of Exp. Bot.* **28**, 729-735.

Bell, J.N.B., Rutter, A.J. and Relton, J.: 1979, 'Studies on the Effects of Low Levels of Sulphur Dioxide on the Growth of *Lolium perenne* L', *New Phyto.* **72**, 1299-1306.

Black, V.J. and Unsworth, M.H.: 1979, 'Effects of Low Concentration of SO_2 on Net Photosynthesis and Dark Respiration of *Vicia faba*', *J. Exp.Bot.* **30**, 473-474.

Bleasdale, J.K.: 1973, 'Effects of Coal Smoke Pollution Gases on the Growth of Ryegrass (*Lolium perenne* L.)', *Environ. Pollut.* **5**, 275-283.

Bytnerowicz, Andrzej, Olszyk, David M., Kats, Gerrit, Dawson, Philip, J., Wolf Joanne and Thompson, C. R. (1987). Effects of SO_2 on Physiology, Elemental Content and Injury Development of Winter Wheat. *Agri. Ecosys Environ.* 20, 37-47.

Chapekar, S.B., Boralkar, D.B. and Shetye, R.P.: 1979, 'Plants for Air Monitoring in Industrial Areas', In Tropical Ecology and Development (ed) J. I. Furtado. *Proc. V Int. Symp. of Trop. Ecol.*, 1383, ISTE, Kuala Lampur, 669-675.

Chauhan, A. : 2013, Effect of Air Pollutants on Wheat Plant Growth and Yield in Urban Area of District Haridwar. In Advances in Agriculture and Ecology. (Eds.) Pawan Kumar Bharti, Avnish Chauhan and Ezeaku Peter Ikemfuna (Discovery Publication House, New Delhi.) pp. 1-15.

Cheng. S., Li, J., Feng, B., Jin, Y. and Hao, R.: 2007, 'A Gussian-box Modeling Approach for Urban Air Quality Management in a Northern Chinese City-I. Model Development', *Water Air Soil and Pollut.* 178, 37-57.

Davies, T. : 1980, 'Grasses More Sensitive to SO_2 Pollution in Conditions of Low Irradiance and Short Days', Nature, London, 284-483-485.S

Davieson, G., Murray, F. & Wilson, S.: 1990, 'Effects of Sulphur Dioxide and Hydrogen Fluoride, Singly and in Combination, on Growth and Yield of Wheat in Open-top Chambers', *Agric. Ecosys. Environ*, 30, 317-325.

Godzik, S. and Krupa, S.V. (1982). Effects of Sulphur Dioxide on Growth and Yield of Agricultural and Horticultural Crops; In *Effects of Gaseous Air Pollution in Agriculture and Horticulture* (eds) M H Unsworth and D P Ormrod (London: Butterworths)247-265

Gomez, K.A. and Gomez, A.A. (1984). In : Statistical Procedures for Agricultural Research (2nd Edition). John Wiley and Sons, New York.

Grosso, J. J., Manser, H.A., Hodges, G. H. and Mickinney, H.H.: 1971, 'Effect of Air Pollutants on Nicotiana Cultivars and Species Used for Various Studies. *Phytopathol.* 61,945-950.

Gupta, G. and Sabratnam, S.: 1980, 'Reduction in Soybean Yield After a Brief Exposure to Nitrogen Dioxide', *J. Agric. Sci. Comb.* 110, 399-400.

Gupta, V., Tomer, Y.S. and Prakash, G.: 1993, 'Effects of SO_2 Pollution', Ph.D. Thesis. Ch. C.S. University, Meerut.

Heggestad, H.E. and Lesser, V.M.: 1990, 'Effects of Ozone, Sulfur Dioxide, Soil Water Deficit and Cultivar on Yields of Soybean, *J. Environ.Quali.* 19, 488-495.

Jacob, M. B. and Hochheiser, S.: 1968, 'Continuous Sampling and Ultra-micro Determination of Nitrogen Dioxide in Air', *Annal. Chem.* 32, 426,

Joshi, P.C., Swami, A. and Gangwar, K.K.: 2006, 'Air Quality Monitoring at Two Selected Traffic Junctions in the City of Haridwar', *Him. J. Env. Zool.* 20(2), 219-221.

Khan, M. R. and Khan, M.W.: 1991, 'Impact of Air Pollution Emanating from a Thermal Power Plant on Tomato', *Journal of Indian Botanica Society*, 70, 239-244.

Khan, M. R. and Khan, M.W.: 1993, 'The Interaction of SO_2 and Root-knot Nematode on Tomato', *Environ. Pollut.* 81, 91-102.

Kumar, P., Jain, S., Gurjar, B.R., Sharma, P., Khare, M., Morawska, L., Britter, R., 2013. New Directions: Can a "Blue Sky" Return to Indian Megacities? Atmos. Environ. 71, 198-201.

Kumar, P., Khare, M., Harrison, R.M., Bloss, W.J., Lewis, A.C., Coe, H., Morawska, L., 2015. New Directions: Air Pollution Challenges for Developing Megacities like Delhi. Atmos. Environ. 122, 657-661.

Kumar, P., de Fatima Andrade, M., Ynoue, R.Y., Fornaro, A., de Freitas, E.D., Martins, J., Martins, L.D., Albuquerque, T., Zhang, Y., Morawska, L., 2016. New Directions: From Biofuels to Wood Stoves: The Modern and Ancient Air Quality Challenges in the Megacity of Sau Paulo. Atmos. Environ. 140, 364-369

Last, F.T. : 1982, 'Effects of Atmospheric Sulphur Compounds of Natural and Man Made Terrestrial and Aquatic Ecosystems', *Agric. Environ.* 7, 299-387.

Locyer, D.R., Cowling, D.W. and Jones, L. H. P.: 1976, 'A System for Exposing Plants to Atmosphere Containing Low Concentrations of Sulphur Dioxide', *Journal of Exp. Bot.* 27,397-409.

Maggs,R., Wahid, A., Shamsi, S.R.A., and Ashmore, M.R.: 1995, 'Effects of Ambient Air Pollution on Wheat and Rice Yield in Pakistan', *Water Air, Soil and Pollut.* 85, 1311-1316.

Matsushima, J. and Brewer, R.F.:1972, 'Influence of Sulphur Dioxide and Hydrogen Fluoride as a Mix or Reciprocal Exposure on Citrus Growth and Development', *J. Air Pollut. Contr. Ass.*, 22, 710-713.

Mandloi, B.L. and Dubey, P.S. : 2000, 'Effects of Different Combinations of SO_2 and Cement Dust on Wheat (*Triticum aestivum* CV-HI-1077)', In: Environmental Pollution and its Management. Edited by Pankaj Shrivastava, A.P.H. Publishing Corp.: New Delhi, 70-75 pp.

Mishra, R.M and Gupta, A.K.: 1993, 'Pollution Oriented Occupational Health Problems of Limestone Crusher Workers', *Conx. and Ecol.* 11(3), 634-637,.

Murray, F. and Wilson, S.: 1988, 'The Joint Action of Sulphur Dioxide and Hydrogen Fluoride on the Yield and Quality of Wheat and Barley', *Environ. Pollut.* 55, 239-249.

Pandey, J., and Agrawal, M.: 1994, 'Elevation of Air Pollution Phytotoxicity in a Seasonally Dry Tropical Urban Environment Using Three Woody Perennials', *New Phytolo.*126, 53-61.

Rajput, M. and Agrawal, M.: 2004, 'Physiological and Yield Responses of Pea Plants to Ambient Air Pollution', *Indian J. Plant Physiol.* 19 (1), 9-14.

Rajput, M. and Agrawal, M.:2005, 'Biomonitoring of Air Pollution in a Seasonally Dry Tropical Suburban Area Using Wheat Transplants', *Environmental Monitoring and Assessment* 101, 39-53.

Roberts, T. M.: 1984, 'Long-term Effects of Sulphur Dioxide on Crops: An Analysis of Dose-response Relations', *Phil. Trans. R. Soc. Lond.*, B 305, 299-316.

Sharma, H.C. and Rao, D.N.: 1983, 'Effect of Sulphur Dioxide, Hydrogen Fluoride and their Combination on Wheat Plants', *Indian J. Environ. Hlth.* 25(3), 169-174.

Shukla, J., Pandey, V., Singh.S.N., Yunus, M., Singh, N., and Ahmad, K.J.: 1990, 'Effects of Cement Dust on the Growth and Yield of *Brassica Campestris* L.', *Environ. Pollut.* 66, 81-88.

Singh, S. P. and Prakash, G.: 1995, 'Ecophysiological Impact of SO_2 Pollution on Crop Plants', *Ad. Plant Sci.* 8(l), 1-19.

Singh, N. and Rao, D.N.: 1981, 'Effects of Ozone and Sulphurdioxide, Singly and in Combination, on the Growth Behaviour of *Oziva sativa*', *Abtr. Symp. Environ.*, Options for Developing Countries, The Institute of Sciences, Bombay.

Temmerman, L. De, Vandermeiren, K & Guns, M.: 1992, 'Effect of Air Filtration on Spring Wheat Grown in Open-top Field Chambers at a Rural Site. I. Effect on Growth, Yield and Dry Matter Partitioning', *Environ. Pollut.* 77, 1-5.

Thomas, M.D.: 1961, 'Effects of Air Pollution on Plants; in Air Pollution WHO Monograph', Series No.46, (Geneva: WHO) pp. 233-278.

Treshow, M.: 1984, 'Air Pollution and Plant Life', John Wiley and Sons, New York.

Trivedy R.K., and Goel, P.K: 1986, 'Chemical and Biological Methods for Water Pollution Studies', Env. Publications. Karad, India.

Vandermeiren, K., De Temmerman, L., O. & Guns, M.: 1989, 'Effects of Aerial Pollutants on Growth and Yield of Spring Wheat and Clover Species Grown in Open-top Chambers in 1987', In *The European Communities Project on Open-top Chambers. Results on Agricultural Crops* 1987-1988, eds J. bonte & P. Mathy. Air Pollution Report 19, CEC, Brussels, pp.73-89.

Wahid A., Maggs, R., Shamsi, S.R.A., Bell, J.N.B. & Ashmore, M.R.: 1995, 'Air Pollution and Its Rice Impacts on Wheat Yield in the Pakistan Punjab', *Environ. Pollut.* 88, 147-154.

West, P.W. and Gaeke, G.C.: 1956, 'Fixation of Sulphur Dioxide as Sulfitomercurate III and Subsequent Colorimetric Determination', *Annal. Chem.*, 28,1816.

Wilson, S. and Murray, F.: 1990, 'SO_2 – Induced Growth Reductions and Sulphur Accumulation in Wheat', *Environ. Pollut.* 66,179-191.

White, K.L.. Hill, A.C. and Bannet, J.H.: 1974, 'Synergistic Inhibition of Apparent Photosynthesis Rate of Alfalfa by Combinations of SO_2 and NO_2', *Envir. Sci. Technol* .8, 574-576.

Pal, A., Kulshrestra, K., Ahmad, K.J. and Yunus, M.: 2000, 'Changes in Leaf Surface Structures of Two Avenue Tree Species Caused by Auto-exhaust pollution', *J. Environ. Biol*, 21 (1), 15-21.

Rao, D.N., Obitaille, G. and Le Blanc, F.: 1977, 'Influence of Heavy Metal Pollution on Lichens and Bryophtes', *J. Hattori.Bot.Lab.* 42, 213-239.

Sprugel, D.G., Muller, R.N., Smith, H.J. and Xerikos, P.B.: 1980, 'Sulphur Dioxide Effects on the Yield and Seed Quality in Field Grown Soybeans', *Phytopatholog*, 70, 1129-1133.

Walkley, A., Black, I.A.: 1934, 'An Examination of the Degtjareff Method for Determining Soil Organic Matter and Prepared Modifications of the Chromic Acid Titration Method', *Soil. Sci* 34, 29-38.

Wellburn, A.R.: 1982, 'Effects of SO_2 and NO_2 in Metabolic Functions; in *Effects of Gaseous Pollutants in Agriculture and Horticulture*', (eds) M.H. Unsworth and D.P. Ormord (London: Butterworths), pp. 167-186.

Ziegler, I. : 1992, 'Effects of SO_2 on the Activity of Ribulose 1, 5-diphosphate Carboxylase in Isolated Spinach Chloroplasts', *Planta.* 103, 155-163.

Plant Response to Environmental Stress **Page: 42-59**
Edited by: Dr. Alka Chauhan; Dr. Pawan Kumar 'Bharti' and Dr. Avnish Chauhan
ISBN: 978-93-86841-58-2
Edition: 2018
Published by: Discovery Publishing House Pvt. Ltd., New Delhi (India)

4

Physiology of Sorghum Antioxidative System in Response to Cadmium Stress

An Overview

Prasann Kumar[1]

ABSTRACT

During their life span, plants can be subjected to a number of abiotic stresses, like drought, temperature (both high and low), radiation, salinity, soil pH, heavy metals, lack of essential nutrients, air pollutants, etc. When affected by one, or a combination of abiotic stresses, a response is induced by changes in the plant metabolism, growth and general development. *Sorghumbicolor* L. is an imperative crop due to its extensive use as food, feed and energy crop. Nearly every government around the world advocates for an environment free from harmful contamination for their citizens. However, the demand for a country's economic, agricultural and industrial development outweighs the demand for a safe, pure and natural environmental.

Keywords: Agriculture, Biology, Cadmium, Sorghum.

INTRODUCTION

Sorghum appears gifted as a cereal crop, which has some non-food uses, particularly for bioethanol production. It comes originally from North Africa, and therefore, is resistant to heat and drought. It is unique due to specific compounds (phytates, tannins), which affect its nutritional value. Increased concentration of essential elements in agricultural soils means higher plant uptake. However, soil also contains toxic elements such as heavy metals; the higher concentrations, the higher are the uptake of nonessential elements. What is more, the concentrations of these metals are so toxic they can cause death of plants or reduced their production. Sorghum is able to accumulate large quantities of metals in shoots grown in hydroponic conditions but in field trails these amounts are lower. Nevertheless, one advantage is the possibility of some economic returns during the process. Sorghum has high production of biomass in comparison to other crops such as sunflowers or corn. Nowadays, there is a huge energy demand; therefore, the growth of energy crops on polluted sites

[1] Assistant Professor, Department of Agronomy, School of Agriculture, Lovely Professional University, Jalandhar, Punjab, 144411, India

can be feasible. Human evolution has led to immense scientific and technological progress (Figure 4.1). Reactive Oxygen Species (ROS) are a natural consequence of the aerobic metabolism, and plants have mechanisms to deal with them in normal conditions, controlling the formation and removal rates. Under stress conditions, cell homeostasis is disrupted and ROS production can increase a lot putting a heavy burden on the thoseantioxidative mechanisms, some of which are activated in order to eliminate the excess ROS (Mittler *et al.*, 2004). Trace element contamination cause abiotic stress in plants and it can affect crop production and quality. Certain metals, like copper, are essential for plants, but at high concentrations (depending on plant species) can be considered toxic. Other elements like cadmium and arsenic (a metalloid), while not essential elements for plants, are widespread pollutants that are present in nature due to both natural and manmade activities. Plants have developed different strategies to cope with these stresses. Some use an avoidance strategy to reduce trace element assimilation while others use internal defence mechanisms to cope with the increasing levels of the toxic species. Phytotoxic amounts of trace elements are known to affect several physiological processes and can cause oxidative stress. Plants have developed several trace element defence mechanisms, that allow them to grow despite the presence of variable concentrations of trace elements, but the threshold concentrations as well as the different response mechanisms strongly depend on the plant species and on the type of metal. Metal toxicity

Fig. 4.1: Grain yield of *Sorghum vulgare* L. in polluted soil with heavy metals, especially cadmium.

(**Source:** Prasann Kumar, based on author research)

can cause a redox imbalance and induce the increase of ROS concentration, activating the antioxidant defence mechanisms of plants (Sharma & Dietz, 2009). These mechanisms are very dependent on the metal and the plant, but usually include the involvement of the ascorbate-glutathione cycle enzymes, which is a major antioxidativedefence mechanism, and of other antioxidant enzymes like catalase, peroxidases, and superoxide dismutase.

Other non-enzymatic substances with reported antioxidant properties can also be involved in plant defence mechanisms, like ascorbate, glutathione, alkaloids, phenolic compounds, non-proteic amino-acids and carotenoids. Oxidative stress and ROS production ROS are produced by all aerobic organisms and are usually kept in balance by the antioxidative mechanisms that exist in all living beings. Because ROS have an important signalling role in plants (Foyer & Noctor, 2003; Vranova *et al.*, 2002), their concentration must be carefully controlled through adequate pathways (Mittler, 2002). ROS can be formed during normal aerobic metabolic processes like photosynthesis and respiration and thus, the majority of ROS are produced in the mitochondria, chloroplast, peroxisomes, plasma membrane and apoplast (Ahmad *et al.*, 2008; Moller, 2001). Other sources of ROS production are NADPH oxidases, amine oxidases and cell-wall peroxidases (Mittler, 2002). Under certain stress conditions (like excess light, cold, heat, drought, heavy metals etc.) the production of ROS can exceed the capacity of the plant's defence mechanisms, an imbalance in intracellular ROS content is established and this results in oxidative stress (Gill & Tuteja, 2010). Thus, oxidative stress can be defined as the physiological changes resulting from the formation of excess quantities of reactive oxygen species (ROS) (Vangronsveld & Clijsters, 1994). This increase in ROS levels induces a metabolic response in the plant in order to eliminate them. This metabolic response is highly dependent on the plant species, plant growing state and the type and duration of the stress. Heavy metals1 are natural elements that are present at different concentrations throughout nature, but whose levels can increase and overtake the toxicity threshold of living beings due to both natural and anthropogenic causes (Sánchez, 2008). As plants must adapt (or die) to the conditions where they grow, the presence of heavy metals can induce oxidative stress and the activation of several defence factors in the plants (Prasad, 2004). It is important to understand how some plants can cope with high concentration of metals in order to produce crops able to grow on contaminated soils (Schröder *et al.*, 2008), to help in environmental cleanup via phytoremediation (Adriano *et al.*, 2004) and to breed plants with higher contents of essential nutrients (Zhao & McGrath, 2009). Types of ROS Molecular oxygen (O2) is in itself a bi-radical, as it has two unpaired electrons that have parallel spins (Halliwell, 2006). The ground state of the oxygen molecule is the triplet oxygen because this is an energetically more favourable state. Due to this electron configuration, it doesn't react easily with organic molecules that have paired electrons with opposite spins. Thus, in order for oxygen to react, it must be activated (Garg & Manchanda, 2009). If the oxygen molecule in its ground state absorbs sufficient energy, the spin of one of the unpaired electrons can be reversed forming singlet oxygen, that can readily react with organic molecules. This can happen during photosynthesis when an excess of light energy cannot be readily dissipated by the photosynthetic machinery (Foyer *et al.*, 1994). Although the term "heavy metal" can be misleading because it includes a whole range of substances, some of which do not conform to the more usual chemical definitions of the term, we use it in this text in its environmental context, where it includes metals that are a cause of pollution concern. Other authors sometimes use the expression "trace elements" in this context, although this definition also has problems on its own. Radicals are usually highly unstable, and thus very reactive, species that have one or more unpaired electrons. Another form of activation is by partial reduction adding one, two or three electrons giving rise to the superoxide radical, hydrogen peroxide and hydroxyl radical, respectively (Mittler, 2002). The complete reduction of oxygen (adding four electrons) results in water, which is the normal reduction of oxygen that occurs in the mitochondrial electron transport chain, catalyzed by cytochrome oxidase. As such, this type of activation can occur in metabolic pathways that involve an electron transport chain and can thus occur in several cell locations (Alscher *et al.*, 2002). Singlet oxygen is mainly produced in the chloroplasts at photosystem II (Asada, 2006) but may also result from lipoxygenase activity and is a highly reactive species that can last for nearly 4 μs in water (Foyer *et al.*, 1994). $^1O_2$ reactivity has as preferred target the conjugated double bonds present on polyunsaturated fatty acids (PUFAs) leaving a specific footprint in the cell (Moller *et al.* 2007) that can be followed by the detection of several aldehydes like malondialdehyde (MDA) formed by PUFA peroxidation. The superoxide radical is mainly produced both in the chloroplasts (photosystems I and II) and mitochondria as sub products and in peroxisomes (del Rio *et al.*, 2006; Moller *et al.*, 2007; Rhoads *et al.*, 2006), has a half-life of 2-4 μs and cannot cross phospholipid membranes (Garg & Manchanda, 2009) and so it is important that the cell has adequate in situ mechanism to scavenge this ROS. Superoxide dismutase can catalyse the conversion of this species into hydrogen peroxide. Superoxide radical can also be produced by NADPH oxidase in the plasma membrane (Moller *et al.* 2007). Hydrogen peroxide is mainly produced in peroxisomes (del Rio *et al.*, 2006) and also in mitochondria (Rhoads *et al.*, 2006), and also results from the dismutation of superoxide. It is not a radical and can easily cross membranes diffusing across the cell and has a half-life of around 1 ms (Garg & Manchanda, 2009). The hydroxyl radical, the most reactive of the species be formed from hydrogen peroxide via Fenton and Fenton-like reactions (catalyzed by iron or other transition metals) and, unlike the previous two ROS mentioned, there are no known enzymatic systems able to degrade it (Freinbichler *et al.*, 2011). Although the superoxide radical and hydrogen peroxide are not as reactive as other species they are produced in large amounts in the cell and can initiate other reactions that lead to more dangerous species (Noctor & Foyer, 1998). In fact, superoxide radical can be converted by specific enzymes into hydrogen peroxide, and this can also be a problem as it cause the occurrence of Fenton reactions (Moller *et al.*, 2007). Heavy metals are known to induce oxidative stress increasing the ROS concentration. Effect of Cd and Cu in hydrogen peroxide content in roots of tobacco plants. As can be seen, there is a good correlation between Cu levels and H_2O_2 content, but the effect of Cd showed only a small non-significant increase. These metals, an essential and a non-essential, do seem to provoke different responses in the plant. The increase in hydrogen peroxide levels with metals is a frequently reported stress indicator (Khatun *et al.*, 2008; Mobin & Khan, 2007). ROS effect in different cellular components (lipids, DNA, proteins, carbohydrates) When cell homeostasis are affected by a given stress, ROS production increases to the point where it can damage cellular components and ultimately lead to cell death. ROS can affect lipids, proteins, carbohydrates and DNA and the detailed mechanisms are well detailed in Moller *et al.* (2007). Unsaturated fatty acids from lipid membranes are particularly susceptible to ROS oxidation, increasing membrane leakage. Lipid peroxidation occurs through a series of chain reactions that start when a ROS like the hydroxyl radical removes one hydrogen from a carbon from the fatty acid molecule (mainly at the unsaturation). An oxygen can then easily bond to that location forming a lipid peroxyl radical, that can continue and propagate the same kind of reactions (Gill & Tuteja, 2010). Proteins can also suffer oxidation by ROS, causing certain enzymes to lose its catalytic function. One of the more susceptible targets in proteins are thiol groups the oxidation of which can lead to protein denaturation and loss of functional conformation (Moller *et al.*, 2007). Also, protein oxidation leads to the production of carbonyl groups and to increased rate of proteolysis as the damaged proteins are targeted by proteolytic enzymes (Palma *et al.*, 2002). Changes in protein content and in protein profile can be found as a consequence of the stress induced by toxic metals. This protein increase could represent the positive balance from the inactivation of some proteins, whereas other proteins are formed in relation to the defense response.

Antioxidant Defence Mechanisms

Enzymatic mechanisms as was said before, enzymatic mechanisms and enzymes involved in specific metabolic pathways are one of the major antioxidative defence strategy of plant defence against excess ROS. Superoxide dismutase (SOD, EC 1.15.1.1), catalyses the dismutation of superoxide molecules into hydrogen peroxide and oxygen (Alscher *et al.*, 2002). SOD has a metal cofactor and depending on the metal can be classified in three different groups, localized in different cell compartments: FeSOD (chloroplasts), MnSOD (mitochondria and peroxisomes), Cu/ZnSOD (chloroplast and cytosol). As SOD produces hydrogen peroxide that is subsequently converted to water by peroxidases and catalases, the activity of all these enzymes must be carefully balanced. Catalase (CAT, EC 1.11.1.6) exists mainly in the peroxisomes and as during stress the number of these organelles increase, CAT can have an important role in H_2O_2 detoxification that can diffuse into the peroxisome from other cell locations where it is produced (Mittler, 2002). CAT catalyses the hydrogen peroxide breakdown to water: $H_2O_2 + H_2O_2 \rightarrow 2H_2O + O_2$ Peroxidases (EC 1.11.1) are a member of a large family of enzymes that are ubiquitous in the cell and have numerous roles in plant metabolism (Passardi *et al.*, 2005), namely to remove hydrogen peroxide formed due to induced stress using different reductants. They have the general reaction: $H_2O_2 + R(OH)_2 \rightarrow 2H_2O + RO_2$ $R(OH)_2$ represents different electron donors: guaiacol peroxidase (GPOD, EC 1.11.1.7) uses mainly phenolic donors, ascorbate peroxidase (APX, EC 1.11.1.11) uses ascorbic acid and glutathione peroxidase (GPX, EC 1.11.1.9) uses glutathione. Besides their role as a scavenger of hydrogen peroxide, cell-wall peroxidases are also involved in ROS formation, both as a defence against biotic stresses and as a signalling process against several stresses, leading to the activation of other defence mechanisms (Mika *et al.*, 2004). APX has a much higher affinity to H_2O_2 than CAT suggesting that they have different roles in the scavenging of this ROS, with APX being responsible for maintaining the low levels of hydrogen peroxide while CAT is responsible for the removal of its excess (Mittler, 2002). The water-water cycle occurs in chloroplasts and is a fundamental mechanism to avoid photooxidative damage (Rizhsky *et al.*, 2003), using SOD and APX to scavenge the superoxide radical and hydrogen peroxide in the location where they are produced avoiding the deleterious effects of their reactivity with other cellular components (Asada, 1999; Shigeoka *et al.*, 2002). The ascorbate-glutathione cycle is an important group of reactions involved in ROS detoxification, as it converts hydrogen peroxide (formed as a consequence of an induced stress or via SOD action) and occurs in several cell compartments, like chloroplasts, cytosol, mitochondria, peroxisomes and apoplast. It uses APX and GPX as well as other enzymes like monodehydroascorbate reductase (MDHAR, EC 1.6.5.4) and dehydroascorbate reductase (DHAR, EC 1.8.5.1) that have a role in the regeneration of the reduced form of ascorbate and glutathione reductase (GR, EC 1.6.4.2), important to maintain the pool of reduced glutathione. Other enzymes like heme oxygenase (HO, EC 1.14.99.3), that catalyzes the stereo specific cleavage of heme to biliverdin (Balestrasse *et al.*, 2005) have been reported to have a role in plant defence mechanisms against oxidative stress. Enzymatic responses to heavy metal stress have been extensive studies on the activities of the enzymes involved in ROS defence on plants subjected to heavy metal stress (Sharma & Dietz, 2009). Although different metals can cause oxidative stress, their mode of action is different. For example, while copper, an essential element toxic at high concentrations, is involved in redox reactions, cadmium, which has no known biological function, cannot. However, they both can induce oxidative stress, through different mechanisms (Cuypers *et al.*, 2010). Of all the main enzymes involved in oxidative stress defence, like SOD, APX, CAT and peroxidases, published reports both describe an increase in its activity and a decrease (or no change), depending on plant species, plant organ, type of metal, duration of the treatment, plant age, and growing media (Gratão *et al.*, 2005). As can be seen, there is a huge variation between the behaviour of the enzymes involved in oxidative stress. In some situations the activity increases in lower concentrations of the metal and then decreases as the defence mechanism breaks down due to excessive concentration. This also shows that different components of the antioxidative defence system described above are active under different conditions. The increase in activity in a given enzyme can be a signal that that enzyme has been activated or its expression upregulated. On the other hand, sometimes the effect of the metal can be so drastic that enzyme structures are being affected with a consequent decrease in activity. Several enzymes have metal cofactor so there could be a link between these enzymes, expression and metal availability (Cohu & Pilon, 2007). Consequently, enzymatic response can be complex to analyse. For example the activity of guaiacol peroxidase in tomato roots growing for 3 days with 50 μM Cu in nutrient solution. As can be seen by the relative activity, no significant changes in POD activity were detected compared to control. However, the isoperoxidase profile showed the appearance of new isoforms in tomato roots (C, D), while other isoforms showed less intensity (A, B). These results indicate that although enzymatic activity can be similar in control and stressed plants it is possible that some isoforms can be activated in response to excess copper. Polyphenol oxidase (PPO, EC 1.10.3.1) is an oxidoreductase that catalyzes the oxidation of phenols to quinones and its activity has been shown to increase under heavy metal stress and has thus been associated to some form of defence mechanism (Ali *et al.*, 2006; L.L. Martins & Mourato, 2006). Kováèik *et al.* (2009) observed an increase in root PPO activity with Cu and Cd and concluded that the formation of polymerized phenols could be used to complex free metal ions. On the other hand PPO has also been associated to a catalase-like activity (Gerdemann *et al.*, 2001), and could thus have a role in direct hydrogen peroxide removal. Peroxiredoxins (PRX, EC 1.11.1.15) are ubiquitous antioxidant enzymes that participate in cellular redox homeostasis and reduce hydrogen peroxide to water. PRX levels have been shown to increase under several abiotic stresses suggesting a role in the defence mechanisms (Barranco-Medina *et al.*, 2007). Non enzymatic mechanisms besides the enzymatic mechanisms described in the two previous chapters, there is a whole range of other substances that have been reported to be involved in antioxidative defence in plants. Some are well known and have been extensively studied (like the role of ascorbate and glutathione) while others are thought to be part of defence mechanism but its role remains to be fully understood. While many studies report the increase in the concentration of some substance in relation to the induction of a stress, this type of correlation is not, by itself, conclusive enough to ascertain the effect of that substance in the plant metabolism. Several organic molecules have been reported to be able to form complexes with heavy metals, like phytochelatins, organic acids and amino acids like proline. But exactly what kind of molecules complex the metals seem to be highly dependent not only on metal type and plant species but also on plant organ and compartment, as different complexes can be formed in the cytoplasm, the xylem and phloem, for example (Sharma & Dietz, 2006). Ascorbate and glutathione are antioxidants that exist in relatively high concentration in cell compartments (Potters *et al.*, 2002), and are involved in the ascorbate-glutathione cycle as described above being also a substrate for APX an enzyme important in H_2O_2 removal. Ascorbate (ASC) is an electron donor that can be oxidized to the radical monodehydroascorbate (MDHA) and this compound can then form dehydroascorbate (DHA). Besides its role as an enzyme substrate, ascorbate also reacts directly with singlet oxygen and superoxide and is important in the regeneration of a-tocopherol and certain carotenoids (Potters *et al.*, 2002). Glutathione is a tripeptide (containing glutamate, cysteine and glycine) that can exist in two predominant forms: the reduced form (usually represented by GSH) and the oxidized form (usually represented by GSSG) (Noctor & Foyer, 1998). It is involved in the sulphur metabolism and in defence reactions against oxidative stress (Potters *et al.*, 2002). It can also lead to the synthesis of phytochelatins that are important sequesters for certain heavy metals (Cobbett & Goldsbrough, 2002). Heat shock proteins (HSP) are proteins that not only showed increased expression under heat stress but are also molecular chaperones that protect other proteins from stress induced damage (Feder & Hofmann, 1999). HSP help proteins maintain or recover their native conformation, and remove potentially harmful polypeptides. HSP expression has been associated to high temperature, cold, drought, light, heavy metals, salt and ozone stresses (Timperio *et al.*, 2008). Kochhar & Kochhar (2005) detected the induction of both high and low molecular weight HSPs in response to combined heat and cadmium stress. ROS also has a signaling role during a stress, in order to induce HSP production (Timperio *et al.*, 2008). Carotenoids have an important protective role during photosynthesis as these molecules can quench the excited states of chlorophyll in order to avoid the production of singlet oxygen. As a consequence, the carotenoid molecules become themselves excited, but this is not a big problem as they don't have enough energy to form this ROS species (Taiz & Zeiger, 2002). Terpenoids are a large class of organic compounds derived from the isoprene unit that could also have an antioxidative role in plants, although that is not yet clear (Grassmann *et al.*, 2002). Flavonoids are organic molecules with a structure similar to flavone, that have been shown to have a protective role against several stresses (Jaakola *et al.*, 2004), both by themselves and in conjugation with peroxidases (Mika *et al.*, 2004). Anthocyanins, a type of flavonoids (they are glucosides of anthocyanidins, present in the vacuoles, have an antioxidative capacity (Kahkonen & Heinonen, 2003) but its location in the cell prevents them to contact directly with ROS production sites, although its levels have been reported to increase under Cd stress (Mobin& Khan, 2007). Thiols can play an important antioxidative role, protecting membrane lipids. Lipoic acid, both in its reduced and oxidized form, is reported to have antioxidative properties due to its direct scavenging of ROS. It is also able to chelate several metal ions that induces oxidative stress (Navari-Izzo *et al.*, 2002) and thus can have an important role in cell protection. Tocopherols are a class of compounds synthesized by photosynthetic organisms that have vitamin E activity. Tocopherol is the most common form in leaves while tocopherol is more common in roots (Abbasi *et al.*, 2007). They have a role in ROS protection as they can quench singlet oxygen (Gill & Tuteja, 2010) and can act as an antioxidant and terminate chain reactions occurring during lipid peroxidation (Garg & Manchanda, 2009). Proline, is a compatible solute that participate in the osmotic adjustment of plant cells being able to balance water stress. Proline has been reported to improve plant resistance to oxidative stress by scavenging ROS (namely by quenching singlet oxygen and hydroxyl radicals), increasing the activity of antioxidative enzymes and protecting them and maintaining redox homeostasis (Matysik *et al.*, 2002), and they could also participate in signalling pathways that regulate stress related genes (Khedr *et al.*, 2003). Although the concentration of proline has been shown to increase under heavy metal stress in certain plants (Martins *et al.*, 2011), its exact role in heavy metal detoxification is unclear as, under certain conditions, it could be only an indirect response due to heavymetal induced disturbances in plant water balance (Schat *et al.*, 1997). Histidine is another amino acid that has been mainly linked to Ni hyperaccumulator plants (Sharma & Dietz, 2006). Glycine betaine (2-trimethylammonioacetate, is another compatible solute that is involved in plant resistance against abiotic stresses, namely salt stress (Banu *et al.*, 2009). It helps not only in controlling water balance but can also help to maintain protein and membrane structure (F.L. Zhang *et al.*, 2008). Nicotianamine is an amino acid that has a known role in heavy metal transport in plants (Stephan & Scholz, 1993), but recent findings have suggested an important role also in heavy metal tolerance namely in relation to hyper accumulating species (Sharma & Dietz, 2006). Mugineic acid is a siderophore (that is, an iron-chelating compound) that promotes iron acquisition from the rhizosphere, but that may also participate in the distribution of other metals in the plant (Haydon & Cobbett, 2007). Meda *et al.* (2007) reports that phytosiderophores can alleviate Cd toxicity in maize. Polyamines are low molecular weight amines that have a role in plant growth and developmental processes (Kakkar & Sawhney, 2002). The concentration of some polyamines has been reported to increase under abiotic stress. Mascher (2002) showed that the concentration of putrescine, spermidine and spermine incresaed when red clover plants were subjected to As toxicity. However, it is still not clear the exact role these compounds play in heavy metal defence, but a participation in the stabilization and protection of the membrane systems has been proposed (Sharma & Dietz, 2006). Although soluble sugars have been linked to metabolic pathways that produce ROS, they can also have an important role in ROS scavenging mechanisms. Increased glucose levels can increase the production of NADPH (via the pentose-phosphate pathway), that is an important intermediate in the ascorbate-glutathione cycle (Couée *et al.*, 2006) as NADPH is the primary electron donor that assures a intracellular reduction status. Both glucose and sucrose levels have been shown to increase in some plant species under certain abiotic stresses but it is not obvious that this happens due to a putative defence mechanism induction (Couée *et al.*, 2006), although these sugars also participate in signalling mechanisms. Van den Ende and Valluru (2009) suggest that sucrose might have a protective role against stress due to its capacity to scavenge ROS. Other sugars like raffinose and fructans (which are fructose polymers) are also reported to have a protective role of membranes against several stresses, namely freezing and drought stress (Van den Ende & Valluru, 2009). Trehalose is a non-reducing disaccharide that can also participate in the stabilization of membranes and protection of proteins under abiotic stresses (Luo *et al.*, 2008). Although trehalose exists in numerous organisms (like bacteria, fungi and nematodes) it is not found widespread in plants, and when it is found is usually in very low concentrations (Wingler, 2002), but several studies have correlated the availability of this disaccharide (or the expression of the genes related to its synthesis) with stress responses. Almeida *et al.* (2005) found that transgenic tobacco plants over-expressing trehalose-6phosphate synthase had higher resistance against different abiotic stresses (like drought and temperature). Nery *et al.* (2008) stated that trehalose participated in protecting cells against hydrogen peroxide, by preventing oxidation of both membranes and proteins. Brassinosteroids are a family of polyhydroxysteroids that have been reported to modify the activity of antioxidant enzymes and the level of non-enzymatic compounds (like ascorbic acid and tocopherols), when plants are subjected to different abiotic stresses, but its effect is still poorly understood (Bajguz & Hayat, 2009). ROS also has a signalling role in hormone responses, like ABA, auxin and ethylene (Kwak *et al.*, 2006). Ionic form in plants but are bound to different types of organic molecules. These include organic acids (like citric and maleic acid) and some amino acids (Haydon & Cobbett, 2007). In fact, organic acids, among other organic solutes of several types, can accumulate in leaves in stress conditions, such as water stress, with an important role on subcellular structures protection acting as osmolytes (Pinheiro *et al.*, 2004). One possible effect of heavy metal stress is that plants restrict water uptake, thus indirectly inducing water stress. Any changes in the concentrations of the intermediate organic acids can reflect an influence of a heavy metal in metabolic pathways as they are involved in primary plant metabolism such as cell respiration and the formation of ATP. Organic acids can have a detoxification role complexing metals, and reducing their availability to the plant, but this role is not yet fully understood (Hall, 2002). The metabolism of several phenols has been reported to change under Cu and Cd stress indicating a putative role of these compounds in heavy metal detoxification by decreasing the presence of the free metal ions (Kováèik *et al.*, 2009). Lignin accumulation has also been described as a consequence of Cu toxicity (Lequeux *et al.*, 2010) but whether this is related to a heavy metal defence mechanism is still not clear. Zorrig *et al.* (2010) suggested a transport role for citrate to translocate Cd from the roots to the shoots of lettuce plants while Panfili *et al.* (2009) also studied the effect of citrate in the uptake of Cd. Citrate and malate have been reported to be major ligands for Zn and Ni in several studies (Haydon & Cobbett, 2007). Phytochelatins (PC) are small metal-binding peptides with the structure (γ-Glu-Cys)n-Gly where n ranges between 2 and 11 (Cobbett & Goldsbrough, 2002). Its synthesis is catalyzed by phytochelatin synthase using glutathione as a substrate (Clemens, 2006; Grill *et al.*, 1989). They form complexes with metals like Cd (due to the high affinity metals have to the thiol group present in cysteine) and sequester them to the vacuoles and are thus an important mechanism that plants use to avoid heavy metal toxicity. Other peptides with a structure similar to phytochelatins have been identified, with the terminal Gly being replaced by other amino acids like serine, glutamic acid and glutamine in the case of isophytochelatins or alanine in homophytochelatins (Oven *et al.*, 2002). All of these peptides have been reported to participate in the detoxification mechanisms of various plant species against several metals or metalloids, besides Cd, like As (Vázquez *et al.*, 2009) and Pb (Z. C. Zhang *et al.*, 2008).

CONCLUSION

With the rapid industrial development, soil environmental pollution in India has become increasingly serious. Cadmium (Cd) is a highly toxic heavy metal in the environment. Cd is a non-essential nutrient for plants, and excessive Cd has not only significant adverse effects, but also endangers human health via food chain. The alleviation or inhibition of Cd damage in plants has, therefore, caused extensive attention of the whole society. Heavy metals have an adverse impact on growth and development of the plants, showing some physiological and biochemical characteristic of damages. To a certain extent, plant growth and physiological characteristic can reflect the adverse impact of heavy metal externally or internally. The research of the poisoning effect of the heavy metal Cd on plant mainly focuses on food crops such as rice, wheat and maize, but less on *Sorghum* plants, which is known often as animal feed sources. Sorghum scientist reported some important changes in growth and physiological characteristic of sorghum plant under cadmium stress. In their experiment, the major physiological parameters for observation were like this, [A] effects of cadmium on height of different species of sorghum; [B] effects of cadmium on chlorophyll contents of different species of sorghum plants; [C] effects of cadmium on root activities in leaves of different species of sorghum plants; [D] effects of cadmium on MDA contents in leaves of different species of sorghum plants. They found several interesting observations and these can be summarized such as, a kind of oxidative stress, heavy metal stress affects the growth of plants.

REFERENCE

Abbasi, A.-R., Hajirezaei, M., Hofius, D., Sonnewald, U., & Voll, L. M. (2007). Specific Roles of {alpha}- and {gamma}-Tocopherol in Abiotic Stress Responses of Transgenic Tobacco. Plant Physiology, Vol. 143, No. 4, 1720-1738.

Adriano, D. C., Wenzel, W. W., Vangronsveld, J., & Bolan, N. S. (2004). Role of Assisted Natural Remediation in Environmental Cleanup. Geoderma, Vol. 122, 121-142.

Ahmad, P., Sarwat, M., & Sharma, S. (2008). Reactive Oxygen Species, Antioxidants and Signaling in Plants. Journal of Plant Biology, Vol. 51, No. 3, 167-173.

Almeida, A. M., Villalobos, E., Araújo, S. S., Leyman, B. V. D. P., Alfaro-Cardoso, L., Fevereiro, P. S., Torné, J. M., & Santos, D. M. (2005). Transformation of Tobacco with an Arabidopsis Thaliana Gene Involved in Trehalose Biosynthesis Increases Tolerance to Several Abiotic Stresses. Euphytica, Vol. 146, 165-176.

Alscher, R. G., Erturk, N., & Heath, L. S. (2002). Role of Superoxide Dismutases (SODs) in Controlling Oxidative Stress in Plants. Journal of Experimental Botany, Vol. 53, No. 372, 1331-1341.

Asada, K. (1999). The Water-Water Cycle in Chloroplasts: Scavenging of Active Oxygens and Dissipation of Excess Photons. Annual Review of Plant Physiology & Plant Molecular Biology, Vol. 50, No. 1, 601.

Asada, K. (2006). Production and Scavenging of Reactive Oxygen Species in Chloroplasts and their Functions. Plant Physiology, Vol. 141, No. 2, 391-396.

Bah, A. M., Dai, H., Zhao, J., Sun, H., Cao, F., Zhang, G., & Wu, F. (2011). Effects of Cadmium, Chromium and Lead on Growth, Metal Uptake and Antioxidative Capacity in Typha Angustifolia. Biological Trace Element Research, Vol. 142, No. 1, 77-92.

Bajguz, A., & Hayat, S. (2009). Effects of Brassinosteroids on the Plant Responses to Environmental Stresses. Plant Physiology and Biochemistry, Vol. 47, No. 1, 1-8.

Balestrasse, K. B., Noriega, G. O., Batlle, A., & Tomaro, M. L. (2005). Involvement of Heme Oxygenase as Antioxidant Defense in Soybean Nodules. Free Radical Research, Vol. 39, No. 2, 145-151.

Banu, M. N. A., Hoque, M. A., Watanabe-Sugimoto, M., Matsuoka, K., Nakamura, Y., Shimoishi, Y., & Murata, Y. (2009). Proline and Glycinebetaine Induce Antioxidant Defense gene Expression and Suppress Cell Death in Cultured Tobacco Cells Under Salt Stress. Journal of Plant Physiology, Vol. 166, No. 2, 146-156.

Barranco-Medina, S., Krell, T., Finkemeier, I., Sevilla, F., Lazaro, J.-J., & Dietz, K.-J. (2007). Biochemical and Molecular Characterization of the Mitochondrial Peroxiredoxin PsPrxII F from Pisum sativum. Plant Physiology and Biochemistry, Vol. 45, No. 10-11, 729-739.

Clemens, S. (2006). Evolution and Function of Phytochelatin Synthases. Journal of Plant Physiology, Vol. 163, No. 3, 319-332. Cobbett, C., & Goldsbrough, P. (2002). Phytochelatins and Metallothioneins: Roles in Heavy Metal Detoxification and Homeostasis. Annual Review of Plant Biology, Vol. 53, 159-182.

Cohu, C. M., & Pilon, M. (2007). Regulation of Superoxide Dismutase Expression by Copper Availability. Physiologia Plantarum, Vol. 129, No. 4, 747-755.

Couée, I., Sulmon, C., Gouesbet, G., & El Amrani, A. (2006). Involvement of Soluble Sugars in Reactive Oxygen Species Balance and Responses to Oxidative Stress in Plants. Journal of Experimental Botany, Vol. 57, No. 3, 449-459.

Cuypers, A., Plusquin, M., Remans, T., Jozefczak, M., Keunen, E., Gielen, H., Opdenakker, K., Nair, A., Munters, E., Artois, T., Nawrot, T., Vangronsveld, J., & Smeets, K. (2010). Cadmium Stress: An Oxidative Challenge. BioMetals, Vol. 23, No. 5, 927-940.

del Rio, L. A., Sandalio, L. M., Corpas, F. J., Palma, J. M., & Barroso, J. B. (2006). Reactive Oxygen Species and Reactive Nitrogen Species in Peroxisomes. Production, Scavenging, and Role in Cell Signaling. Plant Physiology, Vol. 141, No. 2, 330-335.

Ekmekci, Y., Tanyolac, D., & Ayhan, B. (2008). Effects of Cadmium on Antioxidant Enzyme and Photosynthetic Activities in Leaves of Two Maize Cultivars. Journal of Plant Physiology, Vol. 165, No. 6, 600-611.

Feder, M. E., & Hofmann, G. E. (1999). Heat-shock Proteins, Molecular Chaperones, and the Stress Response: Evolutionary and Ecological Physiology. Annual Review of Physiology, Vol. 61, 243-282.

Foyer, C. H., Lelandais, M., & Kunert, K. J. (1994). Photooxidative Stress in Plants. Physiologia Plantarum, Vol. 92, No. 4, 696-717.

Foyer, C. H., & Noctor, G. (2003). Redox Sensing and Signalling Associated with Reactive Oxygen in Chloroplasts, Peroxisomes and Mitochondria. Physiologia Plantarum, Vol. 119, No. 3, 355-364.

Freinbichler, W., Colivicchi, M. A., Stefanini, C., Bianchi, L., Ballini, C., Misini, B., Weinberger, P., Linert, W., Vareslija, D., Tipton, K. F., & Della Corte, L. (2011). Highly Reactive Oxygen Species: Detection, Formation, and Possible Functions. Cellular and Molecular Life Sciences, Vol. 68, No. 12, 2067-2079.

Freisinger, E. (2009). Metallothioneins in Plants. In A. Sigel, H. Sigel & R. K. O. Sigel (Eds.), Metallothioneins and Related Chelators (Vol. 5, pp. 107-153). Cambridge: The Royal Society of Chemistry. Garg, N., & Manchanda, G. (2009). ROS Generation in Plants: Boon or Bane? Plant Biosystems, Vol. 143, No. 1, 81 - 96.

Gill, S. S., & Tuteja, N. (2010). Reactive Oxygen Species and Antioxidant Machinery in Abiotic Stress Tolerance in Crop Plants. Plant Physiology and Biochemistry, Vol. 48, No. 12, 909-930.

Grassmann, J., Hippeli, S., & Elstner, E. F. (2002). Plant's Defence and Its Benefits for Animals and Medicine: Role of Phenolics and Terpenoids in Avoiding Oxygen Stress. Plant Physiology and Biochemistry, Vol. 40, No. 6-8, 471-478.

Gratão, P. L., Polle, A., Lea, P. J., & Azevedo, R. A. (2005). Making the Life of Heavy Metal Stressed Plants a Little Easier. Functional Plant Biology, Vol. 32, 481-494.

Grill, E., Loffler, S., Winnacker, E. L., & Zenk, M. H. (1989). Phytochelatins, the Heavy-MetalBinding Peptides of Plants, Are Synthesized from Glutathione by a Specific Gamma www.intechopen.com

Characterization of Plant Antioxidative System in Response to Abiotic Stresses: A Focus on Heavy Metal Toxicity 41 Glutamylcysteine Dipeptidyl Transpeptidase (Phytochelatin Synthase). Proceedings of the National Academy of Sciences of the United States of America, Vol. 86, No. 18, 6838-6842.

Hall, J. L. (2002). Cellular Mechanisms for Heavy Metal Detoxification and Tolerance. Journal of Experimental Botany, Vol. 53, No. 366, 1-11. Halliwell, B. (2006). Reactive Species and Antioxidants. Redox Biology is a Fundamental Theme of Aerobic Life. Plant Physiology, Vol. 141, No. 2, 312-322.

Hassinen, V. H., Tervahauta, A. I., Schat, H., & Karenlampi, S. O. (2011). Plant Metallothioneins - Metal Chelators with ROS Scavenging Activity? Plant Biology, Vol. 13, No. 2, 225-232.

Haydon, M. J., & Cobbett, C. S. (2007). Transporters of Ligands for Essential Metal Ions in Plants. New Phytologist, Vol. 174, No. 3, 499-506.

Jaakola, L., Määttä-Riihinen, K., Kärenlampi, S., & Hohtola, A. (2004). Activation of Flavonoid Biosynthesis by Solar Radiation in Bilberry (Vaccinium myrtillus L.) leaves. Planta, Vol. 218, No. 5, 721-728.

Kahkonen, M. P., & Heinonen, M. (2003). Antioxidant Activity of Anthocyanins and their Aglycons. Journal of Agricultural and Food Chemistry, Vol. 51, No. 3, 628-633.

Kakkar, R. K., & Sawhney, V. K. (2002). Polyamine Research in Plants - A Changing Perspective. Physiologia Plantarum, Vol. 116, No. 3, 281-292.

Ke, W. S., Xiong, Z. T., Xie, M. J., & Luo, Q. (2007). Accumulation, Subcellular Localization and Ecophysiological Responses to Copper Stress in two Daucus carota L. populations. Plant and Soil, Vol. 292, No. 1-2, 291-304.

Khan, I., Ahmad, A., & Iqbal, M. (2009). Modulation of Antioxidant Defence System for Arsenic Detoxification in Indian Mustard. Ecotoxicology and Environmental Safety, Vol. 72, No. 2, 626-634.

Khatun, S., Ali, M. B., Hahn, E.-J., & Paek, K.-Y. (2008). Copper toxicity in Withania somnifera: Growth and Antioxidant Enzymes Responses of in vitro Grown Plants. Environmental and Experimental Botany, Vol. 64, No. 3, 279-285.

Khedr, A. H. A., Abbas, M. A., Wahid, A. A. A., Quick, W. P., & Abogadallah, G. M. (2003). Proline Induces the Expression of Salt Stress Responsive Proteins and May Improve the Adaptation of Pancratium Maritimum L. to Salt Stress. Journal of Experimental Botany, Vol. 54, No. 392, 2553-2562.

Kochhar, S., & Kochhar, V. K. (2005). Expression of Antioxidant Enzymes and Heat Shock Proteins in Relation to Combined Stress of Cadmium and Heat in Vigna Mungo Seedlings. Plant Science, Vol. 168, No .4, 921-929.

Kovácik, J., & Backor, M. (2008). Oxidative Status of Matricaria Chamomilla Plants Related to Cadmium and Copper Uptake. Ecotoxicology, Vol. 17, No. 6, 471-479.

Kováèik, J., Klejdus, B., Hedbavny, J., Štork, F., & Baèkor, M. (2009). Comparison of Cadmium and Copper Effect on Phenolic Metabolism, Mineral Nutrients and Stress-related Parameters in Matricaria Chamomilla Plants. Plant and Soil, Vol. 320, No. 1, 231-242.

Kwak, J. M., Nguyen, V., & Schroeder, J. I. (2006). The Role of Reactive Oxygen Species in Hormonal Responses. Plant Physiology, Vol. 141, No. 2, 323-329.

Lequeux, H., Hermans, C., Lutts, S., & Verbruggen, N. (2010). Response to Copper Excess in Arabidopsis Thaliana: Impact on the Root System Architecture, Hormone Distribution, Lignin Accumulation and Mineral Profile. Plant Physiology and Biochemistry, Vol. 48, No. 8, 673-682.

Luo, Y., Li, W.-M., & Wang, W. (2008). Trehalose: Protector of Antioxidant Enzymes or Reactive Oxygen Species Scavenger Under Heat Stress? Environmental and Experimental Botany, Vol. 63, No. 1-3, 378-384.

Markovska, Y. K., Gorinova, N. I., Nedkovska, M. P., & Miteva, K. M. (2009). Cadmiuminduced Oxidative Damage and Antioxidant Responses in Brassica Juncea Plants. Biologia Plantarum, Vol. 53, No. 1, 151-154.

Martins, L. L., Mourato, M. P., Cardoso, A. I., Pinto, A. P., Mota, A. M., Goncalves, M. d. L. S., & de Varennes, A. (2011). Oxidative Stress Induced by Cadmium in Nicotiana tabacum L.: Effects on Growth Parameters, Oxidative Damage and Antioxidant Responses in Different Plant Parts. Acta Physiologiae Plantarum, Vol. 33, No. 4, 1375-1383.

Mascher, R., Lippmann, B., Holzinger, S., & Bergmann, H. (2002). Arsenate Toxicity: Effects on Oxidative Stress Response Molecules and Enzymes in Red Clover Plants. Plant Science, Vol. 163, No. 5, 961-969.

Matysik, J., Alia, Bhalu, B., & Mohanty, P. (2002). Molecular Mechanisms of Quenching of Reactive Oxygen Species by Proline Under Stress in Plants. Current Science, Vol. 82, No. 5, 525-532.

Meda, A. R., Scheuermann, E. B., Prechsl, U. E., Erenoglu, B., Schaaf, G., Hayen, H., Weber, G., & von Wiren, N. (2007). Iron Acquisition by Phytosiderophores Contributes to Cadmium Tolerance. Plant Physiology, Vol. 143, No. 4, 1761-1773.

Mijovilovich, A., Leitenmaier, B., Meyer-Klaucke, W., Kroneck, P. M. H., Gotz, B., & Kupper, H. (2009). Complexation and Toxicity of Copper in Higher Plants. II. Different Mechanisms for Copper versus Cadmium Detoxification in the Copper-Sensitive Cadmium/Zinc Hyperaccumulator Thlaspi caerulescens (Ganges Ecotype). Plant Physiology, Vol.151, No.2, 715-731.

Mika, A., Minibayeva, F., Beckett, R., & Lüthje, S. (2004). Possible Functions of Extracellular Peroxidases in Stress-induced Generation and Detoxification of Active Oxygen Species. Phytochemistry Reviews, Vol. 3, No. 1, 173-193.

Mittler, R. (2002). Oxidative Stress, Antioxidants and Stress Tolerance. Trends in Plant Science, Vol. 7, No. 9, 405-410. Mittler, R., Vanderauwera, S., Gollery, M., & Van Breusegem, F. (2004). Reactive Oxygen Gene Network of Plants. Trends in Plant Science, Vol. 9, No. 10, 490-498.

Mobin, M., & Khan, N. A. (2007). Photosynthetic Activity, Pigment Composition and Antioxidative Response of Two Mustard (Brassica juncea) Cultivars Differing in Photosynthetic Capacity Subjected to Cadmium Stress. Journal of Plant Physiology, Vol. 164, No. 5, 601-610.

Moller, I. M. (2001). Plant Mitochondria and Oxidative Stress: Electron Transport, NADPH Turnover and Metabolism of Reactive Oxygen Species. Annual Review of Plant Physiology and Plant Molecular Biology, Vol. 52, 561-591.

Moller, I. M., Jensen, P. E., & Hansson, A. (2007). Oxidative Modifications to Cellular Components in Plants. Annual Review of Plant Biology, Vol. 58, 459-481. Navari-Izzo, F., Quartacci, M. F., & Sgherri, C. (2002). Lipoic Acid: A Unique Antioxidant in the Detoxification of Activated Oxygen Species. Plant Physiology and Biochemistry, Vol. 40, No. 6-8, 463-470.

Nery, D. d. C. M., da Silva, C. G., Mariani, D., Fernandes, P. N., Pereira, M. D., Panek, A. D., & Eleutherio, E. C. A. (2008). The Role of Trehalose and Its Transporter in Protection Against Reactive Oxygen Species. Biochim Biophys Acta, Vol. 1780, No. 12, 1408-1411.

Noctor, G., & Foyer, C. H. (1998). Ascorbate and Glutathione: Keeping Active Oxygen Under Control. Annual Review of Plant Physiology and Plant Molecular Biology, Vol.49, 249-279.

Nouairi, I., Ben Ammar, W., Ben Youssef, N., Ben Miled, D. D., Ghorbal, M., & Zarrouk, M. (2009). Antioxidant Defense System in Leaves of Indian Mustard (Brassica juncea) and rape (Brassica napus) under Cadmium Stress. Acta Physiologiae Plantarum, Vol. 31, No. 2, 237-247.

Oven, M., Page, J. E., Zenk, M. H., & Kutchan, T. M. (2002). Molecular Characterization of the Homo-phytochelatin Synthase of Soybean Glycine Max - Relation to Phytochelatin synthase. Journal of Biological Chemistry, Vol. 277, No. 7, 4747-4754.

Palma, J. M., Sandalio, L. M., Corpas, F. J., Romero-Puertas, M. C., McCarthy, I., & del Rio, L. A. (2002). Plant Proteases, Protein Degradation and Oxidative Stress: Role of Peroxisomes. Plant Physiology and Biochemistry, Vol. 40, No. 6-8, 521-530.

Panfili, F., Schneider, A., Vives, A., Perrot, F., Hubert, P., & Pellerin, S. (2009). Cadmium Uptake by Durum Wheat in Presence of Citrate. Plant and Soil, Vol. 316, No. 1, 299-309.

Passardi, F., Cosio, C., Penel, C., & Dunand, C. (2005). Peroxidases have More Functions than a Swiss Army Knife. Plant Cell Reports, Vol. 24, No. 5, 255-265.

Peng, H. Y., Yang, X. E., Yang, M. J., & Tian, S. K. (2006). Responses of Antioxidant Enzyme System to Copper Toxicity and Copper Detoxification in the Leaves of Elsholtzia Splenden. Journal of Plant Nutrition, Vol. 29, No. 9, 1619-1635.

Pinheiro, C., Passarinho, J. A., & Ricardo, C. P. (2004). Effect of Drought and Rewatering on the Metabolism of Lupinus albus Organs. Journal of Plant Physiology, Vol.161, No.11, 1203-1210.

Pinto, A. P., Alves, A. S., Candeias, A. J., Cardoso, A. I., de Varennes, A., Martins, L. L., Mourato, M. P., Goncalves, M. L. S., & Mota, A. M. (2009). Cadmium Accumulation and Antioxidative Defences in Brassica juncea L. Czern, Nicotiana tabacum L. and Solanum nigrum L. International Journal of Environmental Analytical Chemistry, Vol. 89, No. 8-12, 661-676.

Potters, G., De Gara, L., Asard, H., & Horemans, N. (2002). Ascorbate and Glutathione: Guardians of the Cell Cycle, Partners in Crime? Plant Physiology and Biochemistry, Vol. 40, No. 6-8, 537-548.

Prasad, M. N. V. (2004). Heavy Metal Stress in Plants: Springer. Rhoads, D. M., Umbach, A. L., Subbaiah, C. C., & Siedow, J. N. (2006). Mitochondrial Reactive Oxygen Species. Contribution to Oxidative Stress and Interorganellar Signaling. Plant Physiology, Vol. 141, No. 2, 357-366.

Rizhsky, L., Liang, H. J., & Mittler, R. (2003). The Water-water Cycle is Essential for Chloroplast Protection in the Absence of Stress. Journal of Biological Chemistry, Vol. 278, No. 40, 38921-38925. Sánchez, M. L. (2008). Causes And Effects Of Heavy Metal Pollution. New York: Nova Science Publishers, Inc. Schat, H., Sharma, S. S., & Vooijs, R. (1997). Heavy Metal-induced Accumulation of Free Proline in a Metal-tolerant and a Nontolerant Ecotype of Silene Vulgaris. Physiologia Plantarum, Vol. 101, No. 3, 477-482.

Schröder, P., Herzig, R., Bojinov, B., Ruttens, A., Nehnevajova, E., Stamatiadis, S., Memon, A., Vassilev, A., Caviezel, M., & Vangronsveld, J. (2008). Bioenergy to save the world. Environmental Science and Pollution Research, Vol.15, No.3, 196-204. Sharma, S. S., & Dietz, K.-J. (2009). The relationship between metal toxicity and cellular redox imbalance. Trends in Plant Science, Vol.14, No.1, 43-50.

Sharma, S. S., & Dietz, K. J. (2006). The Significance of Amino Acids and Amino Acid-derived Molecules in Plant Responses and Adaptation to Heavy Metal Stress. Journal of Experimental Botany, Vol. 57, No. 4, 711-726.

Shi, G. R., Cai, Q. S., Liu, Q. Q., & Wu, L. (2009). Salicylic Acid-mediated Alleviation of Cadmium Toxicity in Hemp Plants in Relation to Cadmium Uptake, Photosynthesis and Antioxidant Enzymes. Acta Physiologiae Plantarum, Vol. 31, No. 5, 969-977.

Shigeoka, S., Ishikawa, T., Tamoi, M., Miyagawa, Y., Takeda, T., Yabuta, Y., & Yoshimura, K. (2002). Regulation and Function of Ascorbate Peroxidase Isoenzymes. Journal of Experimental Botany, Vol. 53, No. 372, 1305-1319.

Smeets, K., Ruytinx, J., Semane, B., Van Belleghem, F., Remans, T., Van Sanden, S., Vangronsveld, J., & Cuypers, A. (2008). Cadmium-induced Transcriptional and Enzymatic Alterations Related to Oxidative Stress. Environmental and Experimental Botany, Vol. 63, No. 1-3, 1-8.

Stephan, U. W., & Scholz, G. (1993). Nicotianamine - Mediator of Transport of Iron and Heavy-Metals in the Phloem. Physiologia Plantarum, Vol. 88, No. 3, 522-529.

Taiz, L., & Zeiger, E. (2002). Plant Physiology (3rd ed.). Sunderland, MA: Sinuaer Associates, Inc. Timperio, A. M., Egidi, M. G., & Zolla, L. (2008). Proteomics Applied on Plant Abiotic Stresses: Role of Heat Shock Proteins (HSP). Journal of Proteomics, Vol. 71, No. 4, 391-411.

Tuteja, N., Singh, M. B., Misra, M. K., Bhalla, P. L., & Tuteja, R. (2001). Molecular Mechanisms of DNA Damage and Repair: Progress in Plants. Critical Reviews in Biochemistry and Molecular Biology, Vol. 36, No. 4, 337-397.

Van den Ende, W., & Valluru, R. (2009). Sucrose, Sucrosyl Oligosaccharides, and Oxidative Stress: Scavenging and Salvaging? Journal of Experimental Botany, Vol. 60, No. 1, 9-18.

Vangronsveld, J., & Clijsters, H. (1994). Toxic Effects of Metals. In M. E. Farago (Ed.), Plants and the Chemical Elements. Biochemistry, Uptake, Tolerance and Toxicity (pp. 149-177).

Weinheim: VCH Verlagsgesellschaft. Vázquez, S., Goldsbrough, P., & Carpena, R. O. (2009). Comparative Analysis of the Contribution of Phytochelatins to Cadmium and Arsenic Tolerance in Soybean and White Lupin. Plant Physiology and Biochemistry, Vol. 47, No. 1, 63-67.

Vranova, E., Inze, D., & Van Breusegem, F. (2002). Signal Transduction during Oxidative Stress. Journal of Experimental Botany, Vol. 53, No. 372, 1227-1236.

Wingler, A. (2002). The Function of Trehalose Biosynthesis in Plants. Phytochemistry, Vol. 60, No. 5, 437-440.

Zhang, F.L., Niu, B., Wang, Y.C., Chen, F., Wang, S.H., Xu, Y., Jiang, L.-D., Gao, S., Wu, J., Tang, L., & Jia, Y.J. (2008). A Novel Betaine Aldehyde Dehydrogenase Gene from Jatropha Curcas, Encoding An Enzyme Implicated in Adaptation to Environmental Stress. Plant Science, Vol. 174, No. 5, 510-518.

Zhang, Z. C., Gao, X., & Qiu, B. S. (2008). Detection of Phytochelatins in the Hyperaccumulator Sedum Alfredii Exposed to Cadmium and Lead. Phytochemistry, Vol. 69, No. 4, 911-918.

Zhao, F.-J., & McGrath, S. P. (2009). Biofortification and Phytoremediation. Current Opinion in Plant Biology, Vol. 12, No. 3, 373-380.

Zorrig, W., Rouached, A., Shahzad, Z., Abdelly, C., Davidian, J.-C., & Berthomieu, P. (2010). Identification of Three Relationships Linking Cadmium Accumulation to Cadmium Tolerance and Zinc and Citrate Accumulation in Lettuce. Journal of Plant Physiology, Vol. 167, No. 15, 1239-1247.

Advances in Selected Plant Physiology Aspects Edited by Dr. Giuseppe Montanaro ISBN 978-953-51-0557-2 Hard cover, 388 pages Publisher InTech Published online 25, April, 2012 Published in print edition April, 2012. InTech Europe University Campus STeP Ri Slavka Krautzeka 83/A 51000 Rijeka, Croatia Phone: +385 (51) 770 447 Fax: +385 (51) 686 166 www.intechopen.com

Plant Response to Environmental Stress **Page: 60-89**
Edited by: Dr. Alka Chauhan; Dr. Pawan Kumar 'Bharti' and Dr. Avnish Chauhan
ISBN: 978-93-86841-58-2
Edition: 2018
Published by: Discovery Publishing House Pvt. Ltd., New Delhi (India)

5

Agro Ecosystem Analysis and Ecosystem Service Based Ecologically Sustainable Management of Rice Field Weed, *Ludwigia spp.*, by Its Classical Bio-control Agent *Altica cyanea* Weber

Nayan Roy[1]

ABSTRACT

In the modern era of ecofriendly and sustainable agriculture, ecosystem service based biointensive management of pests and weeds are the central theme in agro ecosystem analysis (AESA) based ecological management of pests or weeds (EPM or EWM). Today, the application of agro-ecology and environmental biotechnology has a great concern for sustainable agriculture as well as environment. Integrated crop management for sustainable agriculture, herbivores is generally used as bio-control agent to regulate weeds without interfering the cropping system. The flae beetle, *Altica cyanea* Weber (Coleoptera:Chrysomelidae) is a wide spread bio-control agent found in rice field and wetland ecosystem for defoliation of the weeds guided by means of their chemical signals. The water primrose, *Ludwigia spp.* (Onagraceae) is a wide spread decumbent weed commonly found in rice field and wetland ecosystem abundantly throughout India and elsewhere. They are highly invasive and common form of weed species in the Indian rice field ecosystems including West Bengal. They induce nutrient partitioning with the rice plants and thus reduce their production along with short and long term allelopathy on the other subsequent economic crops cultivated after rice. The successful use of a classical biocontrol agent for the management of the notorious weeds is fully depending on its host preference and population dynamics in relation with its host phytoconstituents. The host-preference and population growth of the flea beetles were studied to determine its potential value as a biological control agent for ecological management of the beetle against the weed species. In the present study host preference and population dynamics of the beetle, *A. cyanea* on *L. adscendens* has showed superiority relative to the other (*L. prostate* and *L. hyssopifolia*) host plants. The phytochemical constituents were correlated with such type of

[1] Assistant Professor of Zoology, Ecology Research Unit Department of Zoology, M.U.C. Women's College Burdwan-713104, West Bengal, India.

preference and survivability of this beetle. Thus, by knowing such variations in their population growth and host susceptibility, one can make ecological management by time based application of the beetle in the field rather than toxic herbicides against the notorious weed species. It will be the most important biointensive tool towards the judicious use of different control measures mainly environmentally benign chemical herbicides for ecofriendly management of the weed species in our agro ecosystem for better cultivation of rice well as other subsequent crops cultivated rotationally in near future.

Keywords: ecosystem service, biointensive management, *Ludwigia adscendens, L. prostate, L. hyssopifolia, Altica cyanea*, allelopathy, bio-control agent, AESA, EPM, EWM, sustainable agriculture.

INTRODUCTION

In the modern era of ecofriendly and sustainable agriculture ecosystem service based biointensive management of pests and weeds are the central theme in agro ecosystem analysis (AESA) based ecological management of pests or weeds (EPM or EWM). Today, the application of agro-ecology and environmental biotechnology has a great concern for sustainable agriculture as well as environment. The control of weeds through herbivorous bio-control agents without interfering the cropping system is a most effective eco-friendly approach rather than exception. The successful use of a classical biocontrol agent for the management of a notorious weed is fully depending on its host preference and population dynamics in relation with its host phytoconstituents. A number of coleopteran chrysomelid insects have been found in association with aquatic weeds in areas of the native range and can serve the purpose of regulating weeds (Husain and Ahamad, 1977; Satpathi *et al.*, 2005). The chrysomelid, *Altica foeveicollis,* is very effective in the natural control of *Ludwigia spp.* in Thailand (Napompeth, 1992). The search for suitable biological control agents for marshy herbaceous weeds common in rice elds has been conducted by many researchers from the oriental and southeast Asian countries (Stebbing, 1914; Husain and Ahamad, 1977; King, 1974; Lefroy, 1978; Nayek and Banerjee, 1987; Satpathi *et al.*, 2005). The beetle, *Altica cyanea* (Weber) (Coleoptera : Chrysomelidae) also attracted in large numbers for defoliation and feeding on *L. adscendens* (Nayek and Banerjee, 1987; Roy *et al.*, 2012). The larvae and adults of this beetles caused considerable damage to different *Ludwigia spp., Trapanatans, T. bisponsis, Rotala indica,* etc. but no feeding occurred on rice (Nayek and Banerjee, 1987; Shui, 1990). They are multivoltine in nature and completed a generation within 80–84 days (Nayek and Banerjee, 1987; Shui, 1990). One of the predatory species, *Zicrona coerulea* L. (*Hemiptera: Pentatomidae*) along with other natural predators preyed upon *A. cyanea* larvae to reduce their natural population (Nayek and Banerjee, 1987). The beetles may also decline by the usual light traps or bated traps present in the field to control the other insect pests.

Ludwigia spp. (Myrtales :Onagraceae) is a troublesome weed growing abundantly in Indian rice fields and elsewhere (Nayek and Banerjee, 1987; Verheij and Coronel, 1991; Napompeth, 1992; Wagu and Ugborogho, 2000; Roy and Barik, 2010; Roy *et al.*, 2011, 2012, Roy, 2016). Generally *Ludwigia spp.* occurs in moist places while a few is predominantly aquatic, ranging from annual herbs to large shrubs (Verheij and Coronel, 1991; Wogu and Ugborogho, 2000). It is generally common across different districts of West Bengal and also widespread over Bihar and Assam of India (Nayek and Banerjee, 1987; Roy and Barik, 2010; Roy *et al.*, 2011, 2012). They compete with rice plants for nourishment by nutrient partitioning and disturb crop production (Nayek and Banerjee, 1987). In other aspects, allelopathic interactions have been of great concern among many ecologists, agronomists and phytochemists in recent years (Norwal, 1994). Allelochemicals (e.g. flavonoids, terpenoids, phenolic compounds, water soluble glycosides, tannins and lignins, etc.) present in all plant tissues may be released by leaching, root exudation and decomposition of plant residues; and the soil adjacent to the decomposing debris may contain more decomposition products than other areas of the field (Rice, 1984; Norwal, 1994). In multiple cropping system, there is little time gap between the harvest and showing between two successive crops, and also for the decomposition of weed residues. Hence the succeeding crops are cultivated in the weed residues of previous crop, and this crop may be affected by the allelochemicals deposited in the soil by the previous crop's weed (Norwal, 1994; Inderjit *et al.*, 1999; Inderjit and Duke, 2003; Bogatek *et al.*, 2006; Roy and Barik, 2010; Roy *et al.*, 2011). The troublesome weeds, *Ludwigia spp.*, grow abundantly in rice fields and start their life cycle with the germination of rice and complete many generations up to rice harvesting. After rice harvesting, farmers used to cultivate several crops (e.g. green gram,til and dhania, etc.) in the field according to their needs. Usually, farmers do not consider the effect of the weed remains of the previous crop. In the rice field, several weed remnants decompose and may release allelochemicals in the soil that can be phytotoxic towards the other crops (Batish *et al.*, 2002; Bernat *et al.*, 2004; Bogatek *et al.*, 2006). At the same time, *Ludwigia spp.* also inhibit germination and seedling growth of rice due to allelochemicals released by leaching of the weed parts, decomposing weed residues (Mukherjee and Barik, 2013). They also showed long and short term allelopathic effects on different subsequent crops cultivated after rice by deposition of allelochemicals in the rice fields (Roy and Barik, 2010; Roy *et al.*, 2011).

Life table study is a central theme in ecological research which was first applied to insect population by Morris and Miller (1954) and used to calculate the vital statistics on pest population dynamics including comprehensive description of the survivorship, development, fecundity, mortality and life expectancy (Southwood, 1978, 1995; Southwood and Henderson, 2000; Maia *et al.*, 2000; Carey, 2001; Gould *et al.*, 2005; Sarfraz *et al.*, 2007; Ali and Rizvi, 2008,

2009). Life table is widely useful technique in insect pest management, where developmental stages are discrete and mortality rates vary widely from one life stage to another (Sugawe and Bilapate, 2007; Kakde *et al.*, 2014). There is a range of innet capacity for individual of a population but the variation in available food quality (Kim and Lee, 2002; Yasar and Güngör, 2005; Win *et al.*, 2011; Roy and Barik, 2012a, 2012b, 2013) along with environmental factors (Ellers-Kirk and Fleischer, 2006; Schowater, 2006; Ali and Rizvi, 2010) always influence the growth, reproduction, longevity and survival of that population. It is very helpful to determine the key mortality factors responsible in a particular stage within which the maximum mortality of the pest is obtained. Thus, by knowing such most vulnerable stages from life table, one can make time based application of different control measures for proper management of the pest population. The effect of different food sources on population parameters were observed in *Aphis gossypii* (Kocourek *et al.*, 1994); *Maladera matrida* (Harari *et al.*, 1997), *Spilosoma obliqua* (Varatharanjan *et al.*, 1998; Das and Chaudhury, 2005), *Podisus nigrispinus* (Medeiros *et al.*, 2000), *Aphid spiraecola* (Tsai and Wang, 2001), *Helicoverpa armigera* (Liu *et al.*, 2004), *Earias vitella* (Satpute *et al.*, 2005), *Plutella xylostella* (Hemchandra and Singh, 2003; Sarfraz *et al.*, 2007), *Trichoplusia ni* (Jagtap *et al.*, 2007), *Spodoptera litura* (Gedia *et al.*, 2008a, 2008b), *Monochilus sexmaculatus* (Ali and Razvi, 2009), *Coocinella septemounctata* (Ali and Razvi, 2010), *Nilaparvata lugens* (Win *et al.*, 2011), *Calosobruchus chinensis* L. (Chakroborty and Mondal, 2015), *D. casignetum* (Roy, 2015a), *Podontia quatuordecimpunctata* L. (Roy, 2015b), *Leptocorisa acuta* (Thunb.) (Dutta and Roy, 2016), *Epilachna vigintioctopunctata* Fab. (Roy, 2017) and *Altica cyanea* (Roy, 2016) on different host plants. All the variation of these studies could be attributed to differences among nutritional and anti-nutritional factors present in the respective host plants that directly affect potential and achieved herbivore development and fecundity (Awmack and Leather, 2002; Syed and Abro, 2003; Roy and Barik, 2013, Roy, 2014, 2015a, 2015b, 2016, 2017). Rizvi *et al.* (2009) were conducted both, age-specific (horizontal) and stage-specific (vertical) life-table of the cabbage butterfly, *Pieris brassicae* on various cole crops. But, in my current study, I have used only the stage-specifc life table approach as it is with lower biasness and more useful in the field condition. So, the development of life tables for *Altica cyanea* on different types of *Luwigia spp.* will help to assess the relative contribution made by the various phyto-constituents to the adult population pool. On the other hand, there is no report regarding the preferential potency of *A. cyanea* as a bio-control agent against the three *Ludwigia spp.* It is well known that, host-preference by herbivorous insects depends on chemical cues including nutritional requirements of insects and to some extent on secondary metabolites of their host- plants (Banerjee and Haque, 1985; Hamilton *et al.*, 2005; Harborne, 1994; Dicke, 2000; Schoonhoven *et al.*, 2005; Roy and Barik, 2012a and 2013). In this study, the host-preference of the flea beetle, *A. cyanea* were studied to determine its potential value as a biological control agent for one of the commonest and major invasive rice field weed, *L. adscendens* over the other two *Ludwigia spp*. Despite the extensive literature documenting the effects of host plant quality traits on performance of the classical biocontrol agent, *A. cyanea,* and few publications have reflected directly on its population growth parameters. The Knowledge of life table parameters of *A. cyanea* and the resistance-susceptibility characteristics of *Ludwigia spp*. will enable growers to employ the most appropriate biointensive control tactics towards ecosystem service based integrated weed management (IWM) in the form of ecological weed management (EWM) for better production of rice and other subsequent crops.

MATERIALS AND METHODS

Plant Materials

Three types of Fresh *Ludwigia spp.* leaves were collected randomly growing in rice fields near Chinsurah Rice Research Center adjacent to the district Hooghly (22°53′N, 88°23′E, 13m above sea level),West Bengal, India (Figure 5.1). Leaves were initially rinsed with distilled water and dried by paper toweling for phytochemical analysis.

Biochemical Analysis

(a) Extraction and phytochemical screening: The fresh leaves of the three host plants (*L. adscendens, L. prostate, L. hyssopifolia*) were air dried (Figure 5.1) and ground to make fine powder. 10 gm. of dried powdered leaves were successively extracted in to 100 ml of each of 90% methanol, 90% ethanol and distilled water. Then the preliminary microchemical evaluation of the powdered leaf was performed by chemical colour reaction tests with various reagents for detection of various phytochemical groups present in the leaves following different standard methods (Trease and Evans, 1983, 1989; Day and Underwood, 1986; Duke, 1985; Harborne, 1973; Khandelwal, 2000; Aguinaldo *et al.*, 2004; Raman, 2006). The screening test of each biochemical reaction was repeated for three times.

(b) Extraction and phytochemical estimation: The freshly harvested leaves of were dipped in different solvents for extraction of different primary and secondary biochemicals. The variability in nutritional quality of three host-plants were estimated by various biochemical analysis, such as total carbohydrates (DuBois *et al.*, 1956), total proteins (Lowry *et al.*, 1951; Miller, 1959), total lipids (Folch *et al.*, 1957), total amino acids (Moore and Stein 1948; Roy *et al.*, 2013), moisture (Banerjee and Haque, 1984; Roy and Barik, 2013), total phenols (Bray and Thorpe, 1953; Roy and Barik, 2012a), total flavonoids (Zhishen *et al.*, 1999), tannin (Trease and Evans, 1983), saponin (Trease and Evans, 1983), phytate (Reddy and Love, 1999). Each biochemical analysis was repeated for three times and expressed in dry weight basis.

L. adscendens L. prostate L. hyssopifolia

Fig. 5.1: Three most common rice field weeds of *Ludwigia spp.* (Onagraceae)-common host plant of a classical biocontrol agent, *Altica cyanea* (Weber) [Coleoptera: Chrysomelidae].

Insect Rearing

The insects used in this study were collected by light trap from the weed growing in a rice eld near Chinsurah Rice Research Center. The insects were maintained in 1 l glass jars, containing three types of weed leaves, and covered with ne-mesh nylon nets at 27 ± 1°C temperature, 65 ± 10% relative humidity, and a 12 L:12 D photoperiod in a BOD incubator. The F_2 *A. cyanea* insects for oviposition separately in different sterilized glass jars. Fresh leaves were given daily by replacing the previous one until eggs were laid by the test insects, and the eggs with each host-plant leaves were placed in new sterilized glass jars separately. To study the duration of larval and post larval development, the eggs were separated and reared separately in sterilized glass jars containing 40 larvae on each kind of host-plant, and observations were noted during their respective development with three replicates for each host plants.

Life Table Parameters

The construction of *A. cyanea* life table includes several parameters which were calculated with the formulae of Carey (1993), Krebs (1994) and Price (1998). These parameters include probability of survival from birth to age x (*lx*), proportion dying each age (*dx*), mortality (*qx*), survival rate (*sx*) per day per age class from egg to adult stages. Using these parameters, the following statistics like, average population alive in each stage (*Lx*), life expectancy (*ex*), exponential mortality or killing power (*kx*), total generation mortality (*K* or *GM*), generation survival (*GS*), gross reproductive rate (*GRR*), net reproductive rate (NRR or R_0), mean generation time (T_c), doubling time (*DT*), intrinsic rate of population increase (r_m), Euler's corrected *r* (r_c), finite rate of population increase (λ), weekly multiplication rate (λ^7), increase rate per generation (λ^{Tc}), were also computed, using Carey's formulae (Carey, 1993). Some other population parameters like potential fecundity (Pf), total fertility rate (Fx), mortality coefficient (MC), population growth rate (PGR), population momentum factor of increase (PMF), expected population size in 2nd generation (PF_2), expected females in 2nd generation (FF_2), general fertility rate (GFR), crude birth rate (CBR), reproductive value (RV), vital index (VI) and trend index (TI) were also determined by using well defined formulae (Brich, 1948; Southwood, 1978, 1995; Southwood and Henderson, 2000).

Statistical Analysis

All the data of biochemical analyses of the three host plants as well as the data on growth duration (i.e. larval and post larval duration and adult longevity), survivability and fecundity of *A. cyanea* reared on three host-plants were subjected to one way analysis of variance (ANOVA), regression analysis and correlation analysis (Parui and Roy, 2016, Roy, 2014, 2015a, 2015b, 2016, 2017) to compare the effects of the diet regimes. Means associated with all the data for each variable were separated using Tukey's test ("honestly significant difference test") when significant values were obtained (Sokal and Rohlf, 1994; Zar, 1999; Roy, 2015, 2016, 2017). Effect of the host plants on the population dynamics of *A. cyanea* were analyzed using one-way ANOVA, regression and correlation analysis (Sokal and Rohlf, 1994; Zar, 1999; Parui and Roy, 2016, Roy, 2014, 2015a, 2015b, 2016, 2017). Means of different demographic parameters were compared by Tukey's test (HSD) when significant values were obtained (Sokal and Rohlf, 1994; Zar, 1999; Roy, 2014, 2015a, 2015b, 2016, 2017). All the statistical analysis was performed using the statistical program SPSS (version 13.0) computer software program (SPSS, 2004, Roy, 2014, 2015a, 2015b, 2016, 2017).

RESULTS

(a) Host phytochemicals and nutritional ecology: The host preference of the flea beetle, *A.cyanea*, was studied to determine its potential as a biological control agent for the three *Ludwigia spp.*(*L. adscendens, L. prostate, L. hyssopifolia*). The biochemical screening tests followed by quantitative analysis of the three host-plants are presented in Figure 5.2. Total carbohydrates, proteins, lipids and moisture content was varied significantly among the three host-plants, which can be arranged in order of *L. adscendens* > *L. prostate* > *L. hyssopifolia* ($P < 0.0001$). Total amino acid content was highest and significantly differed ($P < 0.001$) in *L. adscendens* than the other two host plants. Phenol concentration was also differed significantly among the three host-plants ($P < 0.0001$) and can be arranged in order of *L. adscendens* > *L. prostate* > *L. hyssopifolia*. The females laid yellowish eggs in masses on the abaxial surface of the weed leaves and larvae passed through three distinct instars along with pre-pupal and pupal stages.

The developmental duration (i.e., total larval, post larval duration and adult longevity) of the different stages of *A. cyanea*on the three species of *Ludwigia*was varied significantly (P < 0.001) and they could be arranged as *L. adscendens* < *L. prostate* < *L. hyssopifolia* whereas, the adult longevity was in the reverse order i.e., *L. adscendens* > *L. prostate* > *L. hyssopifolia* (Figure 5.3).The fecundity was always higher in *L. adscendens* and significantly differed (p < 0.001) than the other two host plants (*L. prostate* and *L. hyssopifolia*) (Figure 5.4). The hatchability percent, larval survivability and adult emergence were significantly differed (p <0.001) among the three selected host plants (Figure 5.5). The beetle showed lower hatchability, larval survivability and adult emergence when they were fed on *L. hyssopifolia* and *L. prostate* instead of *L. adscendens* during the study (Figure 5.5).

(b) Life table and population dynamics: The stage-specific pooled life table of *A. cyanea* was constructed on *L. adscendens* separately for the three cohorts containing 130 eggs each and showed four distinct stages with three larval instars (Table 5.1, 5.2 and 5.3). The demographic data of *A. cyanea* reared on the weed represent similar pattern of development with significant variations (*P*<0.01) within the developmental stages (Table 5.4). The proportion of surviving (lx), average population alive in each stage (Lx), proportion of dying (dx) and mortality (qx) were increased particularly in the early stages and subsequently decreased in advance stages (Table 5.1, 5.2 and 5.3). Life expectancy (ex) also followed the same pattern of lx and Lx. The killing power (kx) was increased and decreased with developmental advancement with lesser values in adults (Table 5.1, 5.2 and 5.3). All the population parameters (lx, dx, qx, sx, Lx and ex) of *A. cyanea* were differed significantly (*P*< 0.0001) in each developmental stage (Table 5.1, 5.2 and 5.3). The observed accumulated survival of *A. cyanea* indicated type-III survivorship curve (Figure 5.5).

Table 5.1. Stage-specific Pooled Life Table (Means of 3 Observations) for 3 Cohorts of *A. cyanea* on *L. adscendens*.

Life stages on *L. adscendens*	lx	dx	qx	sx	Lx	Tx	kx	ex
Egg	1.000	0.077	0.077	0.923	0.962	6.223	0.035	6.223
Instar I	0.923	0.169	0.183	0.817	0.838	5.262	0.088	5.700
Instar II	0.754	0.123	0.163	0.837	0.692	4.423	0.077	5.867
Instar III	0.631	0.108	0.171	0.829	0.577	1.838	0.081	2.915
Prepupa	0.523	0.054	0.103	0.897	0.496	1.262	0.047	2.412
Pupa	0.469	0.069	0.148	0.852	0.435	0.765	0.069	1.631
Adult	0.400	0.138	0.346	0.654	0.331	0.331	0.185	0.827

Table 5.2: Stage-specific Pooled Life Table (means of 3 observations) for 3 Cohorts of *A. cyanea* on *L. prostate*.

Life stages on *L. prostate*	lx	dx	qx	sx	Lx	Tx	kx	ex
Egg	1.000	0.169	0.169	0.831	0.915	5.485	0.081	5.485
Instar I	0.831	0.138	0.167	0.833	0.762	4.569	0.079	5.500
Instar II	0.692	0.146	0.211	0.789	0.619	3.808	0.103	5.500
Instar III	0.546	0.115	0.211	0.789	0.488	1.550	0.103	2.839
Prepupa	0.431	0.046	0.107	0.893	0.408	1.062	0.049	2.464
Pupa	0.385	0.046	0.120	0.880	0.362	0.654	0.056	1.700
Adult	0.338	0.092	0.273	0.727	0.292	0.292	0.138	0.864

Table 5.3: Stage-specific Pooled Life Table (means of 3 observations) for 3 Cohorts of *A. cyanea* on *L. hyssopifolia*.

Life stages on *L. hyssopifolia*	lx	dx	qx	sx	Lx	Tx	kx	ex
Egg	1.000	0.215	0.215	0.785	0.892	5.092	0.105	5.092
Instar I	0.785	0.162	0.206	0.794	0.704	4.200	0.100	5.353
Instar II	0.623	0.100	0.160	0.840	0.573	3.496	0.076	5.611
Instar III	0.523	0.123	0.235	0.765	0.462	1.354	0.117	2.588
Prepupa	0.400	0.069	0.173	0.827	0.365	0.892	0.083	2.231
Pupa	0.331	0.054	0.163	0.837	0.304	0.527	0.077	1.593
Adult	0.277	0.108	0.389	0.611	0.223	0.223	0.214	0.806

Table 5.4: ANOVA Result of Stage-specific Pooled Life Table for the Three Cohorts (Average of 3 Observations each) of *A. cyanea* on the Three Host Plants (*L. adscendens, L. prostate, L. hyssopifolia L. adscendens*).

A. Cyanea on L. adscendens						
ANOVA: Source of Variation	**SS**	**df**	**MS**	**F**	**P-value**	**F crit**
Between Groups	91.218	7.000	13.031	9.698	0.0001	2.207
Within Groups	64.498	48.000	1.344			
Total	155.716	55.000				

A. Cyanea on L. prostate						
ANOVA: Source of Variation	**SS**	**df**	**MS**	**F**	**P-value**	**F crit**
Between Groups	77.295	7.000	11.042	10.490	0.0001	2.207
Within Groups	50.526	48.000	1.053			
Total	127.821	55.000				
A. Cynaea on L. hyssopifolia						
ANOVA: Source of Variation	**SS**	**df**	**MS**	**F**	**P-value**	**F crit**
Between Groups	67.486	7.000	9.641	9.730	0.0001	2.207
Within Groups	47.559	48.000	0.991			
Total	115.044	55.000				

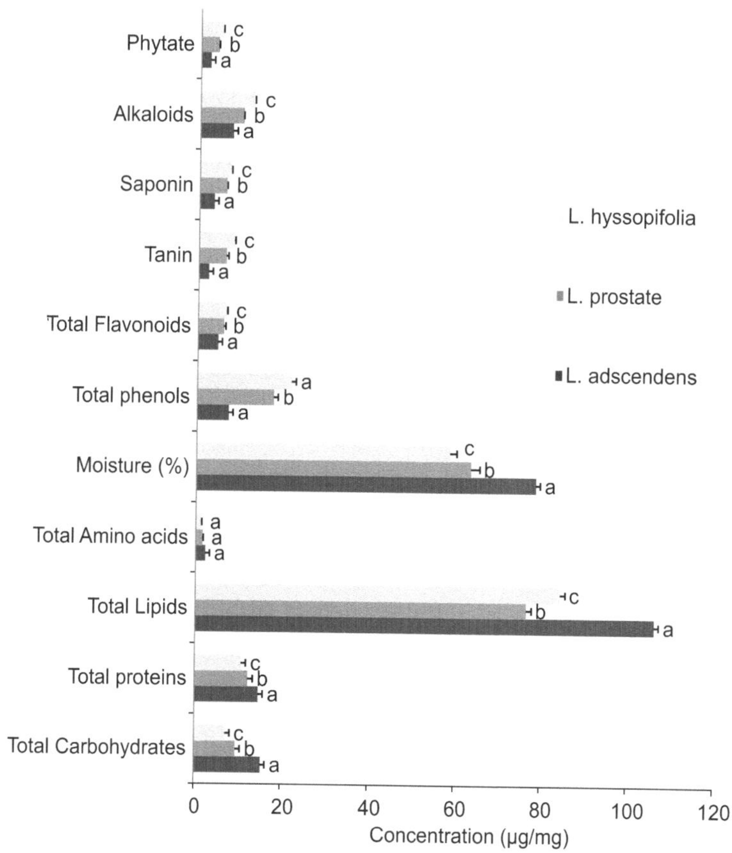

Fig. 5.2: Phytochemical variations of the three *Ludwigia spp.* Different letters over the bars indicate that the means (Mean ± SE of 3 observations) are significantly different ($P < 0.05$), while comparing one type of plants with the other within the column.

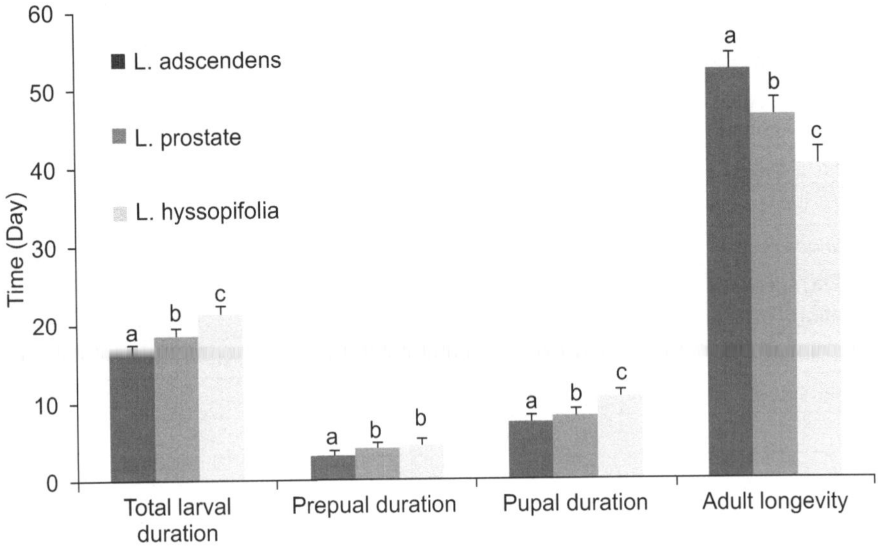

Fig. 5.3: Developmental duration of the different stages of *A.cyanea* on the three species of *Ludwigia*. Different letters over the bars indicate that the means (Mean ± SE of 3 observations) are significantly different (*P* < 0.05), while comparing one type of host plants with the other within the column.

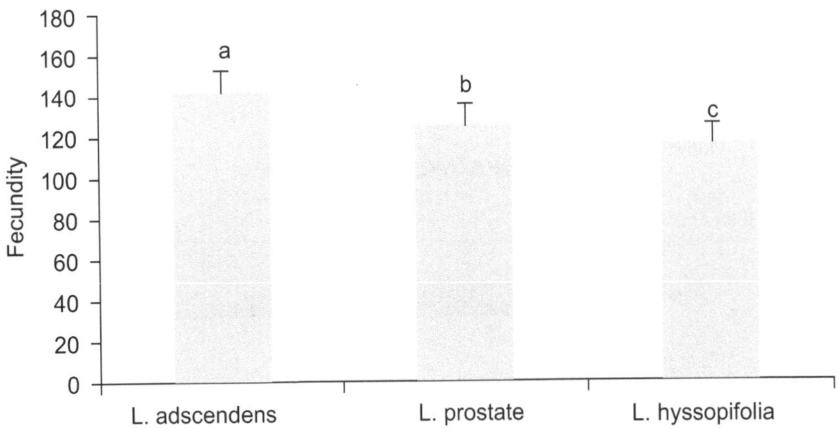

Fig. 5.4: Fecundity of *A.cyanea* on the three species of *Ludwigia spp*. Different letters over the bars indicate that the means (Mean ± SE of 3 observations each) are significantly different (*P* < 0.05), while comparing one type of host plants with the other within the column.

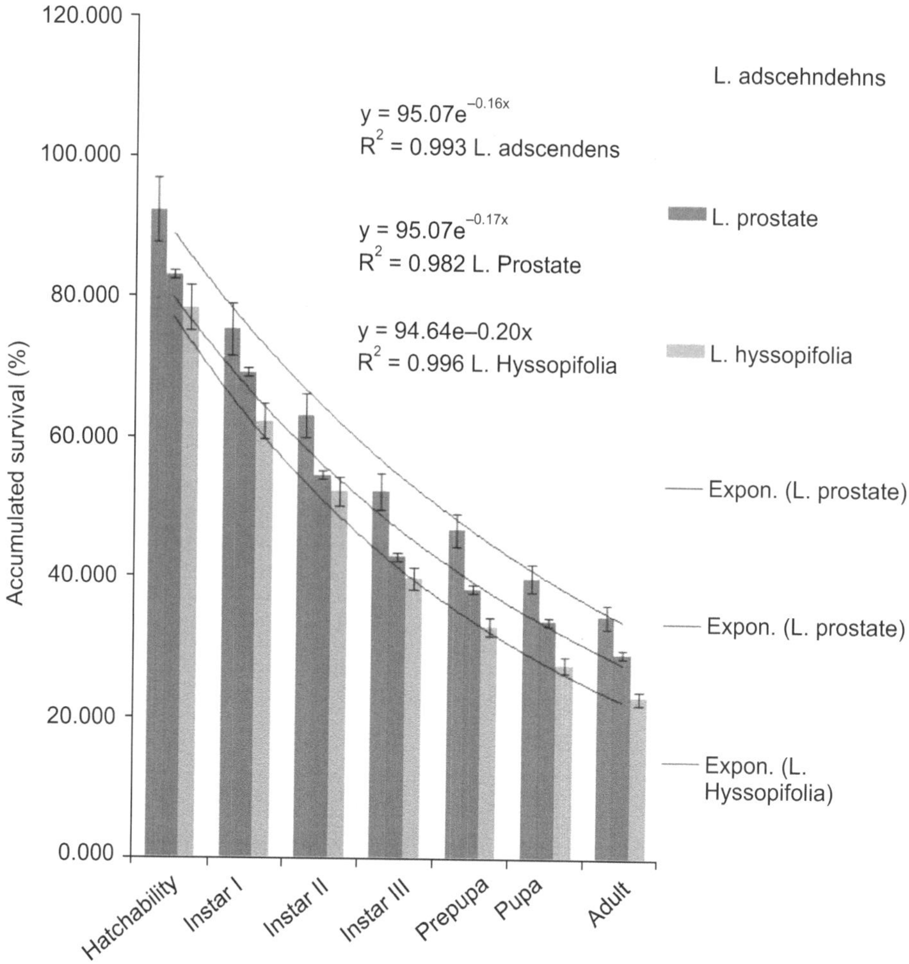

Fig. 5.5: Stage-specific accumulated survival (%) of *A. cyanea* on the three species of *Ludwigia*. The means of three cohorts each on a host (Mean ± SE of 3 observations) are significantly different (P < 0.05), while comparing one type of host plants with the other within the column with exponential trend line, equation and R^2 value.

The average generation fecundity (Fx), gross reproductive rate (GRR), net reproductive rate (R_0), intrinsic rate of natural increase (r_m) and the daily finite rate of increase (λ) always significantly differed ($F_{6,13}$ = 22.592, P<0.001). The average generation time (T_c) of (90.35 days) with the doubling time (DT) of (20.95 days) was also significantly differed (Table 5.5). Thus, the population growth parameters of *A. cyanea* were varied significantly (Table 5.6) in their different developmental stages rather than the cohorts. The reproductive parameters are differentially correlated with each other as well as with their phytoconstituents (Table 5.7 and 5.8).

Table 5.5. Population Dynamics and Reproductive Table of the Nine Cohorts (Average of 3 observations each) of *A. cyanea* on Three Host Plants (*L. adscendens, L. prostate, L. hyssopifolia*).

Population parameters	*L. adscendens*	*L. prostate*	*L. hyssopifolia*	Average	Variance
Potential fecundity (Pf)	142.000	126.000	116.000	128.000	4.432
Total fertility rate (F_x)	1768.000	1664.000	1144.000	1525.333	111765.333
Gross reproductive rate (GRR)	34.000	37.818	31.778	34.532	9.334
Net reproductive rate (NRR)	13.600	12.800	8.800	11.733	6.613
Generation time (T_c)	131.000	133.600	129.400	131.333	4.493
Doubling time (DT)	43.553	46.927	53.291	47.923	24.452
Intrinsic rate of increase (r_m)	0.016	0.015	0.013	0.015	0.000
Euler's corrected r (r_c)	0.078	0.081	0.099	0.086	0.000
Finite rate of increase (ë)	1.016	1.015	1.013	1.015	0.000
Weelkly multiplication rate ($ë^7$)	1.118	1.109	1.095	1.107	0.000
Annual rate of increase (ARI)	333.283	219.499	115.297	222.693	11887.162
Increase rate per generation ($ë^{Tc}$)	13.600	12.800	8.800	11.733	6.613
Generation mortality (GM)	0.582	0.609	0.772	0.654	0.010
Mortality coefficient (MC)	0.105	0.098	0.068	0.090	0.000

Generation survival (GS)	0.433	0.407	0.353	0.398	0.002
Population growth rate (PGR)	0.541	0.473	0.286	0.433	0.017
Population momentum factor of increase (PMF)	7.947	9.479	8.877	8.768	0.596
Population size in 2nd generation (PF_2)	270.205	303.341	195.292	256.279	3064.070
Hypothetical F_2 females (HNf_2)	184.960	163.840	77.440	142.080	3245.261
Realised F_2 females (RNf_2)	108.082	121.336	78.117	102.512	490.251
General fertility rate (GFR)	9.559	10.156	14.773	11.496	8.142
Crude birth rate (CBR)	1.585	1.831	1.912	1.776	0.029
Reproductive value (RV)	68.000	75.636	63.556	69.064	37.336
Vital Indwx (VI)	0.262	0.246	0.169	0.226	0.002
Trend index (TI)	15.961	18.546	14.295	16.267	4.589

Table 5.6: ANOVA Result of Population Dynamics and Reproductive Table of the Nine Cohorts (Average of 3 observations each) of *A. cyanea* on Three Host Plants (*L. adscendens, L. prostate, L. hyssopifolia*).

ANOVA: Source of Variation	SS	df	MS	F	P-value
Between Groups	6654571.446	24.000	277273.810	53.095	0.000
Within Groups	261108.614	50.000	5222.172		
Total	6915680.060	74.000			

Table 5.7: Correlation of Some Selected Population Parameters from Reproductive Table of the Nine Cohorts (Average of 3 observations each) of *A. cyanea* on three host plants (*L. adscendens, L. prostate, L. hyssopifolia*).

Correlation	F_x	GRR	NRR	r_m	r_c	T_c	DT	GM	SG	VI
GRR	0.997									
NRR	1.000	0.997								
r_m	0.999	0.999	0.999							
r_c	0.990	0.976	0.990	0.983						
T_c	0.335	0.404	0.335	0.373	0.196					
DT	-0.992	-0.998	-0.992	-0.996	-0.963	-0.453				
GM	0.844	0.802	0.844	0.821	0.912	-0.223	-0.768			
SG	0.958	0.977	0.958	0.969	0.907	0.590	-0.987	0.655		
VI	0.997	0.988	0.997	0.993	0.998	0.261	-0.979	0.883	0.933	
λ	0.999	0.999	0.999	1.000	0.983	0.372	-0.996	0.822	0.969	0.993

Table 5.8: Correlation of Some Selected Population Parameters from Reproductive Table of the Nine Cohorts (Average of 3 observations each) of *A. cyanea* on the Hosts (*L. adscendens, L. prostate, L. hyssopifolia*) Phytochemicals.

Correlation	F_x	GRR	NRR	r_m	r_c	T_c	DT	GM	SG	VI	λ
Total Carbohydrates	0.983	0.966	0.983	0.975	0.999	0.155	-0.951	0.928	0.889	0.994	0.975
Total proteins	0.996	0.987	0.996	0.992	0.998	0.252	-0.977	0.887	0.930	1.000	0.992
Total Lipids	0.741	0.689	0.741	0.713	0.830	-0.385	-0.648	0.986	0.518	0.790	0.713
Total Amino acids	0.994	0.983	0.994	0.989	0.999	0.231	-0.972	0.897	0.922	1.000	0.989
Moisture (%)	0.971	0.950	0.971	0.960	0.995	0.099	-0.932	0.948	0.862	0.986	0.961
Total phenols	-0.980	-0.963	-0.980	-0.972	-0.999	-0.142	0.947	-0.933	-0.883	-0.993	-0.972
Total Flavonoids	-0.988	-0.973	-0.988	-0.980	-1.000	-0.183	0.959	-0.918	-0.902	-0.997	-0.981
Tanin	-0.987	-0.972	-0.987	-0.979	-1.000	-0.176	0.957	-0.920	-0.899	-0.996	-0.979
Saponin	-0.974	-0.955	-0.974	-0.964	-0.996	-0.113	0.937	-0.943	-0.869	-0.989	-0.964
Alkaloids	-0.998	-1.000	-0.998	-1.000	-0.978	-0.397	0.998	-0.806	-0.975	-0.990	-1.000
Phytate	-0.990	-0.977	-0.990	-0.984	-1.000	-0.202	0.964	-0.910	-0.910	-0.998	-0.984

Thus the beetle, *A. cyanea,* show a preference towards *L. adscendens* over *L. prostate, L. hyssopifolia* and it became a promising biological control agent for *L. adscendens* along with other host plants growing in our rice field (Figure 5.6-5.12). The effect of different population parameters were observed in *A. cyanea* on different host plants due to its different phytoconstituents. The variations in host preference and population dynamics also fully supported in our natural system (Figure 5.6-5.12) which will be a great potential for biointensive management of Ludwigia spp. by the biocontrol agent *A. cyanea*. Thus, this study also informs the growth stages and population parameters of the beetle that may help to use it as a potential bio-control agent in the field condition.

Fig. 5.6: The classical biocontrol agent, *Altica cyanea* (Weber) [Coleoptera: Chrysomelidae] male, female, larva and egg under the leaf of *Ludwigia adscendens* (Onagraceae).

Fig. 5.7: Invasiveness of the most abundant rice field weed, *Ludwigia adscendens* (Onagraceae), a highly preferred host plant of the classical biocontrol agent, *Altica cyanea* (Weber) [Coleoptera: Chrysomelidae].

Fig. 5.8: Biointensive control by defoliation of the most invasive rice field weed, *Ludwigia adscendens* (Onagraceae) by larval stages of the classical biocontrol agent, *Altica cyanea* (Weber) [Coleoptera: Chrysomelidae].

Fig. 5.9: Biointensive control by defoliation of the most invasive rice field weed, *Ludwigia adscendens* (Onagraceae) by the classical biocontrol agent, *Altica cyanea* (Weber) [Coleoptera: Chrysomelidae].

Fig. 5.10: Natural development of a large population of the classical biocontrol agent, *Altica cyanea* (Weber) [Coleoptera: Chrysomelidae] on one of its most preferred host plant, *Ludwigia adscendens* (Onagraceae)- an invasive rice field weed, by complete defoliation.

Fig. 5.11: Complete defoliation of the rice field weed, *Ludwigia adscendens* (Onagraceae) by the classical biocontrol agent, *Altica cyanea* (Weber) [Coleoptera: Chrysomelidae].

Fig. 5.12. The most common predatory blue bug (*Zicrona coerulea*) of the classical biocontrol agent, *Altica cyanea* (Weber) [Coleoptera: Chrysomelidae]-an ecological limiting factor against the biointensive management of rice field weeds, *Ludwigia spp.* (Onagraceae).

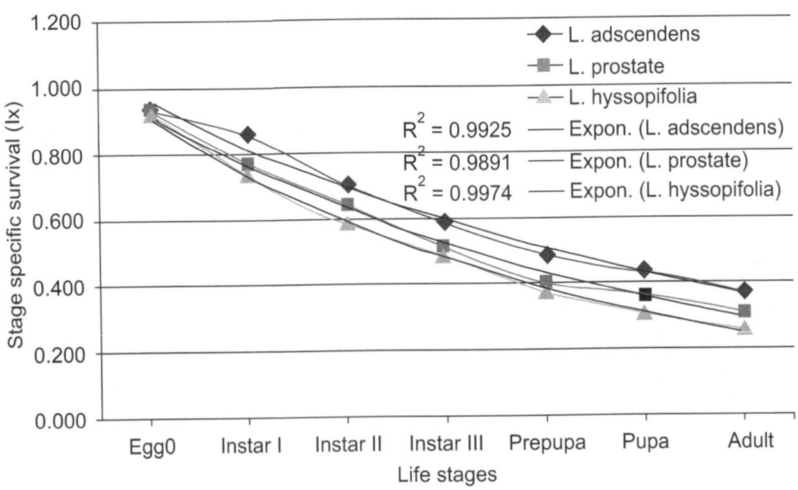

Fig. 5.13: Stage-specific survivorship curve (Type-III) of *A. cyanea* on the three species of *Ludwigia spp.* The means of three cohorts each on a host (Mean ± SE of 3 observations) are significantly different ($P < 0.05$), while comparing one type of host plants with the other within the column with exponential trend line and R^2 value.

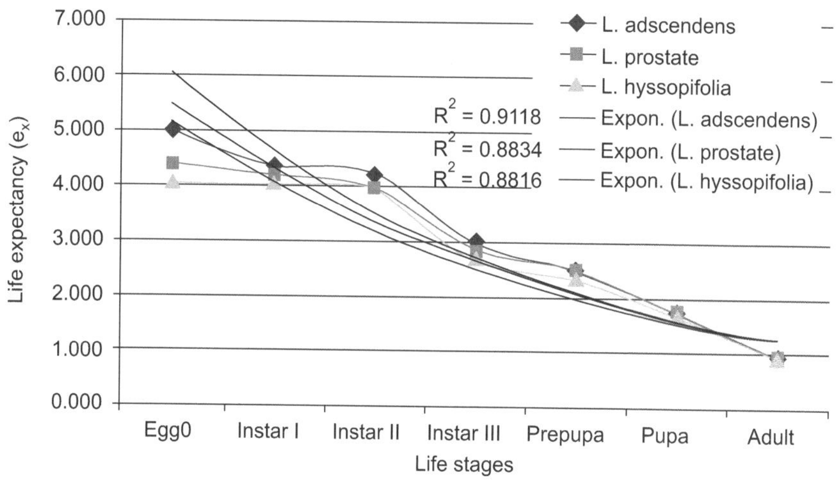

Fig. 5.14: Stage-specific life expectancy (e_x) curve of *A. cyanea* on the three species of *Ludwigia spp.* The means of three cohorts each on a host (Mean ± SE of 3 observations) are significantly different (*P* < 0.05), while comparing one type of host plants with the other within the column with exponential trend line and R^2 value.

DISCUSSION

Host plant availability and quality in terms of their phytochemicals may play a vital role in pest feeding preference as well as population dynamics by affecting immature and adult performance (Applebaum, 1985; Slansky and Scriber, 1985; Dicke, 2000; Hasseb *et al.*, 2001; Schoonhoven *et al.*, 2005; Genc, 2006; Kumar *et al.*, 2009; Shobana *et al.*, 2010; Roy and Barik, 2012a, 2012b, 2013, 2014; Roy *et al.*, 2012, 2013a, 2013b, Roy, 2014). Host-plant utilization is also influenced by the ability of insect to ingest, assimilate and convert food into their body tissues (Scriber and Slansky, 1981; Singh and Singh, 1982; Dadd, 1985; Nation, 2001). Thus, host plant quality during larval growth and development is a key determinant of adult longevity, fecundity, fertility and survivability (Setamou *et al.*, 1999; Awmack and Leather, 2002; Sarfraz *et al.*, 2006; Shobana *et al.*, 2010; Roy and Barik, 2013; Roy, 2014). Ultimately, shorter developmental time along with greater total reproduction of insects on a host indicate greater suitability of a host plant (Thangavelu and Phulon, 1983; Roy and Barik, 2012 and 2013; Roy, 2014).The primary metabolites (carbohydrates, proteins, lipids, amino acids including moisture content) are used for general vitality, growth and reproduction (Mattson, 1980; Dadd, 1985; Slansky and Scriber, 1985; Turunen, 1990; Harborne, 1994; Genc and Nation, 2004; Schoonhoven *et al.*, 2005; Shobana *et al.*, 2010). Whereas, the secondary metabolites govern the suitability of the substrate for herbivoreshost preference and acceptability (Harborne, 1994; Schoonhoven *et al.*, 2005; Roy and Barik, 2012a, 2012b, 2013, 2014; Roy, 2014). Consumption of greater amount of secondary chemicals was also found to significantly reduce the adult longevity, fecundity, and retardation of larval growth (Harborne, 1994; Schoonhoven *et al.*, 2005; Roy and Barik, 2012a, 2012b, 2013, 2014; Roy, 2014) due to higher metabolic costs (Xue *et al.*, 2010).

In ecological research, life table study is a central theme and used to calculate the vital statistics of pest population dynamics including comprehensive description of their survivorship, development, fecundity, mortality and life expectancy (Southwood, 1978; Ricklefs and Miller, 2000; Carey, 2001; Sarfraz *et al.*, 2007; Ali and Rizvi, 2008). It is widely useful technique in insect pest management, where developmental stages are discrete and mortality rates vary widely from one life stage to another (Kakde *et al.*, 2014). There is a range of innet capacity for individual of a population (Gill *et al.*, 1989) but the variation in available food quality (Kim and Lee, 2002; Liu *et al.*, 2004; Yasar and Güngör, 2005; Win *et al.*, 2011; Roy and Barik, 2012 and 2013; Roy, 2014) along with environmental factors (Shirai, 2000; Morgan *et al.*, 2001; Ellers-Kirk and Fleischer, 2006; Schowater, 2006; Ali and Rizvi, 2010) always influence the growth, reproduction, longevity and survival of that population. The effect of different food sources on population parameters were observed in *Plutella xylostella* (Sarfraz *et al.*, 2007) and *Diacrisia casignetum* (Roy and Barik, 2013) on different host plants. Variation between the results of this study could be attributed to differences among nutritional and anti-nutritional factors present in the respective host leaves that directly affect potential and achieved herbivore development and fecundity (Awmack and Leather, 2002; Syed and Abro, 2003; Roy and Barik, 2012a, 2012b, 2013, 2014; Roy, 2014).

The chemical signals and nutritional constituents play an important role in the interactions between plants and phytophagous insects (Dicke, 2000; Zhu *et al.*, 2005; Rahaman and Khan, 2006, 2012; Roy and Barik, 2012a, 2012b, 2013, 2014). The role of host-plant is an important factor in regulating herbivorous insect populations as the concentrations and proportion of nutrients differ greatly among species (Verkerk and Wright, 1996; Baksha, 1997; Howlader, 1993; Schoonhoven *et al.*, 2005). Nutritional requirements for insect growth and reproduction depend on the ability of the insect to ingest, assimilate and convert food into body tissue (Waldbauer, 1968; Dadd, 1985; Nation, 2001). The growth duration such as, developmental time, longevity, fecundity and survival of insects showed significant differences among the three host-plants tested with respect to their food quality (Awmack and Leather, 2002; Shobana *et al.*, 2010; Roy and Barik, 2013). Fecundity of herbivorous insects also depends on host-plant quality, which influences growth rates, developmental time and survivability of herbivores (Ramachandran *et al.*, 1998; Shobana *et al.*, 2010). Clear variation was observed in food consumption and development of *A. cyanea* when fed with these three host-plants. The possible explanation for variation in food consumption and development of this insect is due to significant differences in carbohydrates, proteins, lipids, amino acids and moisture content in the respective host plants. This study indicated higher growth rate, lower developmental time, higher adult longevity, survivability and fecundity of *A. cyanea* when fed with *L. adscendens*, which may be due to the better nutritional quality relative to the other two host plants. Phenols determine the suitability of the substrate for exploitation by the herbivores and thus govern host preferences and acceptability (Harborne, 1994; Schoonhoven *et al.*, 2005). Further, an increase in phenol content indicates reduction in adult longevity and fecundity, and retardation of larval growth (Harborne, 1994). Higher phenol content was observed in *L. hyssopifolia* followed by *L. prostate*, which probably indicates greater resistance in this plant against herbivory. Further, greater content of phenol in *L. hyssopifolia* and *L. prostate* probably caused reduction in fecundity and retardation of larval growth of *A. cyanea* when compared to the host-plant *L. adscendens* used in this study. In this study, higher levels of carbohydrates, proteins, lipids including amino acids, and lower levels of phenol in *L. adscendens* might be the possible explanation for relatively fastest larval development, higher fecundity and survivability when the insects were fed with this host plant relative to the other two host species. Thus in this case, *A. cyanea* show a preference towards *L. adscendens* over *L. prostate* and *L. hyssopifolia* due to higher nutritional quality relative to secondary metabolites. These suggest that, *A. cyanea* may be a promising biological control agent for *L. adscendens* growing in rice-paddies rather than the other two host species.

The difference in different life table parameters and in population dynamics also could be due to the presence of same nutritional factors as well as defensive secondary metabolites that directly affect potential and achieved development and fecundity of *A. cyanea*. Survival rate (lx) of *A. cyanea* during the developmental stages (egg to adult) indicated a gradual decreased rate of survival during early stages and then it gradually increased with aging on all the three host plants. These results suggest that the survival curve of *A. cyanea* is of type III, with high mortality during the immature stages as found in most insect species (Roy, 2015a, 2015b, 2016, 2017). The r_m also known as a bioclimatic index is a fundamental ecological parameter to predict the population growth under a given condition. It would be a most appropriate index to evaluate the performance of an insect on different host plants or plant parts as well as the host plant's resistance. It represents the rate of potential increase of a population under optimal environmental conditions when fecundity and survival are maximal (optimal zone of development) and adequately summarizes the physiological qualities of an animal in relation to its capacity to increase. The high value of R_0 on *L. adscendens* is a reflection of high r_m. The average generation time (*Tc*) and doubling time (DT) of *A. cyanea* was significantly shorter on *L. adscendens* relative to the other (*L. prostate* and *L. hyssopifolia*) host plants. In this study, differences in reproductive period and longevity of *A. cyanea* on the three *Ludwigia spp.* were due to variation in their chemicals as well as their abundance. Thus, the R_0, rm, Tc and DT are useful indices of population growth under a given set of conditions. Other population parameters are also directly or indirectly influence the population dynamics of the biocontrol agent accordingly as in their host preference analysis. Thus population parameters along with life and fecundity table of *A. cyanea* show a preferential facilitation on *L. adscendens* over *L. prostate* and *L. hyssopifolia* for better population growth and dynamics also due to higher nutritional quality relative to secondary metabolites in respective host plants. This knowledge is very important when studying any biocontrol agent or any insect pest population for developing efficient ecological pest management tactics. This study also explain how host quality influences the life table parameters of *A. cyanea* can help one to understand the population dynamics for ecological sustainable management of the biocontrol agent in a manipulated ecosystem towards biointensive control of the notorious weed species (*L. adscendens, L. prostate* and *L. hyssopifolia*) in the rice field. It will be the most important biointensive tool over the judicious use of different control measures mainly chemical herbicides for environmentally safe management in our agro ecosystem towards better cultivation of rice well as other subsequent crops cultivated rotationally.

CONCLUSION

In this modern era with increasing human population there is a need to increase rice production per unit of land through economically and environmentally sustainable strategies. Today, the application of agro-ecology and environmental biotechnology has a great concern for sustainable agriculture as well as environment. In the present study host preference and fundamental population parameters of the beetle, *A. cyanea* on *L. adscendens* relative to the other (*L. prostate* and *L. hyssopifolia*) gives a vivid picture regarding their variations in growth stages and their reproductive potential for understanding of their population dynamics. From the life and fecundity table with different population parameters one can develop a huge gene pool of the beetle, *A. cyanea,* on *L. adscendens* in a manipulated ecosystem to make time based application of the beetle as appropriate biointensive control measures against the notorious weed species (*L. adscendens, L. prostate* and *L. hyssopifolia*) in the rice field by the strategy of ecologically sustainable weed management (ESWM or EWM) in the field condition for better production of rice as well as other subsequent crops cultivated rotationally in near future.

Author's Contributions

NR designed the whole study including sample collection, chemical analysis, index calculation, data analysis and drafts the manuscript with the help of institutional support.

Conflict of Interests

The authors declare that there is no conflict of interests regarding the publication of this paper.

REFERENCES

Aguinaldo, A., Espeso, E. I., Guevara, B. Q. and Nonato, M. G. (2004): A Guidebook to Plant Screening: Phytochemical and Biological. Revised edn. (Manila: UST Publication House), pp. 156.

Ali, A. and Rizvi, P. Q. (2009): Life Table Studies of Special Reference to *Menochilus sexmaculatus* Fabr. (Coleoptera: Coccinellidae) at Varying Temperature on *Lipaphis erysimi* Kalt. World Appl. Sci. J., 7: 897-901.

Ali, A. and Rizvi, P. Q. (2008): Effect of Varying Temperature on the Survival and Fecundity of *Coccinella septempunctata* (Coleoptera: Coccinellidae) fed on *Lipaphis erysimi*. J. Entomol., 5: 133-137.

Ali, A. and Rizvi, P. Q. (2010): Age and Stage Specific Life Table of *Coocinella septemounctata* (Coleoptera: Coccinellidae) at Varying Temperature. World J. Agric. Sci., 6(3): 268-273.

Applebaum, S. W. (1985): Biochemistry of Digestion. In: Kerkot, G. A., and Gillbert, L. I. (eds.), Comprehensiv Insect Physiology, Biochemistry and Pharmacology, Pergamon Press, Oxford, New York, England.

Awmack, C. S. and Leather, S. R. (2002): Host Plant Quality and Fecundity in Herbivorous Insects. Anu. Rev. Ent., 47: 817–844.

Baksha, M. W. (1997): Biology, Ecology and Control of Amra Defoliator, *Podontia quatuordecimpunctata* Linn. (Chrysomelidae: Coleoptera) in Bangladesh. Bangladesh J. Forest Sci., 26: 43-46.

Banerjee, T. C. and Haque, N. (1985): Influence of Host Plants on Development, Fecundity and Egg Hatchability of the Arctiid Moth *Diacrisia casignetum*. Entomol Exp Appl., 37: 193-198.

Banerjee, T. C. and Haque, N. (1984): Dry-matter Budgets for *Diacrisia casignetum* Larvae Fed on Sunflower Leaves. Journal of Insect Physiology, 30 (11): 861-866.

Batish, D. R., Tung, P., Singh, H. P. and Kohli, R. K. (2002): Phytotoxicity of Sunflower Residues against Some Summer Season Crops. J. Agron. Crop Sci., 188: 19-24.

Bernat, W., Gawrońska, H., Janowiak, F. and Gawroński, S. W. (2004): The Effect of Sunflower Allelopathics on Germination and Seedlings Vigour of Winter Wheat and Mustard. Zesz. Probl. Post. Naukroln., 496: 289-299.

Birch, L. C. (1948): The Intrinsic Rate of Natural Increase of an Insect Population. J. Anim. Ecol., 17: 15-26.

Bogatek, R., Gniazdowska, A., Zakrzewska, W., Oracz, K. and Gawronski, S. W. (2006): Allelopathic Effects of Sunflower Extracts on Mustard Seed Germination and Seedling Growth. *Biol.Planta.*, 50(1): 156-158.

Bray, H. G. and Thorpe, W. V. (1954): Analysis of Phenolic Compounds of Interest in Metabolism. Methods of Biochemical Analysis, 1: 27–52.

Carey, J. R. (1993): Applied Demography for Biologists with Special Emphasis on Insects, Oxford University Press, New York, USA.

Carey, J. R. (2001): Insect Biodemography. Annu. Rev. Entomol., 46: 79–110.

Chakrabarty, S. and Mondal, P. (2015): Age Specific and Female Fecundity Life Table of *Calosobruchus chinensis* Linn. on Green Gram. Int. J. Pure App. Biosci., 3(4): 284-291.

Dadd, R. H. (1985): Nutrition: Organisms. In: Kerkut, G. A., Gilbert, L. I. (eds) Comprehensive Insect Physiology, Biochemistry and Pharmacology, pp: 313–390. Pergamon Press, Oxford.

Das, M. and Chaudhuri, N. (2005): Life-fecundity Table on Incidence of *Spilosoma obliqua* on jute. Ann. Plant Protect. Sci., 13(2): 319-323.

Day, R. A. and Underwood, A. L. (1986): Quantitative Analysis. 5th edn., Prentice-Hall Publication, pp. 701.

Dicke, M. (2000): Chemical Ecology of Host-plant Selection by Herbivorous Arthropods: A Multitrophic Perspective. Biochem. Syst. Ecol., 28: 601–617.

DuBois, M., Gilles, K. A., Hamilton, J. K., Rebers, P. A. and Smith, F. (1956): Colorimetric Method for Determination of Sugars and Related Substances. *Analytical Chemistry, 28*(3): 350–356.

Duke, J. A. (1985): Medicinal Plants. Science, 229:1036.

Dutta, S. and Roy, N. (2016): Life Table and Population Dynamics of a Major Pest, *Leptocorisa acuta* (Thunb.) (Hemiptera: Alydidae), on Rice and Non-rice System. International Journal of Pure & Applied Bioscience, 4(1):199-207.

Ellers-Kirk, C. and Fleischer, S. J. (2006): Development and Life Table of *Acalymma vittatum* (Coloptera:Chrysomelidae), a Vector of *Erwinia tracheiphila* in Cucurbits. Env. Entomol., 35: 875–880

Folch, J., Lees, M. and Solane-Stanley, G. H. (1957): A Simple Method for the Isolation and Purification of Total Lipids from Animal Tissues. *Journal of Biological Chemistry*, 226: 497–509.

Gedia, M. V., Vyas, H.J., Acharya, M.F. and Patel, P.V. (2008a): Life Table, Rate of Increase and Stable Age Distribution of *Spodoptera litura* (Fabricius) on Cotton. Ann. Plant Protect. Sci., 16(1): 62-65.

Gedia, M. V., Vyas, H.J., Acharya, M.F. and Patel, P.V. (2008b): Studies on Life Fecundity Tables of *Spodoptera litura* (Fabricius) on Groundnut. Ann. Plant Protect. Sci., 16(1): 74-77.

Genc, H. (2006): General Principles of Insect Nutritional Ecology. Trakya Univ. J. Sci., 7: 53–57.

Genc, H. and Nation, J. L. (2004): Influence of Dietary Lipids on Survival of *Phyciodes phaon* Butterflies (Lepidoptera:Nymphalidae). J. Entomol. Sci., 39: 537– 544.

Gill, J. S., Sidhu, A. S. and Sigh, J. (1989): A Study to Determine Innate Capacity for Increase in Numbers of *Earias insulana* (Boisd) on cotton. J. Insect Sci., 2: 289–295.

Gould, J., Venette, R. and Winograd, D. (2005): Effect of Temperature on Development and Population Parameters of *Copitarsia decolora* (Lepidoptera: Noctuidae). Environ. Entomol., 34: 548-556.

Hamilton, A. J., Endersby, N. M., Ridland, P.M., Zhang, J. and Neal, M. (2005): Effects of Cultivar on Oviposition Preference, Larval Feeding and Development Time of Diamondback Moth, *Plutella xylostella* (L.) (Lepidoptera: Plutellidae), on Some *Brassica oleracea* Vegetables in Victoria. Aust. J. Entomol., 44: 284-287.

Harari, R., Ben-Yakir, D., Chen, M. and Rosen, D. (1997): Life- and Fertility-tables of *Maladera matrida* (Coleoptera: Scarabaeidae). Environ. Entomol., 27: 45-48.

Harborne, J. B. (1994): Introduction to Ecological Biochemistry. Academic Press, London.

Harborne, J. B. (1973): Phytochemical Methods: A Guide to Modern Techniques of Plant Analysis. Edn. 2, Chapman and Hall, New York, pp. 88-185.

Haseeb, M., Kobori, Y., Amano, H. and Nemoto, H. (2001): Population Density of *Plutella xylostella* (Lepidoptera: Plutellidae) and Its Parasitoid *Cotesia plutellae* (Hymenoptera: Braconidae) on Two Varieties of Cabbage in An Urban Environment. Appl. Entomol. Zool., 36: 353-360.

Hemchandra, O. and Singh, T. K. (2003): Life Table, Rate of Increase and Stable-age Distribution of *Plutella xylostella* (Linnaeus) on cauliflower. Ann. Plant Protect. Sci., 11(2): 269-273.

Howlader, M. A. (1993): Growth, Development, and Survival of *Podontia quaturdecempunctata* (Coleoptera: Chrysomelidae) Larvae on Different Parts of Host Plant. Bangladesh J. Zool., 21: 1-7.

Husain, M. and Ahmad, M. (1977): Notes on Chrysomelid Beetles (Coleoptera) of the Bangladesh Agricultural University Area, Mymensingh. Bangladesh J. Zool., 5: 71-75.

Inderjit, K. L. and Duke, K. I. (2003): Ecophysiological Aspects of Allelopathy. Planta, 271: 529-539.

Inderjit, K. L. and Keating, K. I. (1999): Allelopathy: Principals, Procedures, Processes and Promises for Biological Control. Adv. Agron., 67: 141-231.

Jagtap, R., Shetgar, S. S. and Nalwandikar, P. K. (2007): Life-table and Key Mortality Factors of Lepidopterous Foliage Pests of Okra. Indian J. Entomol., 69: 311-314.

Kakde, A. M., Patel, K. G. and Tayade, S. (2014): Role of Life Table in Insect Pest Management-A Review. IOSR J. Agric. Vet. Sci., 7: 40-43.

Khandelwal, K. R. (2000): Textbook of Practical Pharmacognosy. 7th ed. Pune: Nirali Publication, pp. 149-189.

Kim, D. S. and Lee, J. H. (2002). Egg and Larval Survivorship of *Carposina sasakii* (Lepidoptera: Carposinidae) in Apple and Peach and their Effects on Adult Population Dynamics in Orchards. Env. Entomol., 31: 686–692.

King, L. J. (1974). Weeds of the World: Biology and Control. First Wiley Eastern Reprint, Wiley Eastern Private Limited, New Delhi.

Kocourek, F., Havelka, J., Berankova, J. and Jarosik, V. (1994): Effect of Temperature on Development Rate and Intrinsic Rate of Increase of *Aphis gossypii* Reared on Greenhouse Cucumber. Entomol. Exp. Appl., 71: 59-64.

Krebs, C. J. (1994): Ecology: The Experimental Analysis of Distribution and Abundance, Harper Collins College Publishers, New York.

Kumar, S., Saini, R.K. and Ram, P. (2009): Natural Mortality of *Helicoverpa armigera* (Hübner) Eggs in the Cotton Ecosystem. J. Agric. Sci. Technol., 11: 17-25.

Lefroy, H. M. (1978): Indian Insect Life: A Manual of the Insect of Plains (Tropical India). 2nd Reprint, Today and Tomorrow's Printers and Publishers, New Delhi.

Liu, Z., Li, D., Gong, P. and Wu, K. (2004): Life Table Studies of the Cotton Bollworm, *Helicoverpa armigera* (Hübner) (Lepidoptera: Noctuidae), on Different Host Plants. Environ. Entomol., 33: 1570-1576.

Liu, Z., Li, D., Gong, P. and Wu, K. (2004): Life Table Studies of the Cotton Bollworm, *Helicoverpa armigera* (Hübner) (Lepidoptera: Noctuidae), on Different Host Plants, Env. Entomol., 33:1570–1576.

Lowry, A., Rosebrough, N. J., Farr, A. L. and Randall, R. J. (1951): Protein Measurement with the Folin Phenol Reagent. Journal of Biological Chemistry, 193: 265-275.

Maia, A. H. N., Luiz, A. J. B. and Camponhola, C. (2000): Statistical Inference on Associated Fertility Life Table Parameters Using Jacknife Technique: Computational Aspects. J. Econ. Entomol., 93: 511- 518.

Mattson, W. J. Jr. (1980): Herbivory in Relation to Plant Nitrogen Content. Annu. Rev. Ecol. Syst., 11: 119–161.

Medeiros, R. S., Ramalho, F. S., Lemos, W.P. and Zanuncio, J. C. (2000): Age-dependent Fecundity and Life Fertility Tables for *Podisus nigrispinus* (Dallas) (Heteroptera: Pentatomidae). J Appl. Entomol., 124: 319-324.

Miller, G. L. (1959): Protein Determination for Large Numbers of Samples. Anal. Chem., 31: 964.

Moore, R. A. and Stein, W. H. (1948): Photometric Ninhydrin Method for Use in the Chromatography of Amino Acids. J. Biol. Chem., 176: 367–388.

Morgan, D., Walters, K. F. A. and Aegerter, J. N. (2001): Effect of Temperature and Cultivar on Pea Aphid, *Acyrthosiphon pisum* (Hemiptera: Aphididae) Life History. Bull. Entomol. Res., 91: 47-52.

Morris, R. F. and Miller, C. A. (1954): The Development of Life Tables for the Spruce Budworm. Can. J. Zool., 32: 283-301.

Mukherjee, A. and Barik, A. (2013): Potential Allelopathic Effects of *Ludwigia adscendens* on the Seed Germination and Seedling Growth of Rice. Indian J. Agric. Res., 47(1): 1-15.

Napompeth, B. (1992): Brief Overview of Biological Control Activities in Thailand. In: Hirose, Y. (Ed.), Biological Control in South and East Asia. Kyushu University Press, IOBC/SEARS, pp. 51–68.

Narwal, S. S. (1994): Allelopathy in Crop Production. Scientific Publishers, Jodhpur, India.

Nation, J. L. (2001): Insect Physiology and Biochemistry. CRC Press, Boca Raton, FL.

Nayek, T. K. and Banerjee, T. C. (1987): Life History and Host Specificity of *Altica cyanea* (Coleoptera : Chrysomelidae), a Potential Biocontrol Agent for Water Primrose, *Ludwigia adscendens*. Entomp., 32: 407-414.

Parui, A. and Roy, N. (2016): Ecofriendly and Sustainable Management of *Spilosoma obliqua* Walker on Sesame (*Sesamum indicum* L.) Crops by New Botanicals. Journal of Entomology and Zoology Studies, 4 (6): 349-354.

Price, P. W. (1998). Insect ecology. Wiley, New York.

Rahman, S. and Khan, M. R. (2006): Incidence of Pests and Avoidable Yield Loss in Jute, *Corchorus olitorius* L. Ann. Plant Protect. Sci., 14(2): 304-305.

Rahman, S. and Khan, M. R. (2012): Incidence of Pests in Jute (*Corchorus olitorius* L.) Ecosystem and Pest–weather Relationships in West Bengal, India. Arc. Phytopathol. Plant Protect., 45(5): 591-607.

Ramachandran, S., Buntin, G. D., All, J. N. and Raymer, P. L. (1998): Diamondback Moth (Lepidoptera: Plutellidae) Resistance of *Brassica napus* and *B. oleracea* Lines with Differing Leaf Characteristics. J. Econ. Entomol., 91: 987-992.

Raman, N. (2006): Phytochemical Techniques. New Delhi, pp. 19-22.

Reddy, M. B. and Love, M. (1999): The Impacts of Food Processing on the Nutritional Quality of Vitamins and Minerals. Advances in Experimental Medicine and Biology, 459: 99-106.

Rice, E. L. (1984): Allelopathy. Second Edition. Academic Press, Orlando, FL.

[75] Ricklefs, R. E. and Miller, G. L. (2000): Ecology. Edn 4th, Freeman & Company, New York.

Rizvi, P.Q., Ali, A. and Khalid, S. (2009): Age and Stage-specific Life Table of Cabbage Butterfly, *Pieris brassicae* L. (Lepidoptera: Pieridae) on Various Cole Crops. J. Plant Protect. Res., 49(2): 145-150.

Roy N. and Barik A. (2013): Influence of Four Host Plants on Feeding, Growth and Reproduction of *Diacrisia casignetum* (Lepidoptera: Arctiidae). Entomological Science 16: 112–118.

Roy, N. (2014): Role of *Chorchorus capsularis* Phytochemicals on the Feeding Dynamics of *Diacrisia casignetum* Kollar (Lepidoptera: Arctiidae). Journal of Entomology and Zoology Studies, 2: 227–236.

Roy, N. (2015a): Life Table and Population Parameters of *Diacrisia casignetum* Kollar (Lepidoptera: Arctiidae) on Jute, *Chorchorus capsularis* (cv. Sonali; JRC-321), Leaves. International Journal of Fauna and Biological Studies, 2(3): 23-29.

Roy, N. (2015b): Host Phytochemicals in Regulation of Nutritional Ecology and Population Dynamics of *Podontia quatuordecimpunctata* L. (Coleoptera:Chrysomelidae). International Journal of Horticulture, 5(4): 1-11.

Roy, N. (2016). Life Table of a Bio-control Agent *Alticacyanea* on the Weed, *Ludwigia adscendens*. FOCUS: An Annual Multidisciplinary Refereed Journal, 7: 135-144.

Roy, N. (2017): Life Table and Nutritional Ecology of *Epilachna vigintioctopunctata* Fab. (Colioptera: Coccinellidae) on Three Host Plants. International Journal of Horticulture, 7(2): 7-19.

Roy, N. and Barik, A. (2010): Allelopathic Potential of *Ludwigia adscendens* (L.) on Germination and Seedling Growth of Green Gram, *Vigna radiata* (L.) Cultivated After Rice. Agric. Sc. Dig., 30(3): 192–196.

Roy, N. and Barik, A. (2012a): The Impact of Variation in Foliar Constituents of Sunflower on Development and Reproduction of *Diacrisia casignetum* Kollar (Lepidoptera: Arctiidae). Psyche, vol. 2012: Article ID 812091, 9 pages, doi:10.1155/2012/812091.

Roy, N. and Barik, A. (2012b): Alkanes Used for Host Recognition by the Arctiid Moth *Diacrisia casignetum* Kollar. Journal of Entomological Research, 36(4): 345-50.

Roy, N. and Barik, A. (2014): Long-chain Fatty Acids: Semiochemicals for Host Location by the Insect Pest, *Diacrisia casignetum*. *Journal of the Kansas Entomological Society*, 87(1): 22-36.

Roy, N. Basu, M. Chattopadhyay C. and Barik A. (2011): Allelopathic Effects of Rice Field Weed, *Ludwigia adscendens* (L.) on Germination and Seedling Growth of Three Economic Crop Plants. Int. J. Hort. Crop Sc. Res. 1(1): 15–20.

Roy, N., Chattopadhyay, C. and Barik, A. (2013a): Assessing the Attractiveness of Odorous Esterified Fatty Acids to Arctiid Moth, *Diacrisia casignetum* Kollar. The Ecoscan, 3: 87-91.

Roy, N., Laskar, S. and Barik, A. (2012): The Attractiveness of Odorous Esterified Fatty Acids to the Potential Biocontrol Agent, *Altica cyanea*. Journal of Asia-Pacific Entomology, 15(2): 277–282.

Roy, N., Laskar, S. and Barik, A. (2013b): Amino Acids Through Developmental Stages of Sunflower Leaves. Acta Botanica Croatica, 72(1): 41-51.

Sarfraz, M., Dosdall, L. M. and Keddie, B. A. (2006): Diamondback Moth Host Plant Interactions: Implications for Pest Management. Crop Protect., 25: 625-639.

Sarfraz, M., Dosdall, L. M. and Keddie, B. A. (2007): Resistance of Some Cultivated Brassicaceae to Infestations by *Plutella xylostella* (Lepidoptera: Plutellidae). J. Econ. Entomol., 100: 215-224.

Satpathi, C. R., Mukhopadhyay, A. K., Katti, G., Pasalu, I. C. and Venkateswarlu, B. (2005): Quantification of the Role of Natural Biological Control in Farmer's Rice Field in West Bengal. Indian J. Entomol., 67: 211-215.

Satpute, S., Deshmukh, S. D., Rao, N. G. V. and Nimbalkar, S. A. (2005): Life Tables and the Intrinsic Rate of Increase of *Earias vittela* (Lepidoptera: Noctuidae) Reared on Different Hosts. Int. J. Top. Insect Sci., 25(2): 73-79.

Schoonhoven, L. M., Van Loon, J. J. A. and Dicke, M. (2005): Insect-Plant Biology. Oxford University Press, Oxford.

Schowalter, T. D. (2006): Insect Ecology: An Ecosystem Approach. Academic Press, Tokyo.

Scriber, J. M. and Slansky, F. Jr. (1981): The Nutritional Ecology of Immature Insects. Annu. Rev. Entomol., 26:183–211.

Sétamou, M., Schulthess, F., Bosque-Pérez, N. A., Poehling, H. M. and Borgemeister, C. (1999): Bionomics of *Mussidia nigrivenella* (Lepidoptera: Pyralidae) on Three Host Plants, Bull. Entomol. Res., 89: 465–471.

Shirai, Y. (2000): Temperature Tolerance of the Diamondback Moth, *Plutella xylostella* (Lepidoptera: Yponomeutidae) in Tropical and Temperate Regions of Asia. Bull. Entomol. Res., 90: 357-364.

Shobana, K., Murugan, A. and Kumar, N. (2010): Influence of Host Plants on Feeding, Growth and Reproduction of *Papilio polytes* (the common mormon). J. Ins. Physol., 56: 1065–1070.

Shui, W. X. (1990): *Altica cyanea* (Coleoptera: Chrysomelidae) for the Biological Control of *Ludwigia prostrata* (Onagraceae) in China. Tropical Pest Management. 36(4): 368-370.

Singh, P. and Misra, R. M. (1989): Bionomics of the Ambara Defoliator *Podontia 14- punctata* Linn. (Coleoptera:Chrysomelidae). Indian Forester, 115: 910-915.

Singh, S. P. and Singh, D. (1982): Influence of Cruciferous Host Plants on the Survival and Development of *Plutella xylostella* L. J. Res. Punjab Agric. Univ., 19: 100-104.

Slansky, F. and Scriber, J. M. (1985): Food Consumption and Utilization. In: Kerkot, G. A. and Gillbert, L. I. eds, Comprehensive Insect Physiology, Biochemistry and Pharmacology, Pergamon, Oxford, England, pp. 87–113.

Sokal, R. R. and Rohlf. F. J. (1994): Biometry: The Principles and Practices of Statistics in Biological Research. 3rd (edn.), W. H. Freeman and Co., New York. pp. 880.

Southwood, T. R. E. (1978): Ecological Methods Particular Reference to Study of Insect Population. The English Language Book Society and Chapman and Hall, London.

Southwood, T. R. E. and Henderson, P. A. (2000): Ecological Methods, Blackwell Science, Oxford.

Southwood, T. R. E. (1995): Ecological Methods. Edn 2, Chapman & Hall, London, United Kingdom.

SPSS. (2004) SPSS Base 13.0 User's Guide, 2004, SPSS Incorporation, Chicago, IL.

Stebbing, E. P. (1914): Indian Forest Insects of Economic Importance. Eyre and Spottiswoode Ltd., London.

Sugawe, A. G., Bilapate, G. G. (2007): Field Life-table and Key Mortality Factors of Major Lepidopteran Pod Borers on Arhar. J. Maharashtra Agric. Univ., 32(3): 361-364.

Syed, T. S. and Abro, G. H. (2003): Effect of Brassica Vegetable Hosts on Biology and Life Table Parameters of *Plutella Xylostella* Under Laboratory Conditions. Pakisthan J. Biol. Sci., 22: 1891-1896.

Thangavelu, K. and Phulon, J. C. D. (1983): Food Preference of eri Silkworm *Philosamia ricini* Hutt. (Saturniidae:Lepidoptera). Entomon, 8: 311–315.

Trease, G. E. and Evans, W. C. (1983): Textbook of Pharmacognosy. 12th edn. Balliese Tindall and Company Publisher, London. pp. 343-383.

Trease, G. E. and Evans, W.C. (1989): Pharmacognosy. 11th edn. Braillar Tiridel Can. Macmillian publishers.

Tsai, J. H. and Wang, J. J. (2001): Effects of Host Plants on Biology and Life Table Parameters of *Aphid spiraecola* (Homoptera: Aphididae). Environ. Entomol., 30: 45-50.

Turunen, S. (1990): Plant Leaf Lipids As Fatty Acid Sources in Two Species of Lepidoptera. J. Insect Physiol., 36: 665–672.

Varatharajan, R., Singh, S. A., Keisa, T. J., Singh, O. D. and Selvasundaram, R. (1998): Life Table of *Spilosoma obliqua* (Lepidoptera: Arctiidae) on Sunflower. Int. J. Trop. Insect Sci., 18: 383-385.

Verheij, E. W. M. and Coronel, R. E. (1991): Plant Resources of South-east Asia no. 2: Edible Fruits and Nuts. Pudoc Scientific Publishers, Wageningen, Netherlands.

Verkerk, R. H. J. and Wright, D. J. (1996): Multitrophic Interactions and Management of the Diamondback Moth: A Review. Bull. Entomol. Res., 86: 205-216.

Wagu, A. and Ugborogho, R. E. (2000): Seed Morphology, Germination and Seedling Characters in *Ludwigia* Species (Onagraceae) in Nigeria as Aid to Identification. Seed Sci. Technol., 28: 657-697.

Waldbauer, G. P. (1968): The Consumption and Utilization of Food by Insects. Advances in Insect Physiology, 5: 229–288.

Win, S. S., Muhamad, R., Ahmad, Z. A. and Adam, N. A. (2011): Life Table and Population Parameters of *Nilaparvata lugens* Stal. (Homoptera: Delphacidae) on Rice. Trop. Life Sci. Res., 22: 25-35.

Xue, M., Pang, Y-H., Wang, H-T., Li, Q-L. and Liu, T-X. (2010): Effects of Four Host Plants on Biology and Food Utilization of the Cutworm, *Spodoptera litura*. Journal of Insect Science, 10: 1–14.

Yasar, B. and Güngör, M. A. (2005): Determination of Life Table and Biology of Colorado Potato Beetle, *Leptinotarsa decemlineata* Say (Coleoptera: Chrysomelidae), Feeding on Five Different Potato Varieties in Turkey. Appl. Entomol. Zool., 40: 589-596.

Zar, J. H. (1999): Biostatistical Analysis. Prentice Hall, Upper Saddle River, New Jersey, pp. 663.

Zhishen, J., Mengcheng, T. and Jianming, W. (1999): Research on Antioxidant Activity of Flavonoids from Natural Materials. Food Chemistry, 64: 555-559.

Zhu, J. H., Zhang, F. P. and Ren, H. G. (2005): Development and Nutrition of *Prodenia litura* on Four Food Plants. Chinese Bulletin of Entomology, 42: 643–646.

Plant Response to Environmental Stress **Page: 90-104**
Edited by: Dr. Alka Chauhan; Dr. Pawan Kumar 'Bharti' and Dr. Avnish Chauhan
ISBN: 978-93-86841-58-2
Edition: 2018
Published by: Discovery Publishing House Pvt. Ltd., New Delhi (India)

6

Polyamines: Roles In Plant Under Abiotic Stress

Prasann Kumar and Sunil Kumar[1]

ABSTRACT

Environmental changes, irrespective of source, cause a variety of stresses in plants. These stresses affect the growth and development and trigger a series of morphological, physiological, biochemical and molecular changes in plants. Abiotic stress is the primary cause of crop loss worldwide. The most challenging job before the plant biologists is the development of stress tolerant plants and maintenance of sufficient yield of crops in this changing environment. Polyamines can be of great use to enhance stress tolerance in such crop plants. Polyamines are small organic polycations present in all organisms and have a leading role in cell cycle, expression of genes, signaling, plant growth and development and tolerance to a variety of abiotic stresses. High accumulation of polyamines (putrescine, spermidine and spermine) in plants during abiotic stress has been well documented and is correlated with increased tolerance to abiotic stress. Genetic engineering of PA biosynthetic genes in crop plants is the way to create tolerance against different stresses. The present review throws light on the role of polyamines in plants.

Keywords: Agriculture, Cadmium, Diversity, Environment, Polyamines.

INTRODUCTION

Plants are exposed continuously to a variety of adversely changing environmental factors such as heat, cold, light, drought, acidity, alkalinity, oxidative damage and metal damage, which affect plant distribution, growth, development and productivity (Ahmad *et al.* 2008, 2010a, b). These stressful conditions are associated with the losses in the productivity of many of the agriculturally important crops and therefore, affect the economic returns of the

[1] Department of Agronomy, School of Agriculture, Lovely Professional University, Jalandhar, Punjab, 144411, India

country. Thus, concerted efforts are underway worldwide to understand the mechanism of plant resistance against these stresses. There are several natural ways of self-defense in the plants to cope with these stressful conditions: they can induce several functional or regulatory genes (Bartels and Sunkar 2005) or can undergo different physiological or biochemical changes. The accumulation of some functional substances, such as compatible solutes and protective proteins, is an important element of the physiological and biochemical response of plants to the stressful conditions (Liu *et al.* 2007; Ahmad and Sharma 2008; Ahmad *et al.* 2010a, b, 2011). In addition to these responses by the plants, molecules known as 'polyamines', have also been known to be an integral part of plant stress response (Bouchereau *et al.* 1999; Walters 2003a, b; Alcázar *et al.* 2006b).Polyamines (putrescine, spermine, spermidine and cadaverine), are the widely distributed of N containing organic molecules, which were discovered more than 100 years ago and hold their significance from the minutest bacteria to multicellular plants, animals and mammals. In addition to their stabilizing effects, which they confer by binding to the intracellular anions (DNA, RNA, chromatin and proteins), they are also known to possess several regulatory functions (Igarasahi and Kashiwagi 2000; Alcázar *et al.* 2006b, 2010; Kusano *et al.* 2008). In plants, they have been associated with regulating many physiological processes, such as organogenesis, embryogenesis, floral initiation and development, leaf senescence, fruit development and ripening, and abiotic and biotic plant stress responses (Galston and Kaur-Sawhney 1990; Kumar *et al.* 1997; Walden *et al.* 1997; Malmberg *et al.* 1998; Bouchereau *et al.* 1999; Bagni and Tassoni 2001; Alcázar *et al.* 2006b, 2010; Kusano *et al.* 2008). Several changes in concentrations of polyamines in plant cells take place while responding to the stressful conditions (Bouchereau *et al.* 1999; Alcázar *et al.* 2006b, 2010; Groppa and Benavides 2008) . The importance of this process can be exemplified by the fact that the levels of Put may account for 1.2% of the dry matter, representing at least 20% of the nitrogen (Galston 1991) under stressful conditions. Though the exact mechanism of involvement of polyamines during stressful conditions is not fully understood, studies are ongoing to study the molecular mechanisms (Liu *et al.* 2007; Alcazar *et al.* 2010).Evaluating the complete genome sequence of Arabidopsis has facilitated the use of global 'omic' approaches in the identification of target genes in polyamine biosynthesis and signaling pathways (Alcazar *et al.* 2010). The advantages of the progress made in these directions have made possible the generation of Arabidopsis transgenic plants, which are resistant to various stresses (Alcazar *et al.* 2010). Efforts can be made towards the development of such varieties of the agriculturally important crops as well. Such studies add to the economic potential of the agricultural sector touched by the biotechnological advances and hence, further research in these directions is noteworthy (Figure 6.1).

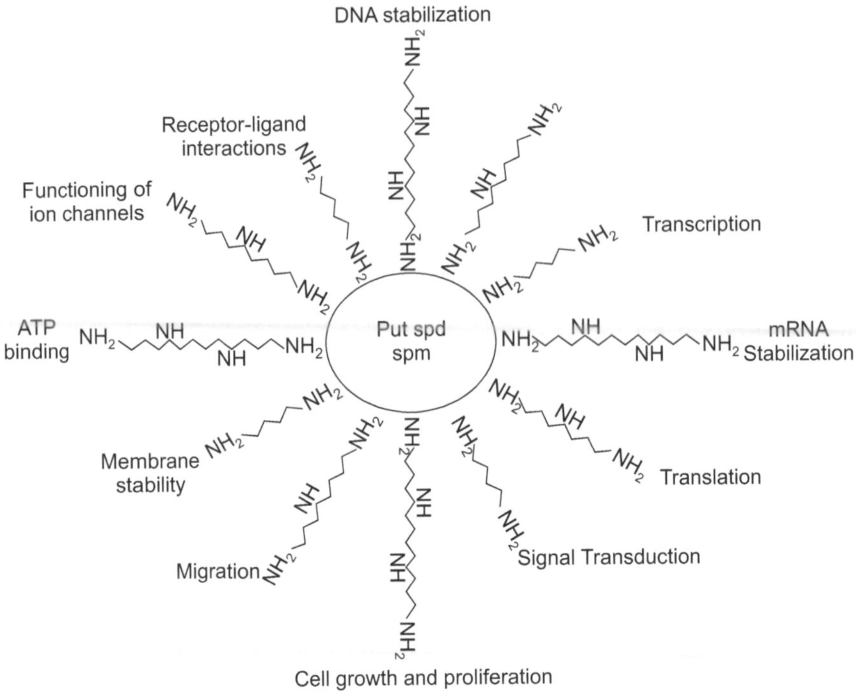

Fig. 6.1: Role of polyamines for mitigation of abiotic stress

(**Source:** Review of Literature)

Polyamine Biosynthesis In Different Organism

The biosynthetic pathways of polyamines have been established for many organisms ranging from bacteria to plants to mammals (Kusano *et al.* 2007). The synthesis essentially starts from the two amino acid precursor molecules, L-arginine and L-methionine. In mammals and fungi, putrescine (Put, 1,4-diaminobutane) is produced by a single pathway catalyzed by ornithine decarboxylase (ODC, EC 4.1.1.17) whereas, in plants two alternative pathways operate, namely the ODC-catalyzed reaction, as in mammals and the second is from arginine (Arg), as a result of the action of Arg decarboxylase (ADC, EC 4.1.1.19), via agmatine. A few plant species, including Arabidopsis thaliana, lack the ODC pathway (Hanfrey *et al.* 2001; Kusano *et al.* 2007).

The polyamines in plants are not only found in the cytoplasm, but also in certain organelles like mitochondria, chloroplasts and vacuoles (Kumar *et al.* 1997; Kusano *et al.* 2008) . The genes encoding enzymes in the polyamine biosynthesis pathway have been cloned and characterized from various plant species (Bell and Malmberg 1990; Michael *et al.* 1996; Bagni and Tassoni 2001; Liu *et al.* 2007; Kusano *et al.* 2008). Briefly, starting from arginine, the diamine putrescine is synthesized via ornithine by arginase (EC 3.5.3.1) and ornithine

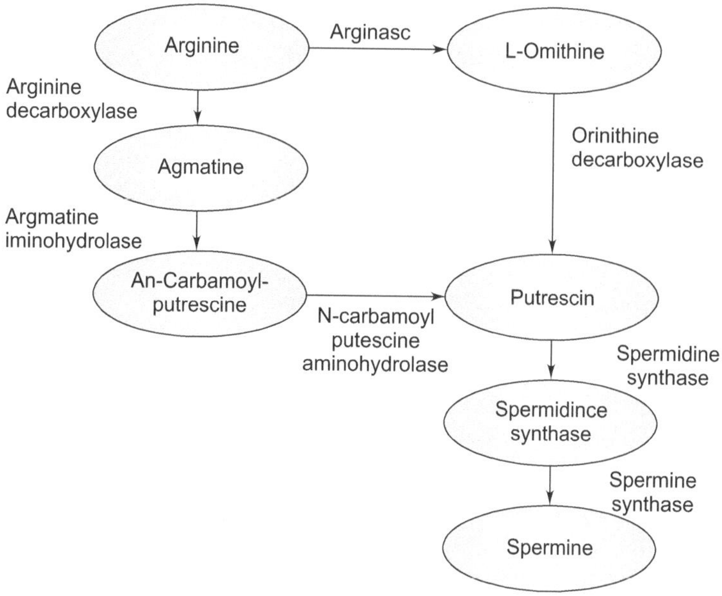

Fig. 6.2: Biosynthetic pathway of polyamines in plants

(**Source:** Review of Literature)

decarboxylase (ODC, EC 4.1.1.17). Putrescine can also be synthesized via agmatine by three sequential reactions catalyzed by arginine decarboxylase (ADC, EC 4.1.1.19), agmatine iminohydrolase (AIH, EC 3.5.3.12), and N -carbamoylputrescine amidohydrolase (CPA, EC 3.5.1.53), respectively (Kusano *et al.* 2008). Putrescine is further transformed to Spd and Spm by successive transfers of aminopropyl groups from decarboxylated S-adenosylmethionine (dSAM) catalysed by specific Spd and Spm synthases. The aminopropyl groups are derived from methionine, which is first converted to S-adenosylmethionine (SAM) by methionine adenosyltransferase (EC 2.5.1.6), and then decarboxylated in a reaction catalyzed by S -adenosylmethionine decarboxylase (SAMDC, EC 4.1.1.50). The resulting decarboxylated SAM is utilized as an aminopropyl donor.The use of the polyamine inhibitors have helped in the evaluation of their respective roles. Four commonly used inhibitors of PA synthesis are: (1) difluoromethylornithine (DFMO), an irreversible inhibitor of ODC; (2) difluoromethylarginine (DFMA), an irreversible inhibitor of ADC; (3) methylglyoxyl- bis-guanylhydrazone (MGBG), a competitive inhibitor of S -adenosyl-methionine decarboxylase (SAMDC); and (4) cyclohexylamine (CHA), a competitive inhibitor of spermidine synthase. Common oxidases are diamine oxidase and polyamine oxidase (PAO), Each PA has been found to be catabolized by a specific oxidase (Kaur-Sawhney *et al.* 2003) .

Polyamine Catabolism

The concentrations of the polyamines in the cells are also maintained by the catabolic pathways (Bagni and Tassoni 2001; Cona *et al.* 2006). Copper containing diamine oxidases (CuAO, EC 1.4.3.6) and flavine-containing polyamine oxidases (PAO, EC 1.5.3.11) catalyse the oxidative de-amination of PAs. CuAO, which prefers diamine substrates, oxidizes Put and cadaverine (1,5-diaminopentane) with concomitant production of pyrroline, NH_3 and H_2O_2, and the resulting aldehyde is further metabolized to g-aminobutyric acid via Δ 1-1-pyrroline (Bagni and Tassoni 2001; Kusano *et al.* 2008). On the other hand, PAO oxidizes Spd and Spm, producing 4-aminobutanal and N-(3-aminopropyl)-4-aminobutanal, respectively, in addition to 1,3-diaminopropane and H_2O_2 (Kusano *et al.* 2007) . This means that plant PAOs are involved in the terminal catabolism of polyamines (Kusano *et al.* 2008) . These enzymes are associated with the cell walls of tissues, where lignification, suberization and wall stiffening occur (Slocum 1991). Spermine oxidase (SMO), a FAD-dependent amine oxidase, which directs the back-conversion of spermine to spermidine with concomitant production of 3-aminopropanal and H_2O_2, was initially identified in mammalian cells (Wang *et al.* 2001; Vujcic *et al.* 2002; Cervelli *et al.* 2003; Kusano *et al.* 2008) . Diaminopropane can be converted into b-alanine, whereas pyrroline can be further catabolized to g-aminobutyric acid (GABA) in a reaction catalysed by pyrroline dehydrogenase (PDH). The g-aminobutyric acid is subsequently transaminated and oxidised to succinic acid, which is incorporated into the Krebs cycle. Thus, this pathway ensures the recycling of carbon and nitrogen from Put. Far from being only a means of eliminating cellular PAs, the enzymes involved in PA catabolism and the products deriving from their action, have been demonstrated to be involved in important physiological processes (Bouchereau *et al.* 1999).

Role of Polyamine In Plants

The first reference of the polyamines in plants can probably be dated back to 1911 when Ciamician and Ravenna demonstrated the presence of putrescine in Datura stramonium (Bagni and Tassoni 2001). In plant cells, the diamine putrescine (Put),triamine spermidine (Spd) and tetramine spermine (Spm) constitute the major PAs. Cadaverine is also present in legumes. These occur either in the free form or as conjugates bound to phenolic acids and other low molecular weight compounds or to macromolecules such as proteins and nucleic acids owing to their positive charge (Kaur-Sawhney *et al.* 2003).

Besides stimulating DNA replication, transcription and translation, they have contributed to various biological processes in plant morphogenesis, growth, embryogenesis, organ development, leaf senescence, abiotic and biotic stress response and infection by fungi and viruses (Kumar *et al.* 1997; Walden *et al.* 1997; Malmberg *et al.* 1998; Bouchereau *et al.* 1999; Liu *et al.* 2000,

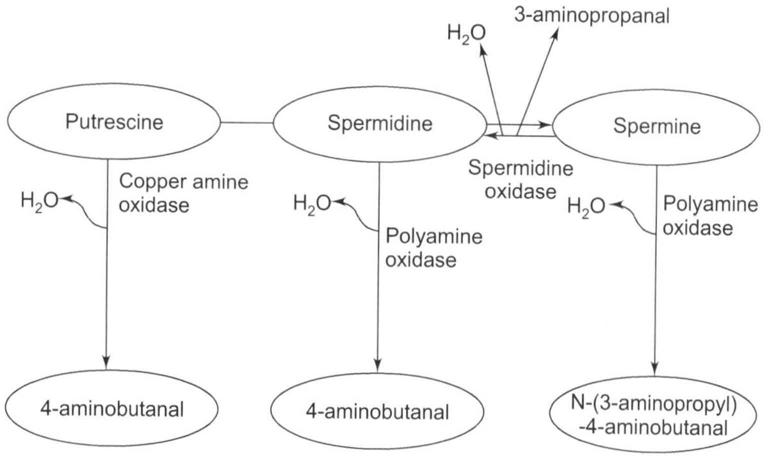

Fig. 6.3: Polyamines degradation in plants

(**Source:** Review of Literature)

2010; Alcázar *et al.* 2006a, b; Groppa *et al.* 2008; Kusano *et al.* 2007, 2008). Their biological activity has been attributed to their cationic nature. Plant polyamines also contribute towards several characteristics of agro-economical importance, such as phytonutrient content, fruiting and fruit quality, vine life, flowering and carnation plants (Kakkar and Rai 1993; Mehta *et al.* 2002; Piqueras *et al.* 2002; Matto *et al.* 2006; Paschalidis and Roubelakis-Angelakis 2005). Some of the observations suggest that PAs can act by stabilizing membranes, scavenging free radicals, affecting nucleic acids and protein synthesis, RNAse, protease and other enzyme activities, and interacting with hormones, phytochromes, and ethylene biosynthesis (Slocum *et al.* 1984; Galston and Tiburcio 1991). Because ofthese numerous biological interactions of PAs in plant systems, it has been difficult to determine theirprecise role in plant growth and development (Kaur-Sawhney *et al.* 2003). However, the recentuse of genomic and proteomic approaches will lead to a better understanding of the functioning in the plants (Kaur-Sawhney *et al.* 2003; Franceschetti *et al.* 2004). The mechanisms involved in the polyamine interactions have been unveiled, at least to some extent with the help of specific polyamine inhibitors, thus explaining their physiological roles in plant growth and development. Clearly, PAs are involved in many plant developmental processes, including cell division, embryogenesis, reproductive organ development, root growth, tuberization, floral initiation and development, fruit development and ripening as well as leaf senescence and abiotic stresses as mentioned above (Evans and Malmberg 1989; Galston *et al.* 1997; Bais and Ravishankar 2002; Kaur-Sawhney *et al.* 2003; Cona *et al.* 2006; Rhee *et al.* 2007; Groppa *et al.* 2008; Alcazar *et al.* 2010). During these developmental processes, changes in the concentrations of the free and conjugated PA's and the enzymes associated with their biosynthesis (ADC, ODC, SAMDC, etc.) take place. Many authors have reported that the increase in the PA levels and the associated biosynthetic enzymes are associated with the rapid cell division in many plant systems e.g., carrot embryogenesis (Montague *et al.* 1978; Feirer *et al.* 1984), tomato ovaries (Heimer and Mizrahi 1982; Neily *et al.* 2011), tobacco ovaries (Slocum and Galston 1985; Franceschetti *et al.* 2004), and fruit development (Kakkar and Rai 1993; Paschalidis and Roubelakis-Angelakis 2005; Falasca *et al.* 2010) . It has been observed that cells undergoing division (apical shoots, meristems, flowers, etc) contain higher levels of PAs whereas cells undergoing expansion and elongation contain lower levels of PA synthesized via ADC (Kaur-Sawhney *et al.* 2003). This has been further exemplified as follows: higher levels of endogenous PAs were found in flowers and siliques as compared to their levels in leaves and bolts of certain strains of Arabidopsis; additions of the PA biosynthetic inhibitors, DFMA and CHA to the culture medium, at the time of seed germination, inhibited bolting and flower formation and this were partially reversed by addition of exogenous Spd (Applewhite *et al.* 2000 ; Kaur-Sawhney *et al.* 2003). These results clearly show that Spd is involved in flower initiation and development. Similar results have been reported in other plants also (reviewed by Galston *et al.* 1997; Bais and Ravishankar 2002). The regulation of many important plant hormones such as auxins, gibberellins, ethylene, etc., which play a vital role in plant growth and developmental processes has been correlated with the changes in the PA metabolism. Of the important plant hormones, ethylene is of particular interest as PAs and ethylene are said to play antagonist roles (Kaur Sawhney *et al.* 2003) . While PAs inhibit senescence of leaves (Kaur-Sawhney *et al.* 1982), cell cultures of many monocot and dicot species (Muhitch *et al.* 1983) and fruit ripening (Kakkar and Rai 1993), ethylene promotes all these processes. The most commonly held view is that ethylene is an effective inhibitor of ADC and SAMDC, the key enzymes in PAbiosynthetic pathway, and on the other hand, PAs tend to inhibit ethylene synthesis from SAM (Kaur-Sawhney *et al.* 2003). Plants are exposed to continuous and rapid changing environmental factors (biotic and abiotic) such as light, temperature, water, nutrient availability, and water. These have a major impact on plant growth and productivity and PAs play an important role in these stresses as briefly discussed below.

Role of Polyamines in Plant Tolerance to Abiotic Stress

Richards and Coleman (1952) observed the presence of a predominant unknown ninhydrin positive spot that accumulated in barley plants when exposed to potassium starvation. This compound was identified as putrescine. Later on, it was shownthat K- deficient shoots fed with L-14 C-arginine produced, labeled Put in a more rapid way compared to feeding with labeled ornithine (Alcazar *et al.* 2010). These resultssuggested that decarboxylation of arginine was the main way of the accumulation of Put under K deficiency (Smith and Richards 1962). The relevance of the ADC pathway in plant responses to abiotic stress was later on established by Galston *et al.* at Yale University (Flores and Galston 1982). It has been observed that polyamines accumulate in plants during various stressful conditions (see Bouchereau *et al.* 1999; Alcázar *et al.* 2006b, 2010; Groppa and Benavides 2008). These all reports support the fact that polyamines do play a protective role during the stressful conditions. Several examples have been quoted by Alcazar *et al.* (2010) in which genetic modification of the genes involved in the PA biosynthetic pathway have proven useful in developing plant tolerance against abiotic stresses. The different stress factors have been briefly discussed below (Figure 6.4).

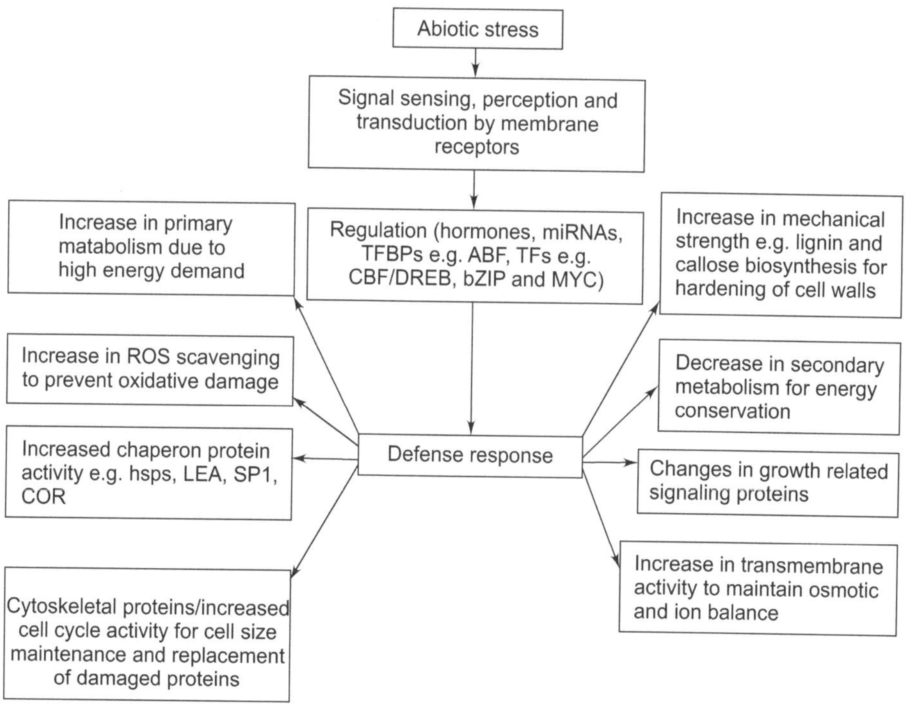

Fig. 6.4: Abiotic stress and its cross talk mechanism

(**Source:** Review Literature)

Mineral Deficiency

This is one of the most common stress related factors affecting plants almost everywhere. However, studies related to this type of stress are often performed on leaves and/or seedlings, as the external symptoms of deficiency become acute. The accumulation of Put. in leaves of K-deficient barley plants were first reported by Richards and Coleman (1952) and subsequent studies by others have established that specific role of Put. in maintaining a cation-anion balance in plant tissues. As a result of K starvation, this diamine accumulation (via ADC activation), is widespread among mono- and di-cotyledonous species and may well be a universal response (Bouchereau *et al.* 1999) . The exact reason behind the increase in Put is unclear. The induced high levels of Put might be the cause of the stress injury. Put might also be beneficial for plants. Alternatively, high levels of Put could be one of the many physiological changes induced by a mineral nutrient deficiency without any specific significance (Bouchereau *et al.* 1999). There are several other examples listing the changes in the polyamine content while responding to the mineral deficiencies (Geny *et al.* 1997). However, the changes differed according to the tissue and the stage of development.

Cold Stress

The injury due to cold causes alteration in the membrane structure, and the chilling injury involves a phase transition in the molecular ordering of membrane lipids (Raison and Lyons 1970). This can cause several deleterious effects like increased membrane permeability and alteration of the activity of membrane proteins. Cold treatment has been reported to increase the levels of Put, and this correlates with the increase in the induction of arginine decarboxylase (ADC) genes (ADC1, ADC2 19 Polyamines: Role of Plants Under Abiotic Stress 499 and SAMDC2) (Urano *et al.* 2003; Cuevas *et al.* 2008, 2009). On the other hand, levels of free Spd and Spm remain constant or even decrease in response to cold treatment (Alcazar *et al.* 2010). The absence of correlation between enhanced SAMDC2 expression and the decrease Spm levels may be a result of increased Spm catabolism (Cuevas *et al.* 2008; Alcazar *et al.* 2010). Boucereau *et al.* (1999) reported that in the chilling-tolerant-cultivar, chilling induced an increase in free abscisic acid (ABA) levels first, then ADC activity and finally free Put levels. Fluridone, an inhibitor of ABA synthesis, inhibited the increase of free ABA levels, ADC activity and free Put levels in chilled seedlings of a chilling-tolerant cultivar. These effects resulted in a reduced tolerance to chilling and could be reversed by the pre-chilling treatment with ABA. All these results suggest that Put and ABA are integrated in a positive feedback loop, in which ABA and Put reciprocally promote each other's biosynthesis in response to abiotic stress. This highlights a novel mode of action of polyamines as regulators of ABA biosynthesis (Alcazar *et al.* 2010).

Thermal Stress

When exposed to heat stress, plants have the ability to synthesize uncommon long chain PAs (caldine, thermine). The levels of free and bound PAs, as well as ADC and polyamine oxidases (PAO) activities, were higher in more tolerant than in sensitive cultures of different crop. (Kuehn *et al.* 1990; Philipps and Kuehn 1991; Roy and Ghosh 1996; Bouchereau *et al.* 1999) . The increased activities of the transglutaminases indicated the high content of the polyamines. This indicates a correlation between heat-stress tolerance, ADC, PAO and transglutaminase activities (Bouchereau *et al.* 1999).

Drought Stress

Certain plants during water scarcity tend to accumulate putrescine (Put) which is supported by the fact that transcript profiling under these conditions induces the expression of certain genes involved in the biosynthetic pathway. The expression of some of these genes is also induced by ABA treatment (Perez-Amador *et al.* 2002; Urano *et al.* 2003; Alcazar *et al.* 2010) . This throws light upon the fact that up- regulation of PA-biosynthetic genes and accumulation of Put under water stress are mainly ABA-dependent responses (Alcazar *et al.* 2010)

Salt Stress

Differences in PA (Put, Spd, Spm) response under salt-stress have been reported among and within species. For example, according to Prakash and Prathapsenan (1988), the endogenous levels of PAs (Put, Spd and Spm) decreased in rice seedlings under NaCl stress, whereas Basu *et al.* (1988) reported that salinity resulted in accumulation of these compounds in the same material (Bouchereau *et al.* 1999). SantaCruz *et al.* (1997) reported that the (Spd + Spm):Put ratios increased with salinity in the salt-tolerant tomato species (Lycopersicon pennellii, Carrel D'Arcy) but not in the salt-sensitive tomato species (L. esculentum). In both species, stress treatments decreased the levels of Put and Spd. The Spm levels did not decrease with salinity in L. pennellii over the salinization period, whereas they greatly decreased in L. esculentum. The effects of different NaCl concentrations in maize embryogenic cells derived from immature embryo cultures of a salt-sensitive inbred line (cv. w64) and a resistant hybrid (cv, Arizona) have also been reported where increased salt concentration remarkably decreased the growth of the calluses and showed a significant increase in the total PA (Put, Spd) content, especially caused by a rise in Put. It has been reported by Bouchereau *et al.* (1999) that using the inhibitors of Put synthesis, the ADC pathway in tomato plants operates in both stress and control conditions, whereas the ODC pathway is stimulated only under the stress conditions. These findings arefurther supported by the studies of Urano *et al.* (2003) who concluded that the expressions of the arginine decarboxylase 2(ADC 2) and spermine synthases (SPMS) during the 24 h stress treatment maintained and hence, increased the levels of Put and Spm. Yamaguchi *et al.* (2006) also suggested the protective role of Spm when its addition suppressed the salt sensitivity in Spm deficient mutants. Bouchereau *et al.* (1999) suggested that polyamine responses to salt stress are also ABA-dependent, since both ADC2 and SPMS are induced by ABA. In fact, Alcazar *et al.* (2006a) reported that stress-responsive, drought responsive (DRE), low temperature-responsive (LTR) and ABA-responsive elements (ABRE and/or ABRE-related motifs) are present in the promoters of the polyamine biosynthetic genes. This also reinforces the view that in response to drought and salt treatments, the expression of some of the genes involved in polyamine biosynthesis is regulated by ABA (Alcazar *et al.* 2010) . The study of the Arabidopsis thaliana flowers by Tassoni *et al.* (2010) has also supported the hypothesis that polyamine levels (mainly Spm) increase with the increase in the salt concentration and therefore, contribute to plant tolerance during the stressful conditions.

Osmotic Stress

Osmotic treatments using sorbitol induced high levels of Put and ADC in detached oat leaves (Flores and Galston 1984), whereas, Spd and Spm show a dramatic decrease. Bouchereau *et al.* (1999) reported that osmotica with widely different assimilation routes, such as sorbitol, mannitol, proline, betaine and sucrose, all induce a rise in Put. These changes are coincident with measurable signs of a stress, such as wilting and protein loss. Tiburcio *et al.* (1995) reported that when peeled oat leaves are incubated with sorbitol in the dark, they lose chlorophyll and senescence rapidly. Senescence could be delayed by including Spm in the incubation medium.The senescence-retarding effect of Spm was correlated with increase in the incorporation of labeled precursors into proteins, RNA and DNA. They also concluded that generally observed as an increase in putrescine level, and in particular its bound form to thylakoid membranes. A study by Schraudner *et al.* (1990) also discovered a relationship between ethylene emission and PA biosynthesis was found in O_3-treated potato and tobacco plants, the leaves of which show early senescence in response to the pollutant. In the presence of O_3, all compounds of ethylene biosynthetic pathway in tobacco leaves were up-regulated. Put and Spd levels also increased, as did ornithine decarboxylase (ODC) activity (Bouchereau *et al.* 1999) .

Polyamine Biosynthesis Genes and Stress Tolerance

The expression of genes responsible for the PA synthesis has benefited the plants to withstand environmental stresses. The over-expression or the down-regulation of the genes for PA metabolism in transgenic plants have been reported by many workers during environmental stress (Kumar *et al.* 1997; Walden *et al.* 1997; Malmberg *et al.* 1998; Capell *et al.* 1998; Rajam *et al.* 1998; Roy and Wu 2001; Bhatnagar *et al.* 2002). The genes which have been reported to be involved in the PA metabolism are ODC, ADC or SAMDC. Bhatnagar *et al.* (2002) have demonstrated that the cellular levels of Put increases by overexpressing ODC or ADC cDNA. Panicot *et al.* (2002a) have also reported that overexpression of ODC or ADC cDNA increases the Put levels in plants. Cheng *et al.* (2009) reported that transformation of yeast SAMDC in tomato increased Spm and Spd under high temperature stress. Overexpression of SPDS in Arabidopsis (Kasukabe *et al.* 2004); tobacco (Franceschetti *et al.* 2004) and sweet potato (Kasukabe *et al.* 2006) plants have conferred tolerance to multiple stresses. Polyamineshave been proved to act as antioxidants and protect the plants from oxidative damage and maintain homeostasis in plant cells (Rodrýguez-Kessler *et al.* 2006).Accumulation of polyamines during environmental stresses in plants has been associated with an increase in the levels of antioxidant enzyme activities like SOD, CAT, etc. Increase in MDA content has been observed during temperature stress in tomato, which leads to lipid peroxidation (Cheng *et al.* 2009). Overexpression of ySAMDC in transgenic tomato increases the Spm and Spd levels, which in turn decreases MDA content (Cheng *et al.* 2009). The overexpression of SAMDCgene in transgenic rice and tobacco showed increased levels of PA and confers tolerance to drought and salinity (Roy and Wu 2002; Waie and Rajam 2003).

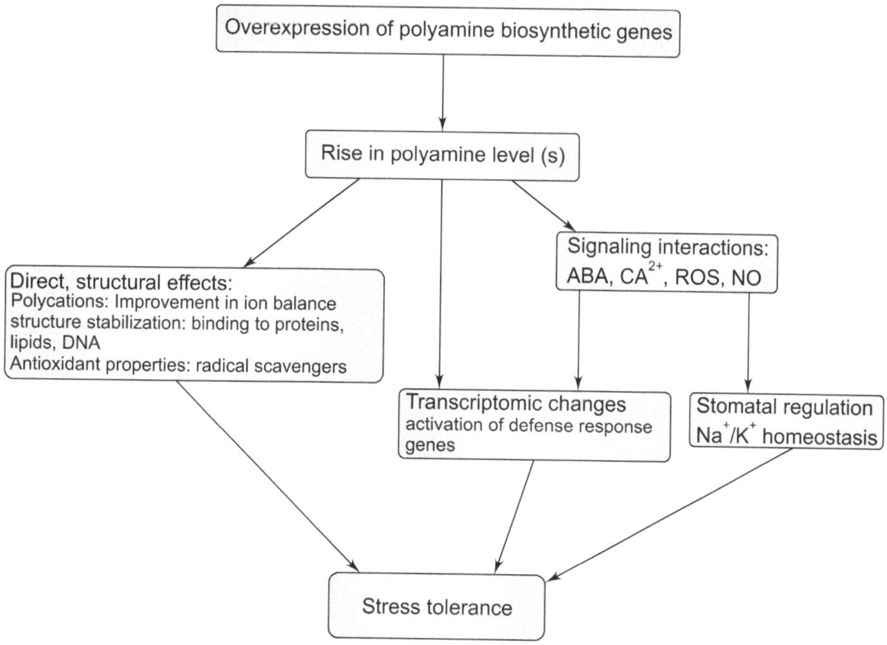

Fig. 6.5: Overexpression of polyamines biosynthesis of polyamines

(**Source:** Review of Literature)

Integration of Polyamines with Other Molecules During Stress Conditions

Polyamines affect several physiological processes in plants by activating the biosynthesis of signaling molecules like NO, H_2O_2; they affect ABA synthesis and signaling and are involved in Ca^{2+} homeostasis and ion channel signaling during the abiotic stress conditions (Table 6.1).

Table 6.1: Polyamine Genes that can be Expressed in Plants for Abiotic Stress Tolerance

Gene over expressed	Plant	Response	Reference
ADC	*Oryza sativa*	Salt tolerance	Roy and Wu (2001)
ADC	*Brassica juncea*	Chilling and salt	Mo and Pua (2002)

ADC1, ADC2	*Oryza sativa*	Drought tolerance	Capell et. al. (2004)
ADC1, ADC 2	*Arabidopsis thaliana*	Freezing	Cuevas et. al. (2008)
ADC	*Malus domestica*	Chilling, Salt and Dehydration	hao et al. (2005)
ADC	*Oryza sativa*	Chilling	Akiyama and Jin (2007)
At ADC2	*Arabidopsis thaliana*	Salt tolerance	Urano et al. (2004)
ADC	*Solamum melongena*	Chilling, Salt and Dehydration	Prabhavathi and Rajam (2007)
MdADC	*Malus sylvestris* (L.) Mill. var. domestica	Salt tolerance	Liu et. al. (2006)
PaADC2	*Pringlea antiscorbutica*	Chilling and salt	Hummel et. al. (2004)
Mouse ODC cDNA	*Populous nigra* X maximowiczil cells	Stress tolerance	Bhatnagar et. al. (2001)
Mouse ODC cDNA	Tobacco	Salt stress	Kumria and Rajam (2002)
MdSAMDC2	*Malus sylvestrix*	Cold and salt	Hao et al. (2005)
MdSAMDC2	*Pyrus communits*	salt	He et al. (2008)
SPDS cDNA from cucurbnita fleifolia	Arabidopsis	Chilling, salinity, drought	Kasukabe et al., (2004)
SPDS cDNA from Cucurbita fleifolia	*Sweet potato*	Increase in Spd	Kasukabe et al. (2006)
MdSPDSI	*Pyrus communits*	Salt, Heavy metal and osmotie stress	Wen et al. (2008)

(**Source:** Review of Literature)

Abscisic acid (ABA) is an anti-transpirant that reduces water loss through stomatal pores on the leaf surface in response to water deficit, resulting in the redistribution and accumulation of ABA in guard cells and final closure of the stomata (Bray 1997). Many authors (Liu *et al.* 2000; An *et al.* 2008; Alcazar *et al.* 2010) have reported that Put, Spd and Spm also regulate stomatal responses by reducing their aperture and inducing closure, and Put modulates ABA biosynthesis in response to abiotic stress. Thus, polyamines are involved in the ABA mediated stress responses which affect the stomatal closure. Polyamines are also linked with reactive oxygen species (ROS) and NO signaling as amino oxidases during the catabolic process generate H_2O_2 which is a ROS (associated with plant defense and abiotic stress) and also there is evidence in which polyamines are reported to enhance the production of NO (Tun *et al.* 2006). NO is also known to enhance the salt stress tolerance in plants by regulating the content and proportions of the different types of free polyamines. According to Neill *et al.* (2008), both H_2O_2 and NO are involved in theAbscisic acid (ABA) is an anti-transpirant that reduces water loss through stomatal pores on the leaf surface in response to water deficit, resulting in the redistribution and accumulation of ABA in guard cells and finally closure of the stomata (Bray 1997). Many authors (Liu *et al.* 2000; An *et al.* 2008; Alcazar *et al.* 2010) have reported that Put, Spd and Spm also regulate stomatal responses by reducing their aperture and inducing closure, and Put modulates ABA biosynthesis in response to abiotic stress. Thus, polyamines are involved in the ABA mediated stress responses which affect the stomatal closure. Polyamines are also linked with reactive oxygen species (ROS) and NO signaling as amino oxidases during the catabolic process generate H_2O_2 which is a ROS (associated with plant defense and abiotic stress) and also there is evidence in which polyamines are reported to enhance the production of NO (Tun *et al.* 2006). NO is also known to enhance the salt stress tolerance in plants by regulating the content and proportions of the different types of free polyamines. According to Neill *et al.* (2008), both H_2O_2 and NO are involved in the regulation of stomatal movements in response to ABA, in such a way that NO generation depends on H_2O_2 production. Thus, altogether, the available data indicate that polyamines, ROS (H_2O_2) and NO act synergistically in promoting ABA responses in guard cells (Alcazar *et al.* 2010). Polyamines are positively charged compounds, which can interact electrostatically with negatively charged proteins, including ion channels. Indeed, polyamines at their physiological concentration block the fast-activating vacuolar (FV) cation channel in a charge-dependent manner (Spm 4^+ > Spd $^{3+}$ >> Put $^{2+}$), at both whole-cell and single-channel levels, thus indicating a direct blockage of the channel by polyamines (Bruggemann *et al.* 1998). According to Alacazar *et al.* (2010), in response to different abiotic stresses, such as potassium deficiency, Put levels are increased drastically(reaching millimolar concentrations), whereas the levels of Spd and Spm are not significantly affected, and this increase of Put may significantly reduce FV channel activity. Bruggemann *et al.* (1998) have also reported that all PA levels increase in amount, and the enhanced Spm concentration probably blocks FV channel activity under salinity stress. These observations can be explained by the fact that polyamines in plants may thus modulate ion channel activities through direct binding to the channel proteins and/or their associated membrane components (Delavega and Delcour 1995; Johnson 1996; Alcazar *et al.* 2010). Phosphorylation and dephosphorylation of ion channel proteins are closely related to their activities. Thus, polyamines could also affect protein kinase and/or phosphatase activities to regulate ion channel functions (Bethke and Jones 1997; Michard *et al.* 2005; Alcazar *et al.* 2010). However, Zhao *et al.* (2007) points out that for elucidating the molecular mechanisms underlying polyamine action, identification of ion channel structural elements and/or receptor molecules regulated by polyamines would be of great importance.

Polyamines also tend to maintain Ca^{2+} homeostasis. Several examples have been reported by Alcazar *et al.* (2010) . Yamaguchi *et al.* (2006, 2007) proposed that the protective role of Spm against high salt and drought stress is a consequence of altered control of Ca^{2+} allocation through regulating Ca^{2+} permeable channels. The increase in cytoplasmic Ca^{2+} results in prevention of Na^+ /K^+ entry into the cytoplasm, enhancement of Na^+ /K^+ influx to the vacuole or suppression of Na+ /K+ release from the vacuole, which in turn increases salt tolerance (Yamaguchi *et al.* 2006; Kusano *et al.* 2007; Alcazar *et al.* 2010). Thus, polyamines have a definite role in calcium homeostasis during stress conditions.

CONCLUSION

Plants are exposed continuously to a variety of adversely changing environmental factors such as heat, cold, light, drought, acidity, alkalinity, oxidative damage and metal damage, which affect plant distribution, growth, development and productivity. These stressful conditions are associated with the losses in the productivity of many of the agriculturally important crops and therefore, affect the economic returns of the country.

REFERENCES

Ahmad P, Sharma S (2008) Salt Stress and Phyto-biochemical Responses of Plants. Plant Soil, Environ 54:89–99.

Ahmad P, Sarwat M, Sharma S (2008) Reactive Oxygen Species, Antioxidants and Signaling in Plants. J Plant Biol 51:167–173.

Ahmad P, Jaleel CA, Salem MA, Nabi GH, Sharma S (2010a) Roles of Enzymatic and Nonenzymatic Antioxidants in Plants During Abiotic Stress. Crit Rev Biotechnol 30:161–175.

Ahmad P, Umar S, Sharma S (2010b) Mechanism of Free Radical Scavenging and Role of Phytohormones during Abiotic Stress in Plants. In: Ashraf M, Ozturk M, Ahmad MSA (eds) Plant Adaptation and Phytoremediation. Springer, Dordrecht/Heidelberg/London/New York, pp. 99–108.

Ahmad P, Ashraf M, Younis M, Hu X, Kumar A, Akram NA, Al-Qurainy F (2011) Role of Transgenic Plants in Agriculture and Biopharming. Biotechnol Adv. doi:10.1016/j.biotechadv. 2011.09.006.

Akiyama T, Jin S (2007) Molecular Cloning and Characterization of An Arginine Decarboxylase Gene Up-regulated by Chilling Stress in Rice Seedlings. J Plant Physiol 164:645–654.

Alcázar R, Cuevas JC, Patrón M, Altabella T, Tiburcio AF (2006a) Abscisic Acid Modulates Polyamine Metabolism Under Water Stress in Arabidopsis thaliana. Plant Physiol 128:448–455.

Alcázar R, Marco F, Cuevas JC, Patrón M, Ferrando A, Carrasco P, Tiburcio AF, Altabella T (2006b) Involvement of Polyamines in Plant Response to Abiotic Stress. Biotechnol Lett 28:1867–1876.

Alcazar R, Altabella T, Marco F, Bortolotti C, Reymond M, Koncz C, Carrasco P, Tiburcio AF (2010) Polyamines: Molecules with Regulatory Functions in Plant Abiotic Stress Tolerance. Planta 231:1237–1249.

Plant Response to Environmental Stress **Page: 105-120**
Edited by: Dr. Alka Chauhan; Dr. Pawan Kumar 'Bharti' and Dr. Avnish Chauhan
ISBN: 978-93-86841-58-2
Edition: 2018
Published by: Discovery Publishing House Pvt. Ltd., New Delhi (India)

7

Effects of Cadmium and Its Role in Triticum Aestivum L.

Prasann Kumar[1]

ABSTRACT

Wheat (*Triticum aestivum* L.) is one of the most important cereal crops, grown extensively throughout the world. It is second important staple food crop of India next to rice. It is consumed in the form of chapati, puris and suji or rawa. Beside their significance in nutrition, they are principally concerned in providing the "glutein" which provide spongy cellular texture of bread and backed products.

Keywords: Agriculture, Biotic, Cadmium, Diffusion, Efficient, Forage, Gap.

INTRODUCTION

Wheat straw is a good source of feed for a large population of cattle in our country. Wheat occupies an area of 217.2 million hectares globally with the production of 161.9 million tons and productivity of 2.84 q ha^{-1}. In case of India, it occupies an area of 26.6 million hectares with the production of 72.1 million tons and productivity 2.71q ha^{-1} during 2003-04 and an area of 25.5 million hectares with the production of 73.3 million tons and productivity 2.76q ha^{-1} during 2004-05. India has been the second largest producer of wheat in the world. About 91% of wheat is produced in six states,i.e. Uttar Pradesh, Punjab, Haryana, Madhya Pradesh, Rajasthan and Bihar in India. Utter Pradesh is the highest producer of wheat (25.6 million tons). This increase in production is possible by increasing per unit produced, either by maintaining optimal agronomic and environmental conditions by manipulating physiological and biological processes or by genetic engineering (Slafer *et al.*,1991). In India four species of wheat namely *Triticum aestivum* L., *T. Durum Defs., T. dicoccum Schubt and T. sphaerococcum* were under cultivation. But now last two have gone out of cultivation due to low productivity and disease susceptibility. Wheat consumption as food grains is estimated to be 35% of world population. The world demand of wheat by 2020 is expected to be 680-1050 million tons. This

[1] Department of Agronomy, School of Agriculture, Lovely Professional University, Jalandhar, Punjab-144411

challenging task requires concentrating our efforts to increase the productivity of wheat from current levels by 2.5 to 3.8 tonnes ha^{-1}. Whereas, last five years total wheat production was declined and during 2001 only 570 million tons of wheat was produced in the world (Nagarajan, 2002).Water is the main constituent of the plant cell. The water content varies from 60-95% of the fresh weight of tissues and organs. The structure of water induced mechanical and physiological functions in the plant. Water pressure on the cell wall is responsible for turgidity and allows the rigidity of plants. Water gives rise to membrane structure and helps in the orientation of protoplasmic molecules in hydrophobic and hydrophilic poles. Being a polar solvent, water is a medium for biochemical reactions in addition to its involvement as a reactant in several processes. The whole water is the driver of saps containing food and hormones (Monneveux and Behassen, 1977). In water deficit condition, a slowdown in biological activities quickly observed at different levels of organization; metabolisms, growth and rigidity all these depend upon the time and range of water deficit conditions to plant and show their effect from germination to formation of final sink. Metal toxicity can affect the plasma membrane permeability, causing a reduction in water content; in particular cadmium has been reported to interact with the water balance (Balrcelo *et al.*, 1988; Poschenrieder *et al.*, 1989; Costa and Morel, 1994) (Figure 7.2). Cd treatments have been shown to reduce the ATPase activity of the plasma membrane fraction of wheat and Sunflower roots (Fodor *et al.*, 1995). Cadmium produces alterations in the functionality of membranes by inducing lipid peroxidation (Fodor *et al.*, 1995) and disturbances in chloroplast metabolism by inhibiting chlorophyll biosynthesis and reducing the activity of enzyme involved in CO_2 fixation (Stobart *et al.*, 1985; De Filippis and Zeigler, 1993). Several studies have suggested that an oxidative stress could be involved in cadmium toxicity, by either inducing oxygen free radical production or by decreasing enzymatic and non enzymatic antioxidants (Somashekaraiah *et al.*, 1992; Stohs and Bagchi, 1995; Shaw, 1995; Gallego *et al.*, 1996; Sandalio *et al.*, 2001; Cho and Seo, 2005) (Figure 7.1).

Heavy metal toxicity and the danger of their bioaccumulation in the food chain represent one of the major environmental and health problems of our modern society. Primary sources of pollution is from the burning of fossil fuels, mining and smelting of metallic ferrous ores, municipal wastes, fertilizers, pesticides and sewage sludge (Xiong, 1998). The most common heavy metal contaminants are: Cadmium (Cd), Chromium (Cr), Copper (Cu), Mercury (Hg), Lead (Pb), Nickel (Ni) and Zinc (Zn) (USEPA, 1997). The term heavy metals refers to metals and metalloids having densities greater than 5 g cm^{-3} and is usually associated with pollution and toxicity although some of these elements (essential metals) are required by organisms at low concentrations (Adriano, 2001). For example, zinc (Zn) is the component of a variety of enzymes (Dehydrogenases,

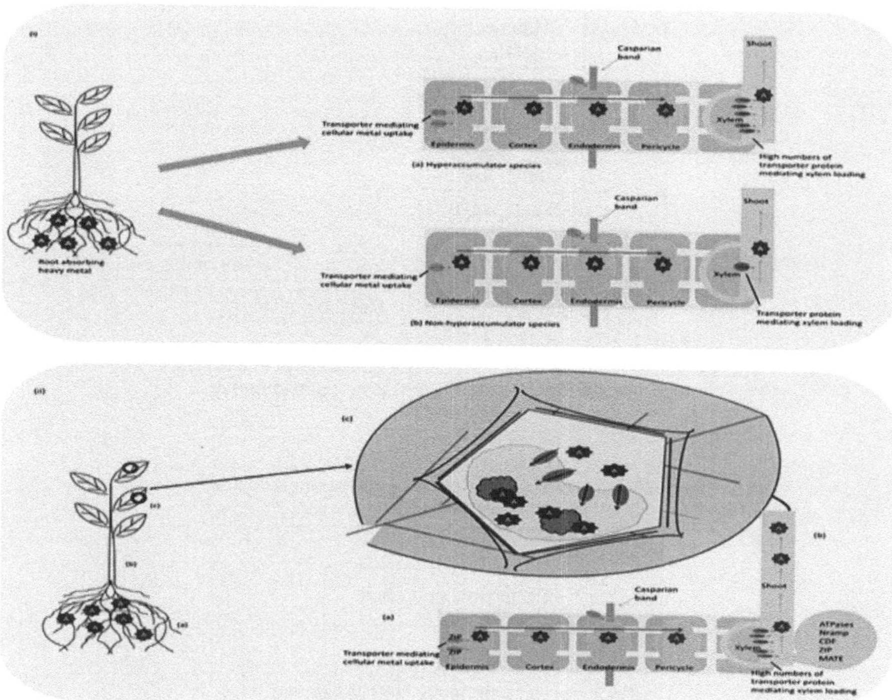

Fig. 7.1: Expression of genes in hyperaccumulator plant of cadmium

(**Source:** Review of Literature)

Proteinases, Peptidases) but is also involved in the metabolism of carbohydrates, proteins, phosphate, auxins, in RNA and ribosome formation in plants (Mengel and Kirkby, 1982). However, at high concentrations, these metals exhibit toxic effects on cells (Baker & Walker, 1990). On the contrary, cadmium (Cd) is not involved in any known biological processes (non essential metal) and may be quite toxic as it is accumulated bio organisms (Suziki *et al.*, 2001). It is known to disturb enzyme activities, to inhibit the DNA-mediated transformation in microorganisms, to interfere in the symbiosis between microbes and plants, as well as to increase plant predisposition to fungal invasion (Kabata-Pendias and Pendias, 2001).The regulatory limit of cadmium (Cd) in agricultural soil is 100 mg/kg soil (Salt *et al.*, 1995) and 0.1 to 0.2 mg per kg fresh weight in plants (by Codex Alimentarius) but this threshold is continuously exceeding because of several human activities. Plants exposed to high levels of Cd causes reduction in photosynthesis, water uptake, and nutrient uptake thus reduction in plant growth. Plants grown in soil containing high levels of cadmium show visible symptoms of injury reflected in terms of chlorosis, growth inhibition, browning of root tips, and finally death (Wojcik and Tukiendorf, 2004) (Figure 7.2).

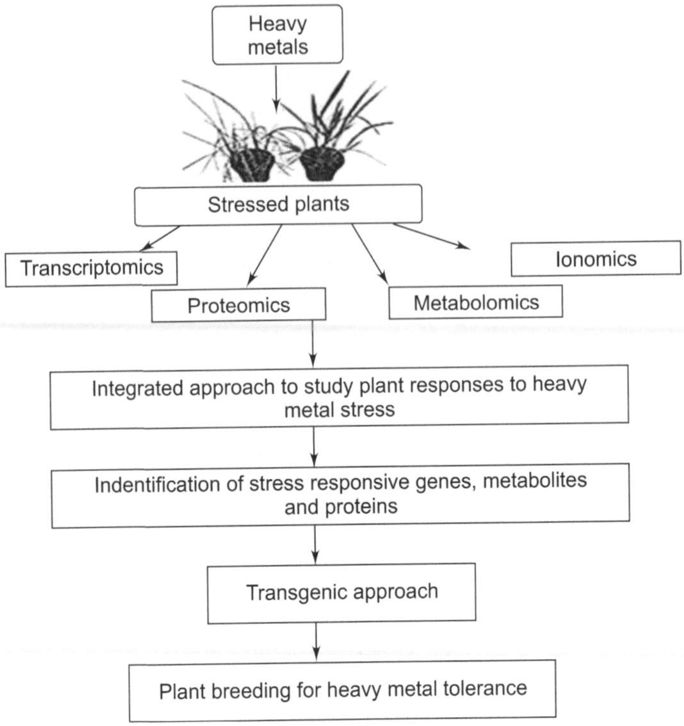

Fig. 7.2: Integrated approach to study plant response to heavy metal

(**Source:** Review of Literature)

The mechanisms involved in heavy metal tolerance may range from exclusion, inclusion and accumulation of heavy metals depending on the plant species. The widespread use of cadmium in a large number of products and industrial process has resulted in severe environmental contamination. The reason of reduced seedling length in metal treatments could be the reduction in meristematic cells present in this region and some enzymes contained in the cotyledon and endosperms. So when the activities of hydrolytic enzyme are affected, the food does not reach to the radical and plumule affecting the seedling length. Cadmium treatment showed significant effect on seedling dry weight, which was evident in the poor growth of roots and aerial parts.The concentration of accumulated Cd is usually highest in the roots, followed by shoots and the reproductive structures (Van Bruwaene *et al.*, 1984) (Figure 7.3).

Cadmium treatment at 25 ppm, 50 ppm, 75 ppm, 100 ppm concentration showed gradual reduction in root and stem growth. Dry weight is also reduced in seedlings with increasing Cd concentration. Seedlings also showed significant reduction in Chlorophyll as well as increase in Proline (stress amino acid) content. Our knowledge is still insufficient to explain the mechanism of cadmium toxicity and more especially the interaction of cadmium with important

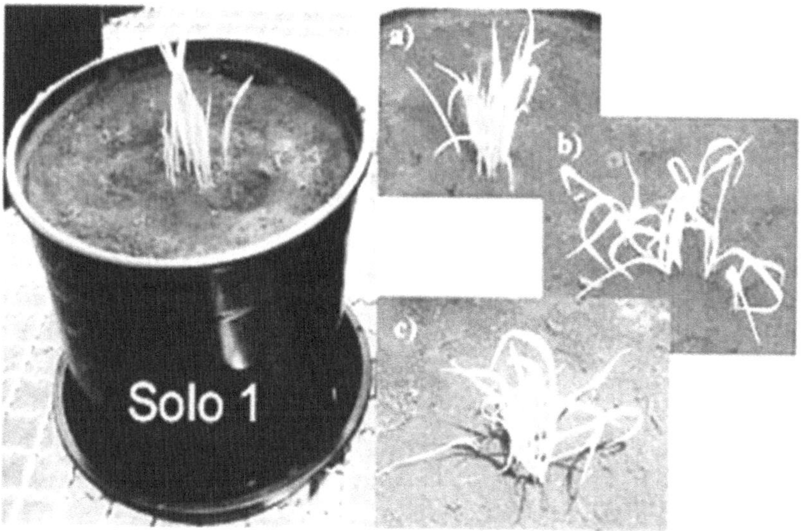

Fig. 7.3: Cadmium induced albinism in plant

(**Source:** Review of Literature)

biochemical processes in plant growth. An attempt has been made to evaluate the effect of increasing levels of cadmium toxicity on germination and seedling growth of wheat. On the basis of mentioned work following objectives were taken into consideration.The heavy metal causes some toxic effects on plants. This fact has been established since long. Cadmium is non essential for plant, but release by human activities in the environment and affects the plant life. The toxicity was monitored at the level of physiological and biochemical changes. Keeping these points in mind the following literatures are consulted. Seed germination and seedling growth are important events in the life cycle of higher plants. Number of workers have described physiology and biochemistry of seed germination (Khan, 1977, Bewley and Black, 1982). The seed germination and seedling growth are controlled by number of factors. Soil is one of the important factors for germination of seeds and growth of the seedlings. The soil, contaminated with toxic metals is considered as stress for germination as well as further growth of the plants. Heydecker (1977) discussed the seed germination in relation to stress. Little information is available on heavy metal stress and seed germination and seedling growth. Dubey and Dwivedi (1987) An attempt have been made to review the relevant literature available on heavy metals in relation to seed germination and seedling growth. The effect of heavy metals on seed germination and seedling growth is reported.Wang and Keturi, (1990) Metal toxicity was assessed by the seed germination test. Seeds of ten plant species, namely cabbage, carrot, cucumber, lettuce, Japanese millet, white proso millet, oat, rice, tomato and wheat were germinated in effluent collected from the acid bath of a metal engraving plant. The sample was adjusted to pH 7.25 and diluted to a series of solutions using hard standard water. The percent germination was decreased. Cucumber and white proso millet were relatively insensitive to the effluent toxicity. Rice, lettuce and tomato were sensitive to toxicity. Moral *et al.*, (1994) studied the effects of Cd on growth of tomato grown in soilless culture. Two Cd treatments were imposed by adding 10 or 30 mg Cd/L Cd to the culture solution as cadmium chloride. Plant growth was affected negatively by Cd. Root, stem length and fresh weight were decreasing with each increment of Cd added to the nutrient solution.Beri and Setia (1995) studied the effects of increasing concentrations of Cd on the growth of lentil. Lentil plants were raised in acid free sand with Hoagland nutrient media and Cd $(NO_3)_2$ (1, 4 and 8 mM). Vegetative growth parameters like shoot length, root and shoot dry weight, number of nodes, leaves and branch net primary productivity decreased with increasing concentration. The decrease in produc-tivity was due to decrease in chlorophyll content. Nagoor and Vyas (1997) studied the effects of increasing concentrations of cadmium on the growth of wheat seedlings. Root length, shoot length, fresh weight and dry weight were decreased with increasing concentration of cadmium. Root growth suffered more than that of the shoot. Simon (1998) studied the cadmium accumulation, distribution as well as the effects of cadmium in sunflower plants. A greenhouse pot experiment was conducted with sunflower. After 21 days of growth, plants were treated with cadmium sulfate; the concentration of cadmium sulfate was 1mg and 10 mg. The fresh weight, dry matter accumulation, elemental composition and cadmium accumulation of sunflower plants were evaluated. After 35 days of cadmium application, leaves of sunflower plants did not show cadmium toxicity symptoms. Lagriffoul *et al.*, (1998) studied the cadmium toxicity on growth of maize plants. Maize plants were grown in nutrient solution with increasing cadmium concentrations (0.001 – 25 mM), 14 days old plants were studied. 25 mM Cd significantly decreased shoot length and leaf dry weight were recorded at an interval of 30 days till 90 days after sowing. Lower concentrations promoted shoot length as compared to control, higher concentration significantly decreased it. Root and shoot dry weight was also suppressed with increasing concentrations. Shoot root ratio on dry weight basis was more than control after 90 days. Numbers of nodes were more in treated plants. Similar numbers of branches were also more. Plant receiving 8 mM Cd did not show branching at all. The number and dry weight of leaves were also reduced. These were considered as toxic effects of Cd. Keltjens and Van Beusichen, (1998) Root length and shoot dry weight of maize plants were decreased after 5 days exposure to cadmium. Root became black in colour which indicates th oxidative stress process, i.e. there may be lipid peroxidation in the root of cadmium treated plants. Haghiri (1973) cadmium is a heavy metal pollutant. It is absorbed through the root system and gets accumulated in various plant parts which ultimately affect the yield.Narwal and Singh (1993) reported that dry matter yield of maize was significantly decreased with increasing levels of cadmium in soil. Salim *et al.*, (1992) studied the effects of cadmium toxicity on the growth of carrot plants. Foliar or root application of 0-10.9 ppm Cd in once a week for 12 weeks was given to the plants. Cd toxicity was more and the symptoms were more severe in foliar treated plants than that in root treated Plants. Cd decreased dry matter of whole plant, shoot and root by 14-71%, 18-79% and 11-64% in root treated plants and by 67-73%, 5-80% and 7-68% in foliar treated plants. The dry matter was decreased with increasing cadmium concentration. Keshan and Mukherji (1994) reported the effects of foliar spray of cadmium sulphate on mungbean. 21 days old potted plants of mung bean were sprayed with 40, 60, 80 and 100 mM concentrations of cadmium sulphate. Control set was sprayed with DW, spraying was done once a week, dry weight of 56 days old plants were observed. All the concentrations of cadmium sulphate showed inhibitory effects on shoot length, leaf area and length of pods as compared to control. The effect was significant in older plants and it was correlated with concentration. Salim *et al.*, (1993) reported the effects of root and foliar treatment with cadmium on the growth of radish plants. Radish seedlings after 2 weeks of transplantation were treated via the soil or by foliar application with three different concentrations of Cd. Cd was inhibitory to growth. Foliar application was more harmful to plants than treatment via the soil. Shoots tended to accumulate Cd. Radish plants treated with a solution containing more than 1 mg cadmium/literposed a health hazard to human. Ferretti *et al.*, (1993) Three days old seedlings of *Zeamays* L. were exposed to 10, 100 and 250 pM cadmium nitrate. The 14 days old seedlings were studied for effects of cadmium. Cadmium decreased the dry matter and leaf area. Pasquale *et al.*, (1995) investigated the effects of high levels of cadmium in soil and in the atmosphere on *Coriandrum sativum* plants. Plants grown in contaminated soil (0, 10 or 100 ppm Cd) showed a significant reduction in the length of the stem and root and number of umbels, yellowing and ultra structural alterations of the leaves and significant decreases in the contents of essential oil components in the fruits. Mehindirata *et al.*, (2000) Brinjal (*Solatium melongena*)seeds were germinated in the pots. The seedlings were transplanted in the pots and Cd in the form of $CdCl_2$ in doses of 5, 15, 30, 75, and 150 pg/g dry weight of soil was applied. The untreated plants were used as control. Sampling was done 20 days after treatment. The length of root and shoot was in generally smaller in the cadmium treated plants than in the control (Figure 7.4).

The decrease in length was quite significant at higher cadmium concentrations. Similarly, significant decrease in the biomass of shoot and root was evident with an increase in the cadmium dose. The shoot was most prominently affected than the root, with the maximum variation being about 59% and 43% respectively. Seedlings raised under cadmium treatment were generally smaller. Bharti *et al.*, (2001) Cadmium associate more than 2.0mM, decreased the fresh

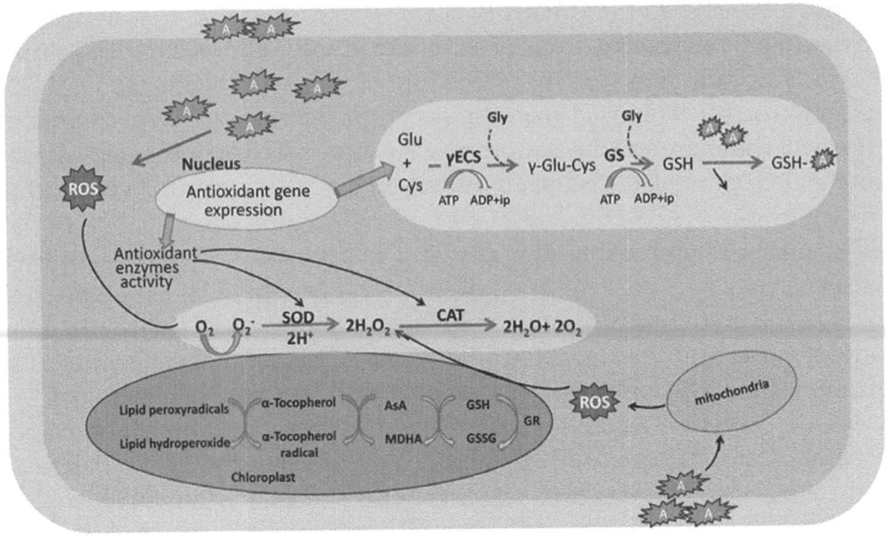

Fig. 7.4: Heavy metal induced-oxidative stress and its tolerance mechanism in plants

(**Source:** Review of Literature)

weight and dry weight of the root, shoot, and leaf of 10 day old *Pisum* seedlings. Root length and shoot length were also reduced.Vediya and Vyas (2002 a) reported the physiological effects of cadmium on cumin. Earthen pots were filled with garden soil. Graded doses of $CdCl_2$ i.e. 10, 50 and 100 ppm were added to the garden soil. The pots without $CdCl_2$ were considered as control. The seeds of cumin var. Guj-1 were sown in the pots. Plants were cultivated using the normal practice. Various growth parameters were studied regularly from control and cadmium treated plants. Cadmium decreased the root and stem elongation, leaf was also decreased by cadmium treatment. The root shoot ratio was also decreased in older plants. Fresh weight and dry weight of root, stem and leaf was decreased by cadmium. Reproductive growth in terms of fruit number, fresh and dry weight was adversely affected by cadmium. Harvest index value was also decreased by cadmium. The stress index value was less than 100% for root, stem and leaf, inflorescence, flower and fruit number as well as fresh and dry weight of various organs. Ewais (1997) revealed the effect of cadmium, nickel and lead on growth, chlorophyll content. These three heavy metals inhibited the shoot growth but were less suppressive to root growth. They also lowered leaf chlorophyll content. The heavy metal additions to soil increased their contents in both roots and shoots, several times more in the roots than in shoots. Fargasova (2001) studied the phytotoxic effects of Cd, Zn, Pb, Cu and Fe on *Sinapis alba* seedlings and their accumulation in roots and shoots. All the metals, except Fe, were accumulated in significantly higher amount in the roots than in the shoots. Cd, Zn, Cu and Pb reduced chlorophyll *a*, and especially chlorophyll *b* content.Tsakou *et al.*, (2001) reported the effect of heavy metal accumulation on the growth of cotton plants and reported growth inhibition due to heavy metals such as cadmium and lead. Ozyigit and Akinci, (2009) Reported that some heavy metals such as Pb, Cd and Al have effects on plant, including: decrease in total leaf number and size, a decrease in shoot biomass, inhibition of root elongation, chlorosis and necrosis of leaves leading to decreased photosynthetic activity and reduces stomata aperture.Lamai *et al.*, (2005) studied the toxicity and accumulation of the heavy metals lead and cadmium in a common filamentous green alga *Cladophora fracta* and found a significant decrease in the relative growth and the total chlorophyll content. The bioaccumulation factor (BCF) of Pb was higher than that of Cd. Zengin and Munzuromglu (2005) observed the effect of some heavy metals on chlorophyll content, proline and some antioxidant chemicals in Bean (*Phaseolus vulgaris* L.) seedlings. Total chlorophyll content declined progressively with increasing concentrations of heavy metals. The heavy metals have effects on chlorophyll content in plants. Heavy metals are known to interfere with chlorophyll synthesis either through direct inhibition of an enzyme step or by inducing deficiency of an essential nutrient (Assche and Clíjsters, 1990). Phetsombat *et al.*, (2006) reported the toxicity and bioaccumulation of cadmium and lead in *Salvinia cucullata*. The toxic symptoms of Cd and Pb to *S. cucullata* showed chlorosis on leaves. There were significant decreases in the relative growth, biomass productivity and total chlorophyll content when the exposure time and concentration were increased. The accumulation study showed the significant increase of both metals when the exposure time and concentration were increased. The roots of *S. cucullata* had higher Cd and Pb contents than leaves, suggesting that the metals were bound to the root cells and were partially transported to the leaves. Shafiq *et al.*, (2008) observed the effect of lead and cadmium on germination and seedling growth of *Leucaena leucocephala*. Both lead and cadmium treatments showed toxic effects on various growth indices of *L. leucocephala*. Increasing the concentration of lead to 75 ppm, significantly ($p < 0.05$) decreased seed germination as compared to control. Seedling and root growth was significant ($p < 0.05$) reduced at 50 ppm treatment of lead. Seed germination and root length significantly ($p < 0.05$) decreased at 50 ppm treatment of cadmium as compared to control. The seedling dry weight also significantly ($p < 0.05$) reduced at 25 ppm treatment of lead and cadmium. Cadmium treatment at 100 ppm showed comparatively pronounced effects in *L. leucocephala* seedlings as compared to lead. John *et al.*, (2009) studied the effect on plant growth, pigment concentration, biochemical parameters and uptake of heavy metals for *Brassica junceas* in response to cadmium and lead stress. The plant exhibited a decline in growth, chlorophyll content and carotenoids with Cd and Pb but Cd was found to be more detrimental than Pb treatment in *B. juncea*. More accumulation of Cd and Pb was observed in roots than shoots in *B. juncea*.Bhardwaj *et al.*, (2009) observed the effect of enhanced lead and cadmium in soil on physiological and biochemical attributes of *Phaseolusvulgaris* L. growth was decreased as concentration of metals was increased as compared to control plants. Photosynthetic pigments, total soluble sugar, starch content as well as soluble protein content decreased as the concentration of metals was increased in comparison of control plants. Heidar and Sarani (2011) observed the effect of lead and cadmium on seed germination, seedling growth and antioxidant enzyme activities of musturd (*Sinapis arvensis*). The results revealed that Cd and Pb adversely influenced the seed germination. The effect of Cd and Pb concentrations causing 5.6% and 10.23% inhibition of germination of seeds, respectively. The root and shoot growth in length of mustard plants were also decreased with increasing concentrations of Cd and Pb metals.Pandey and Tripathi (2011) observed the effect of heavy metals on morphological and biochemical characteristics of *Albizia procera* seedlings and these heavy metals at all concentration (1, 5 and 10 ppm) exhibited significant reduction in chlorophyll, crude protein, amino acid and soluble sugar quantity in leaves. These biochemical parameters showed a positive correlation with leaf area, root length, shoot length and biomass of the plant. Poly phenol, proline and ascorbic acid of leaves significantly increased over control, but revealed a negative correlation with root-shoot length, leaf area and biomass of the plant at all treatment levels. Concentration dependent changes were observed in most of the parameters. Moya *et al.*, (1993) The presence of excessive amounts of Cd in soil commonly elicits many stress symptoms in plants, such as reduction of growth, especially root growth, disturbances in mineral nutrition and carbohydrate metabolism. Chugh and Sawhney, (1999) In *Pisum sativum* seedlings, cadmium caused a sharp decline inchlorophyll content, photosynthetic rates, and activity of thephotosystems and photosynthetic enzymes. Neelima and Reddy (2003) The present investigation reports the results of the effect of cadmium and mercury individually on seed germination, seedling growth, number of lateral roots, fresh and dry weights and seedling metabolism in *Solanum melongena*. Effect of different concentrations of these two heavy metals (Cadmium—50, 100, 300, 500, 700, 1000, 3000, 5000, 7000 and 9000 ppm and Mercury—5, 10, 15, 20, 25, 30, 35, 40, 45 and 50 ppm) and durations for 6, 12 and 24 h were employed for all seedling parameters of brinjal. Both Cd and Hg showed drastic effects at high concentrations and longer duration with regard to seedling growth and metabolism.Patel *et al.*, (2005) studied the effect of cadmium on the growth and the activity of H_2O_2 scavenging enzymes in *Colocassia esculentum*. Cadmium depressed dry matter production of the plant up to 33%. Plant accumulated larger portion of the heavy metal in the roots followed by stem and leaf. Chlorophyll content of the plant declined on treatment with heavy metal.Kiran and Sahin (2006) studied the effect of cadmium on seed germination, root development and mitotic of root tip cells of lentil

(Lensculinaris) and it determines that the germination of seeds and the growth of roots inhibited and mitotic abnormalities increased with the increasing of Cd concentration. Zhang *et al.*, (2007)Heavy metal Cd severely inhibits plant growth and even causesplant death by disturbing the uptake of nutrients and inhibitingphotosynthesis via degradation of chlorophyll.Chen *et al.*, (2011) studied the effects of cadmium on the growth and photosynthetic activities in pakchoi and mustard. Both shoot and root weight decreased progressively with increasing Cd concentration for pakchoi and mustard. Negative linear relationships were observed between total Chlorophyll contents and Cd concentrations in soils in pakchoi ($r^2 = -0.681$, $P < 0.01$) and mustard ($r^2 = -0.463$, $P < 0.05$). In comparison to the controls (Cd = 0 mg·kg-1), significant reductions of chlorophyll-a and chlorophyll-b were both observed at 24 mg Cd kg/soil. Gonzalez *et al.*, (2012) studied the effect of Cd on the growth and chlorophyll content of barley plants *(Hordeum vulgare)*, the amount of metal accumulated in the plant increased by increasing the concentration of the applied metal, and the roots accumulated more metal than did the aerial part of the plant. For plants treated with the highest metal concentrations, the most significant differences were found in chlorophyll content. Siddhu and Khan (2012) reported the effect of cadmium on the growth and metabolism of *Phaseolus mungo*. The highestconcentration of Cd was found to have deleterious effects on seed germination, length and dry weight of root and shoot, plant height, phytomass, number of leaves and branches, leaf area and chlorophyll contents.Iftikhar Ahmad *et al.*, (2012) Study was conducted to evaluate the effect of various Cd levels 0, 5, 20, 50 and 80 mg L^{-1} on seed germination and seedling growth of four wheat cultivars (Sehar-06, Fareed-06, Inqlab-91, Chakwal-50). Cadmium showed toxicity at 5 mg L^{-1} in case of root and shoot growth, whereas 20 mg L^{-1} in the case of seed germination and germination energy which is aggravated on further addition of Cd the from 50 to 80 mg L-1. Sehar-06 performed better under Cd stress while Inqlab-91 had poor performance. Later had a maximum decrease in root length (70.4%), shoot length (81.2%), percent germination (68%) and germination index (76.8%) at 80 mg L-1 Cd compared to control. Mane *et al.*, (2015) Reported that the plants were treated with increasing concentrations of cadmium chloride i.e. 25, 50 and 75 ppm. Wet and dry biomass of the shoots and roots was decreased linearly with increase in concentrations of cadmium chloride in the rooting medium. It was also observed that cadmium chloride had a clear-cut negative effect on the shoot length of T. aestivum showing perfect negative correlation with the increasing concentration of cadmium chloride to the rooting medium. Similarly, reduction in root length was negatively correlated with the increasing cadmium concentration and might be due to the toxicity of cadmium. It was also accumulated in increasing levels in root and shoot parts of wheat seedlings and might be associated with the low molecular weight organic acids secreted by the roots. Chhotu *et al.*, 2008.A greenhouse experiment

was conducted to determine the phytotoxic effect of heavy metals such as Cd, Cu, Ni, Pb and Zn on the growth of Sunflower (*Helianthus annuus*): on the seed germination, root/shoot growth and uptake of metals in soil-vermicompost media. The selected metals were dosed at various concentrations ranging from 0, 5, 10, 20, 40 and 50 ppm separately in soil - vermicompost media (3:1) in pot experiment. The seed germination, root and shoot growth were found significantly affected by these metals at higher concentration of 40 and 50 ppm. However, the lower concentration of heavy metals ranging from 5 to 20ppm doses was observed to be stimulating the root and shoot length and increase biomass of the sunflower plant. Sunflower

CONCLUSION

The heavy metal contamination is of great concern in India and abroad. Its remediation is the major issue for the developed an developing countries. In the case of wheatthe decrease in length was quite significant at higher cadmium concentrations. Similarly, significant decrease in the biomass of shoot and root evident with an increase in the cadmium dose.

REFERENCES

Abdul-Baki, A. A. and Anderson, J. D. (1973). Vigour Determination in Soybean Seed by Multiple Criteria. *Crop Sci.*, 13: 630-633.

Adriano, D. C. (2001). Trace elements in Terrestrial Environments; Biochemistry, Bioavailability and Risks of Metals. Springer Verlag, New York, pp. 150–159.

Baker, A. J. M. and Walker, P. L. (1990). Ecophysiology of Metal Uptake by Tolerant Plants. In: Shaw, AJ, ed. Heavy Metal Tolerance in Plants: Evolutionary Aspects. Boca Raton, FL, USA: CRC Press, 155-177.

Barcelo, J. Vazquez, M. D. and Poschenrieder, C. (1988). Structural and Ultrastructural Disorders in Cadmium-treated Bush Bean Plants (*Phaseolus vulgaris* L.)[J]. *New Phytologist*, 108: 37–49.

Bates, L. S., Waldren, R. P. and Teare, I. D. (1973). Rapid Determination of Proline for Water Stress Studies. *Plant and Soil*, 39: 205-208.

Beri, A. and Setia, R. C. (1995). Assessment of Growth and Yield Lens Culilaris Medic var. Massar 9-12 Treated with Heavy Metals under N-supplied Condition, *J. Indian Bot. Soc.*, 74: 293-297.

Bewley, J. D. and Black, M. (1982). Physiology and Biochemistry of Seed in Relation to Germination. Volume-2 Springer Verlag, Berlin.

Bhardwaj, P., Chaturvedi, A. K. and Prasad, P. (2009). Effect of Enhanced Lead and Cadmium in Soil on Physiological and Biochemical Attributes of *Phaseolus vulgaris* L. *Nature and Science*, 7(8): 63-75.

Bharti, N., Sriva&tav, S. and Srivastav, P. S. (2001). Allevation of Cadmium Induced Decrease in Biomass of Pisum and Sesamum by Inorganic Nutrients. Bull Environ Contain. Toxicol. Springer Verlag, New York. 67: 496 – 502.

Chandel, S.R.S. (1984). A Hand Book of Agricultural Statistics (third ed.), Achal Publication, Kanpur, India.

Chen, Xin., Wang, J., Shi, Y., Zhao, M.Q. and Chi, G. Y. (2011). Effects of Cadmium on Growth and Photosynthetic Activities in Pakchoi and Mustard. *Botanical Studies*, 52: 41-46.

Chhotu, D. Jadia, Madhusudan. Fulekar, H. (2008). Phytoremediation: The Application of Vermicompost to Remove Zinc, Cadmium, Copper, Nickel and Lead by Sunflower Plant. *Environmental Engineering and Management Journal*, 5: 547-558.

Costa, G. and Morel, J. L. (1994). Water Relations Gas Exchange and Amino Acid Content in Cd Treated lettuca. *Plant Physiol. Biochem.*, 32: 561–570.

De Filippis, L. F. and Zeigler, H. (1993). The Effect of Sub Lethal Concentrations of Zn, Cadmium and Mercury on the Photosynthetic Carbon Reduction Cycle of Euglena. *J. Plant Physiology*, 142:167-172.

Dhindsa, R. S., Plumb-Dhindsa, P. and Thorne, T. A. (1981) Leaf Senescence Correlated with Increased Levels of Membrane Permeability and Lipid Peroxidation and Decreased Levels of Superoxide Dismutase and Catalase. *J. Exp. Bot.*, 32: 93–101.

Dubey, R. C. and Dwivedi, R. S. (1973). Effect of Heavy Metals on Seed Germination on Seedling Growth of Soybean. *Nat. Acad. Sci. Let.*, 10 (4): 121-123.

Ewais, E. A. (1997). Effects of Cadmium Nickel and Lead on Growth, Chlorophyll Content and Protein of Weed. *Biol. Plant.*,39(3):403-410.

Fargašová, A. (2001). Phytotoxic Effects of Cd, Zn, Pb, Cu and Fe on Sinapis Alba L. Seedlings and their Accumulation in Roots and Shoots. *Biol. Plant.*, 44(3): 471-473

Ferretti, M. Ghisi, R. Merlo, L. Vecchia, F. D. and Passera, C. (1993). Effect of Cadmium on Photosynthesis and Enzymes of Photosynthetic Sulphate and Nitrate Assimilation Pathways in Maize (*Zea mays* L.). *Photosynthetica*, 29: 49-54.

Fodor, A., Sajabo-Nagy, A. and Erdie, L. (1995). The Effect of Cadmium on the Fluidity and H+ ATPase Activity of Plasma Membrane from Sunflower and Wheat Roots. *J. Plant Physiology*, 14:787-792.

Gallego, S. M., Benavides, M. P. and Tomaro, M. L. (1996). Effect of Heavy Metal Ion Excess on Sunflower Leaves: Evidence for Involvement of Oxidative Stress. *Plant Science*, 121: 151-159.

Haghiri, F. (1973). Cadmium Uptake by Plants. *Journal of Environmental Quality*. 2: 93-96.

Heydecker, W. (1977). Stress and Seed Germination: An Agronomic View. In: Khan, A. A. The Physiology and Biochemistry of Seed Dormancy and Germination. New York : North-Holland Publ. Co. pp. 237-282.

Iftikhar Ahmad, Muhammad Javed Akhtar, Zahir Ahmad Zahir and Amer Jamil (2012). Effect of Cadmium on Seed Germination and Seedling Growth of Four Wheat (T*riticum aestivum*) Cultivars. *Pak. J. Bot.*, 44(5): 1569-1574.

Intawongse, M. & Dean, J. (2006). Uptake of Heavy Metals by Vegetable Plants Grown on Contaminated Soil and their Bioavailability in the Human Gastrointestinal Tract. *Food Additives and Contaminants*, *23*(1): 36-48.

John, R., Ahmad, P., Gadgil, K. and Sharma, S. (2009). Heavy metal toxicity: effect on plant growth, biochemical parameters and metal accumulation by Brassica juncea L. *International Journal of Plant Production*, 3: 65-75.

Kabata-Pendias, A. and Pendias, H. (2000). Trace Elements in Soil and Plants. Boca Raton, FL: CRC Press.

Keltjens, W. G., Beusichem, M. and Van, L. (1998). Phytochelatins as Biomarkers for Heavy Metal Stress in Maize (*Zea mays* L.) and Wheat (*Triticum aestivum* L.): Combined Effects of Copper and Cadmium, *Plant and Soil*, 203: 119-126.

Keshan, U. and Mukherji, S. (1994). Phytotoxic Effects of Cadmium Sulphate on Nitrogen Content, Nitrogen Fixation, Nitrate Reductase and Leghemoglobin Content in Root Nodules of Mungbean (*Vigna radiata* L.). *Indian J. Exp. Biol.*, 32: 351-353.

Khan, A. A. (1977). The Physiology and Biochemistry of Seed Dormancy and Germination. North-Holland, Amsterdam.

Kiran Y, and Sahin A. (2006). The Effect of Cadmium on Seed Germination, Root Development and Mitotic of Root Tip Cells of Lentil (*Lens culinaris* Medic). *World Journal of Agricultural Science*, 2(2):196-200.

Lagriffoul, A., Mocquot, B., Mench, M. and Vangronsveld, J. (1998). Cadmium Toxicity Effects on Growth and Chlorophyll Contents and Activities of Stress Related Enzymes in Young Maize Plants (*Zea mays* L.). *Plant Soil*, 200: 241-250.

Lakshaman Kumar Chughand Surinder Kumar Sawhney (1999). Photosynthetic Activities of *Pisum sativum* Seedlings Grown in Presence of Cadmium. *Plant Physiology and Biochemistry*, 37(4): 297-303.

Lamai, C., Kruatrachue, M., Pokethitiyook, P., Upatham, E. S. and Soonthornsarathool, V. (2005). Toxicity and Accumulation of Lead and Cadmium in Filamentous Green Alga *Cladophora fracta* (O.F. Müller ex Vahl): A Laboratory Study. Sci. Asian, 31, pp. 121–127.

Mane, A. V., Sankpal, R. R., Mane, L. A., and Ambawade, M. S. (2010). Cadmium Chloride Induced Alteration in Growth and Cadmium Accumulation in *Triticum aestivum* (l.) var. MP LOK 1. *J. Chem. Pharm. Res.*, 2(5): 206-215.

.Mehindirata Shalini, Mahmooduzzafar, Siddiqi, T. and Iqbal, M, (2000). Cadmium Induced Changes in Growth and Structure of Root and Stem of *Solanum melongena* L. *Phytomorphology*. 50: 243 - 251.

Mengel, K. and and Kirkby, E. A. (1982). Principles of Plant Nutrition. 3rd Edition, International Potash Institute, Bern.

Monneveux, P. and Behassen, E. (1977). The Diversity of Drought Adaptation in the Wide in: E. Behassen (ed.) Drought Tolerance in Higher Plants: Genetical Physiological and Molecular Biological Analysis. Kluwer Academic Publisher Dordrecht, pp. 7-14.

Moral, R., Gomez, I., Navarro Pedreno, J. and Mataix J. (1994). Effects of Cadmium on Nutrient Distribution, Yield and Growth of Tomato Grown in Soil Less Culture. *J. Plant Nutrition*, 17(6): 953-962.

Moya, J. L., Ros, R. and Picazo, I. (1993). Influence of Cadmium and Nickel on Growth, Net Photosynthesis and Carbohydrate Distribution in Rice Plants. *Photosynthesis Res.*,36:75–80

Nagoor, S. and Vyas, V. (1997). Heavy Metal Induced Changes in Growth and Carbohydrate Metabolism in Wheat Seedlings. *Indian J. Envir. Toxic.*, 7: 98-103.

Nagrajan, S. (2002). Physiological Traits Associated with Yield Performance of Spring Wheat (*Triticum aestivum*) Under Late Sown Condition. *Indian J. of Agri. Sci.*, 72:135-140.

Narwal, R. P., Mahendra, S., Singh, J. P. and Dahiya, J. D. (1993). Cadmiumzinc Interaction in Maize Grown on Sewer Water Irrigated Soil, Arid Land Research and Management, 7(2):125-131.

Neelima, P., Jaganmohan,K. Reddy (2003). Differential Effect of Cadmium and Mercury on Growth and Metabolism of Selenium Melongena L. Seedlings.*J. of Environ. Biol.*, 4: 453-460.

Ozyigit, I. and Akinci, S. (2009). Effects of Some Stress Factors (Aluminum, Cadmium and Drought) on Stomata of Roman Nettle (*Urtica pilulifera* L.). *Not. Bot. Hort. Agrobot*, 37: 108-115.

Pandey, P. and Tripathi, A. K (2011). Effect of Heavy Metals on Morphological and Biochemical Characteristics of Albizia procera (Roxb.) Benth, Seedlings. *International Journal of Environmental Science,* 1(5): 1009-1018.

Pasquale R de, Rapisarda A, Germano M P, Ragusa S, Kirjavainen S, Galati EM and De Pasquale R, (1995). Effects of Cadmium on Growth and Pharmacologically Active Constituents of the Medicinal Plant Coriandrum Sativum L. Water Air and Soil Poll. 84 : K7 – 157.

Patel, J., Patel, N., Mandakini J. & Subramanian1, R.B. (2005). Effect of Cadmium on Growth and the Activity of H_2O_2 Scavenging Enzymes in *Colocassia esculentum. Plant and Soil,* 273: 183–188.

Phetsombat, S., Kruatrachue, M. Pokethitiyook, P. and Upatham, S. (2006). Toxicity and Bioaccumulation of Cadmium and Lead in Salvinia cucullata. J Environ Biol., 27(4):645-52.

Poschenrieder, C., Gunse, B. and Barcelo, J. (1989). Influence of Cadmium on Water Relation, Stomatal Resistance, and ABA Content in Expanding Bean Leave. *Plant Physiology,* 90:1365-1371.

Priti Bhardwaj, Ashish K. Chaturvedi and Prasad, P. (2009). Effect of Enhanced Lead and Cadmium in Soil on Physiological and Biochemical Attributes of *Phaseolus vulgaris* L. *Nature and Science,* 7(8): 63-75.

Salim, R., Al-Subu, M.M. and Attallah, A. (1993). Effects of Root and Foliar Treatments with Lead, Cadmium and Copper on the Uptake, Distribution and Growth of Radish Plants. *Environment International,* 19: 393-404.

Salim, R., Al Subu, M.M., Douleh, A., Chenavier, L. & Hagemeyer, J. (1992). Effects of Root and Foliar Treatments of Carrot Plants with Lead and Cadmium on the Growth, Uptake and the Distribution of Uptake of Metals in Treated Plants, *Journal of Environmental Science and Health,* 27(7): 1793-1758.

Salt, D.E., Blaylock, M., Kumar, N., Dushenkov, S., Ensley, B., Chet, I. and Raskin, I. (1995) Phytoremediation: A Novel Strategy for Removal of Toxic Metals from the Environment Using Plants. *Biotechnol.,* 13: 468-474.

Sandalio, L.M., Dalurzo, H.C., Gomez, M.C., Romero Puertas, M.C. and del Río, L.A. (2001). Cadmium-induced Changes in the Growth and Oxidative Metabolism of Pea Plants. *J. Exp. Bot.,* 52: 2115-2126.

Shafiq, M., Iqbal, M. Z. and Mohammad, A. (2008). Effect of Lead and Cadmium on Germination and Seedling Growth of *Leucaena leucocephala. J. Appl. Sci. Environ. Manage.,* 12 (2): 61-66.

Shaw, B. P. (1995). Effects of Mercury and Cadmium on the Activities of Antioxidative Enzymes in the Seedlings of Phaseolus Aureus. *Biologia Plantarum,* 37, 587-596 (1995).

Siddhu, G. and Khan, Ali (2012). Effect of Cadmium on Growth and Metabolism of *Phaseolus Mungo. Journal of Environmental Biology,* 33: 173-179.

Simon L. (1998). Cadmium Accumulation and Distribution in Sunflower Plant. *Journal of Plant Nutrition,* 21: 341–352.

Slafer, G. A. and Savin, R. (1991). Development Base Temperature in Different Homological Phases of Wheat (*Triticum aestivum* L*). J. Exp. Bot.* 42 (241): 1077-1082.

Somashekaraiah, B.V., Padmaja, K. and Prasad, A. R. K. (1992). Phytotoxicity of Cadmium Ions on Germinating Seedlings of Mung Bean (*Phaseolus vulgaris*): Involvement of Lipid Peroxides in Chlorophyll Degradation. *Physiologia Plantarum,* 85: 85-89 (1992).

Stobart, A. K. Griffiths, W. T., Ameen-Bukhari, I. and Sheerwood, R. P. (1985). The Effect of Cadmium on the Biosynthesis of Chlorophyll in Leave of Barley. *Phyiology of Plant,* 63:

293-298.

Stohs, S. J., Bagchi, D. (1995) Oxidative Mechanisms in the Toxicity of Metal Ions. *Free Rad. Biol. Med.*, 18: 321-336.

Suzuki N., Koizumi N. Sano H., (2001), Screening of Cadmium-responsive Genes in Arabidopsis Thaliana. *Plant Cell Environ.*, 24: 1177-1188.

Tsakou, A., Maria, Roulia and Christodoulakis, N. S. (2001). Growth of Cotton Plants (*Gossypium hirsutum*) as Affected by Water and Sludge from a Sewage Treatment Plant: II. Seed and Fiber Yield and Heavy Metal Accumulation. Bulletin of Environmental Contamination and Toxicology, 66(6):743-7 47.

USEPA, (1997), Cleaning Up the Nation's Waste Sites: Markets and Technology Trends, United States Environmental Protection Agency EPA/542/R-96/005, Office of Solid Waste and Emergency Response, Washington, DC.

Van Bruwaene, R., Kirchmann, R. and Impens, R. (1984). Cadmium Contamination in Agriculture and Zootechnology. *Experientia.* 40: 43-52.

Vediya, S. and Vyas, A. V. (2002a). Physiological Effects on Cumin. *Anarta,* 9: 9 -18.

Wang, W. and Paul H. Keturi (1990). Comparative Seed Germination Tests Using Ten Plant Species for Toxicity Assessment of a Metal Engraving Effluent Sample, *Water Air and Soil Pollution,* 52 (3): 369-376.

Weatherly, P.E. (1962). Studies in Water Relation of the Cotton Plant- I. The Field Measurement of Water Deficit in Leave. - *New Phytol.*, 49: 81-87.

Witham, F. H., Blaydes, B. F. and Devlin, R. M. (1971) Experiments in Plant Physiology, Van Nostrand Reinhold, New York, USA, 1971, pp. 167-200.

Wo´ jcik, M. and Tukiendorf, A. (2004). Phytochelatin Synthesis and Cadmium Localization in wild Type of Arabidopsis Thaliana. *Plant Growth Regulation*, 44: 71–80.

Xin Chen, Wang, J., Shi, Y., Zhao, M.Q. and Chi, G.Y. (2011). Effects of Cadmium on Growth and Photosynthetic Activities in Pakchoi and Mustard. *Botanical Studies*, 52: 41-46.

Xiong, Z. (1998). Heavy Metal Concentration of Urban Soils and Plants in Relation to Traffic in Wuhan City, China. *Toxicol. Environ. Chem.*, 65:31–39.

Zengin F, and Munzuroglu, O. (2005). Effect of Some Heavy Metals on Content of Chlorophyll, Proline and Some Antioxidant Chemicals in Bean (*Phaseolus vulgaris L.*) Seedlings. *Acta Biol Crac.*, 47(2):157–164.

Zhang, P., Zhou, Q. and Jiang, H. (2007). Alleviate Effects of Exogenous Ascorbate Acid on Cd Stress of Rape Seedlings. *Plant Physiology,* 46:73-77.

Heidari, M. and Sarani, S. (2011). Effects of Lead and Cadmium on Seed Germination, Seedling Growth and Antioxidant Enzymes Activities of Mustard (*Sinapis arvensis* L.). *Agricultural and Biological Science,* 6:44-47.

Plant Response to Environmental Stress
Edited by: Dr. Alka Chauhan; Dr. Pawan Kumar 'Bharti' and Dr. Avnish Chauhan
ISBN: 978-93-86841-58-2
Edition: 2018
Published by: Discovery Publishing House Pvt. Ltd., New Delhi (India)

8

Role of Polyamines and Mycorrhiza for the Mitigation of Drought Stress in Solanum Tuberosum

Prasann Kumar and Sunil Kumar[1]

ABSTRACT

The potato is a starchy tuberous crop from the perennial nightshade Solanum tuberosum. The word "potato" may refer either to the plant itself or to the edible tuber. In the Andes, where the species is indigenous, some other closely related species are cultivated. Potatoes were introduced to Europe in the second half of the 16th century by the Spanish.

Keywords: Agriculture, Biotic, Cadmium, Potato

INTRODUCTION

Potato has become a staple food in many parts of the world and an integral part of much of the world's food supply. It is the world's fourth-largest food crop, following maize, wheat, and rice. The green leaves and green skins of tubers exposed to the light are toxic. Wild potato species can be found throughout the Americas from the United States to southern chile. The potato was originally believed to have been domesticated independently in multiple locations, but later genetic testing of the wide variety of cultivars and wild species proved a single origin for potatoes in the area of present-day southern Peru and extreme north-western bolivia (from a species in the *Solanum brevicaule* complex), where they were domesticated approximately 7,000–10,000 years ago. Following millennia of selective breeding, there are now over a thousand different types of potatoes. Over 99% of the presently cultivated potatoes worldwide descended from varieties that originated in the lowlands of south-central Chile, which have displaced formerly popular varieties from the Andes. However, the local importance of the potato is variable and changing rapidly. It remains an essential crop in Europe (especially eastern and central Europe), where per capita production is still the highest in the world, but the most rapid expansion over the past few decades has occurred in southern and eastern Asia. As of 2014, China led the world in potato production and together with India produced

[1] Department of Agronomy, School of Agriculture, Lovely Professional University, Jalandhar, Punjab, 144411, India

37% of the world's potatoes.Potato plants are herbaceous perennials that grow about 60 cm (24 in) high, depending on variety, with the leaves dying back after flowering, fruiting and tuber formation. They bear white, pink, red, blue, or purple flowers with yellow stamens. In general, the tubers of varieties with white flowers have white skins, while those of varieties with colored flowers tend to have pinkish skins. Potatoes are mostly cross-pollinated by insects such as bumblebees, which carry pollen from other potato plants, though a substantial amount of self-fertilizing occurs as well. Tubers form in response to decreasing day length, although this tendency has been minimized in commercial varieties (Figure 8.1).

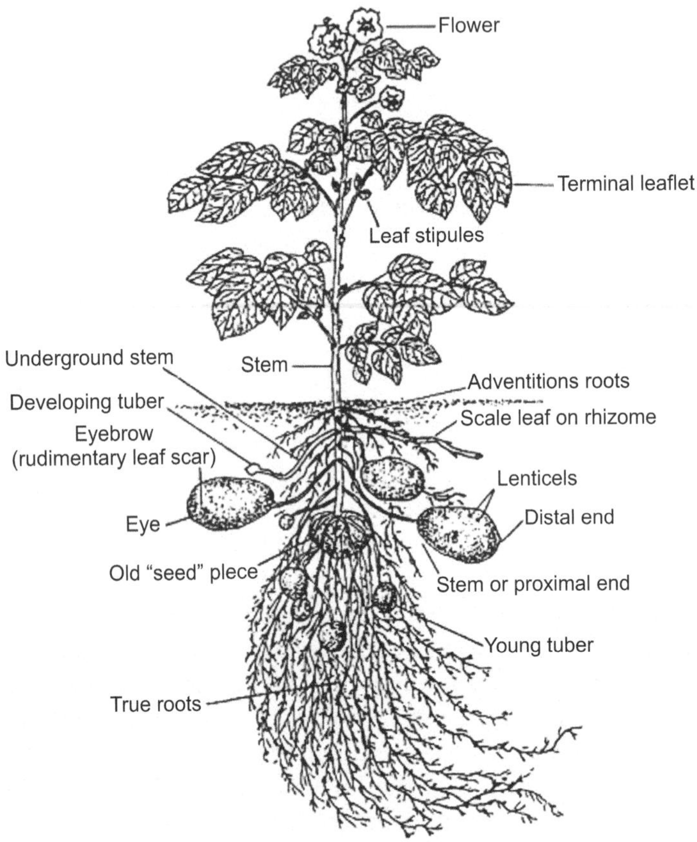

Fig. 8.1: Schematic diagram of potato plants

(**Source:** Review of Literature)

After flowering, potato plants produce small green fruits that resemble green cherry tomatoes, each containing about 300 seeds. Like all parts of the plant except the tubers, the fruit contain the toxic alkaloid solanine and are therefore unsuitable for consumption. All new potato varieties are grown from seeds, also called "true potato seed", "TPS" or "botanical seed" to distinguish it from seed tubers. New varieties grown from seed can be propagated vegetatively by planting tubers, pieces of tubers cut to include at least one or two eyes, or cuttings, a practice used in greenhouses for the production of healthy seed tubers. Plants propagated from tubers are clones of the parent, whereas those propagated from seed produce a range of different varieties. There are about 5,000 potato varieties worldwide. Three thousand of them are found in the Andes alone, mainly in Peru, Bolivia, Ecuador, Chile, and Colombia. They belong to eight or nine species, depending on the taxonomic school. Apart from the 5,000 cultivated varieties, there are about 200 wild species and subspecies, many of which can be cross-bred with cultivated varieties. Cross-breeding has been done repeatedly to transfer resistances to certain pests and diseases from the gene pool of wild species to the gene pool of cultivated potato species.Genetically modified varieties have met public resistance in the United States and in the European Union. The major species grown worldwide is *Solanum tuberosum* (a tetraploid with 48 chromosomes), and modern varieties of this species are the most widely cultivated.There are also four diploid species (with24chromosomes): *S. stenotomum, S. phureja, S. goniocalyx*, and *S.ajanhuiri* There are two triploid species (with 36 chromosomes) *S. chaucha* and *S.juzepczukii*. There is one pentaploid cultivated species (with 60 chromosomes)*S.curtilobum*. There are two major subspecies of *Solanum tuberosum*: *andigena*, or Andean; and *tuberosum*, or Chilean.The Andean potato is adapted to the short-day conditions prevalent in the mountainous equatorial and tropical regions where it originated; the Chilean potato, however, native to the Chiloé Archipelago, is adapted to the long-day conditions prevalent in the higher latitude region of southern Chile. In 2014, world production of potatoes was 382 million tonnes, an increase of 4% over 2013 amounts and led by China with 25% of the world total. Other major producers were India, Russia, Ukraine and the United States.Just over two thirds of the global production is eaten directly by humans with the rest being fed to animals or used to produce starch. This means that the annual diet of an average global citizen in the first decade of the 21st century included about 33 kg (or 73 lb) of potato. However, the local importance of potato is variable and rapidly changing. It remains an essential crop in Europe (especially eastern and central Europe), where per capita production is still the highest in the world, but the most rapid expansion over the past few decades has occurred in southern and eastern Asia. The geographic shift of potato production has been away from wealthier countries toward lower-income areas of the world (although the degree of this trend is ambiguous), leading to 2008 being named as the International Year of the Potato.Raw potato is 79% water, 17% carbohydrates (88% of which is starch), 2% protein, contains negligible fat (table). In a 100 gram amount, raw potato provides 77 calories and is a rich source of vitamin B6 and vitamin C (23% and 24% of the Daily Value, respectively), with no other nutrients in significant amount (table). When a potato is baked, contents of vitamin B6 and vitamin C decline with little significant change in other nutrients. Potatoes contain toxic compounds known as glycoalkaloids, of which the most prevalent are solanine and chaconine. Solanine is also found in other plants in the family Solanaceae, which includes such plants as the deadly nightshade (*Atropa belladonna*), henbane (*Hyoscyamus niger*) and tobacco (*Nicotiana*), as well as eggplant and tomato. These compounds, which protect the plant from its predators, are, in general, concentrated in its leaves, stems, sprouts, and fruits (in contrast to the roots). Potatoes contain toxic compounds known as glycoalkaloids, of which the most prevalent are solanine and chaconine. Solanine is also found in other plants in the family Solanaceae, which includes such plants as the deadly nightshade (*Atropa belladonna*), henbane (*Hyoscyamus niger*) and tobacco (*Nicotiana*), as well as eggplant and tomato. These compounds, which protect the plant from its predators, are, in general, concentrated in its leaves, stems, sprouts, and fruits (in contrast to the roots). Potatoes are generally grown from seed potatoes – these are tubers specifically grown to be disease free and provide consistent and healthy plants. To be disease free, the areas where seed potatoes are grown are selected with care. Potato growth has been divided into five phases. During the first phase, sprouts emerge from the seed potatoes and root growth begins. During the second, photosynthesis begins as the plant develops leaves and branches. In the third phase stolons develop from lower leaf axils on the stem and grow downwards into the ground and on these stolons new tubers develop as swellings of the stolon. This phase is often (but not always) associated with flowering. Tuber formation halts when soil temperatures reach 27°C (81°F); hence potatoes are considered a cool-season crop. At harvest time, gardeners usually dig up potatoes with a long-handled, three-prong "grape" (or graip), i.e., a spading fork, or a potato hook, which is similar to the graip but with tines at a 90° angle to the handle. In larger plots, the plow is the fastest implement for unearthing potatoes. Commercial harvesting is typically done with large potato harvesters, which scoop up the plant and surrounding earth. This is transported up an apron chain consisting of steel links several feet wide, which separates some of the dirt. The chain deposits into an area where further separation occurs. Different designs use different systems at this point. The most complex designs use vine choppers and shakers, along with a blower system to separate the potatoes from the plant. The result is then usually run past workers who continue to sort out plant material, stones, and rotten potatoes before the potatoes are continuously delivered to a wagon or truck. Further inspection and separation occurs when the potatoes are unloaded from the field vehicles and put into storage.Potatoes are usually cured after harvest to improve skin-set. Skin-set is the process by which the skin of the potato becomes resistant to skinning damage. Potato tubers may be susceptible to skinning at harvest and suffer skinning damage during harvest and handling operations. Curing allows the skin to fully set and any wounds to heal. Wound-healing prevents infection and water-loss from the tubers during storage. Curing is normally done at relatively warm temperatures 50 to 60°F (10 to 16°C) with high humidity and good gas-exchange if at all possible. Storage facilities need to be carefully designed to keep the potatoes alive and slow the natural process of decomposition, which involves the breakdown of starch. It is crucial that the storage area is dark, well ventilated and for long-term storage maintained at temperatures near 4°C (39°F). For short-term storage before cooking, temperatures of about 7 to 10°C (45 to 50°F) are preferred. On the other hand, temperatures below 4°C (39°F) convert potatoes' starch into sugar, which alters their taste and cooking qualities and leads to higher acrylamide levels in the cooked product, especially in deep-fried dishes—the discovery of acrylamides in starchy foods in 2002 has led to many international health concerns as they are believed to be possible carcinogens and their occurrence in cooked foods is currently under study as a possible influence in potential health problems. Under optimum conditions possible in commercial warehouses, potatoes can be stored for up to ten to twelve months. When stored in homes, the shelf life is usually only a few weeks. If potatoes develop green areas or start to sprout, these areas should be trimmed before using. Trimming or peeling green areas are inadequate to remove copresent toxins, and such potatoes are no longer suitable as animal food. Commercial storage of potatoes involves several phases: drying of surface moisture; a wound healing phase at 85% to 95% relative humidity and temperatures below 25 °C (77 °F); a staged cooling phase; a holding phase; and a reconditioning phase, during which the tubers are slowly warmed. Mechanical ventilation is used at various points during the process to prevent condensation and accumulation of carbon dioxide.

Uses of Potato

- Potatoes are used to brew alcoholic beverages such as vodka, potcheen, or akvavit.
- They are also used as food for domestic animals.
- Potato starch is used in the food industry as, for example, thickeners and binders of soups and sauces, in the textile industry, as adhesives, and for the manufacturing of papers and boards.
- Maine companies are exploring the possibilities of using waste potatoes to obtain polylactic acid for use in plastic products; other research projects seek ways to use the starch as a base for biodegradable packaging.
- Potato skins, along with honey, are a folk remedy for burns in India. Burn centers in India have experimented with the use of the thin outer skin layer to protect burns while healing.
- Potatoes (mainly Russets) are commonly used in plant research. The consistent parenchyma tissue, the clonal nature of the plant and the low

metabolic activity provide a very nice "model tissue" for experimentation. Wound-response studies are often done on potato tuber tissue, as are electron transport experiments. In this respect, potato tuber tissue is similar to *Drosophila melanogaster*, *Caenorhabditis elegans* and *Escherichia coli*: they are all "standard" research organisms.

- Potatoes have been delivered with personalized messages as a novelty. Potato delivery services include Potato Parcel and Mail A Spud.

Importance Of Potato For National Economy

Generally, potato is characterized as a high-input and high-output crop. The great responsiveness of yields to inputs such as good quality seed, fertilizers, additional labor etc. motivates farmers to use inputs more heavily on potatoes than on other crops. Because of high level of yields, short growing period, and remunerative market value, the potato crop generates larger returns per unit land and time. A joint survey conducted in Farrukhabad district of Utta~ Pradesh by the Central Potato Research Institute, Shimla and the Indian Agricultural Statistics Research Institute, New Delhi in 1984 indicated that, the cost of potato cultivation in this area was ₹ 11,804/ha. Seed alone accounted for 40 per cent of total cost, followed by 23 per cent on human labor, 18 per cent on manure, fertilizers and agro-chemicals, and remaining 19 percent on irrigation, bullocks, tractors etc. The gross and net returns from the potatoes produced on one hectare were ₹ 16,480, and ₹ 4,676, respectively. In other words, investment of one rupee on potato cultivation gives a gross return of ₹ 1.40 in a short period of 80-100 days. The importance of potato in agricultural economy can be judged from the fact that, in 1970-71 potato was cultivated in 0.3 per cent of total cropped area in the country that contributed 1.4 per cent of the total value of agricultural output. In contrast, paddy and wheat widely known to be responsible for green revolution occupied 22.7 and 11.0 per cent of the total cropped area and contributed only 26.2 and 10.4 per cent of total value of agricultural output, respectively. The picture has not changed over the last two and half decades and potato has continued to contribute significantly to the national economy. It was cultivated on 0.6 per cent of the total cropped area in 1995-96 and contributed 1.8 per cent of the total value of agricultural output. In the same year contributions to value output by wheat and paddy were 12.2 per cent from 13.5 per cent area and 21.4 per cent from 23.1 per cent area, respectively. The average ratio of per cent value output to the per cent cropped area for potato, wheat, and paddy during the period 1978-79 to 1995-96 were 3.3:1, 0.92:1, and 0.96:1, respectively. This indicates that potato contributes about 3.5 times more than both wheat and paddy from unit area to the national economy in agricultural sub-sector. For a developing country like India, where labor is surplus and capital limited, high yielding and labor-intensive crops have added advantage in increasing food production and employment generation.

Potato is both a labor and capital intensive crop. In the experiments conducted by the All India Coordinated Agronomic Research Project of the ICAR, it was observed that person-days requirement per hectare in different crop sequences was highest when potato was included in the crop rotation. It ranged from 313 person-days/ha in rice-potato-okra rotation in the central region to 488 person-days for maize-potato-greengram in the north-west region. Potato alone contributed 251 person-days/ha of employment as indicated by a comprehensive study in Farrukhabad district of Uttar Pradesh. Potato industry also generates several other economic activities in the postharvest handling and utilization through cold storage, transportation, marketing, and manufacture of value-added processed products like chips, French fries etc.

Effects of Drought on Potato Plant

A drought is a period of below-average precipitation in a given region, resulting in prolonged shortages in the water supply, whether atmospheric, surface water or ground water. A drought can last for months or years, or may be declared after as few as 15 days. It can have a substantial impact on the ecosystem and agriculture of the affected region and harm to the local economy. Annual dry seasons in the tropics significantly increase the chances of a drought developing and subsequent bush fires. Periods of heat can significantly worsen drought conditions by hastening evaporation of water vapour. Many plant species, such as those in the family Cactaceae (or cacti), have drought tolerance adaptations like reduced leaf area and waxy cuticles to enhance their ability to tolerate drought. Some others survive dry periods as buried seeds. Semi-permanent drought produces arid biomes such as deserts and grasslands. Prolonged droughts have caused mass migrations and humanitarian crises. Most arid ecosystems have inherently low productivity.Drought already poses one of the most important constraints to plant growth and terrestrial ecosystem productivity in many regions all over the world (Chaves *et al.*, 2003) and water availability is becoming even scarcer for agricultural communities. The influencing factors include inadequate rainfall, excessive levels of salts in the soil solution or the increasing diversion of limited fresh-water resources to competing urban and industrial uses (Neumann, 2008). Climatic model predict that global warming will further escalate drought as a result of increasing evapotranspiration (Salinger *et al.*, 2005; Cook *et al.*, 2007) though there are likely to be large regional differences (Metz *et al.*, 2007) with frequency and intensity increasing from 1 to 30% in extreme drought land area by 2100 (Fischlin *et al.*, 2007). These negative consequences of climate change in agriculture will drastically affect poor and marginalized groups who depend on agriculture for their livelihoods coupled with limited potentials to cope. Impact of climate change on potato production in Ireland using simulation models (in the DSSAT package) showed an expected relatively uniform increase in temperature of about 1.6°C over the country by the 2075 climate period (Holden *et al.*, 2003) and potato yield in 2055 and 2075 is expected to fall for non-irrigated tubers resulting in severe loss of yield over most of the country by 2055 (Holden *et al.*, 2003). In northern temperate regions there will be more heterogeneity in weather events with northern Europe influencing more rain in winter and significantly less in summer (Haverkort and Verhagen, 2008) affecting both agriculture production and adaptation. In the Mediterranean and Sahel regions during the heat-free periods of the year potato yields will go down as the suitable periods become shorter. Higher evaporative demand will result to water being use less efficiently and only irrigation may hold the keys for yield increments in potato in the temperate (Haverkort and Verhagen, 2008). Globally, for potato, drought will decrease potential potato yield by 18–32% in the projected period of 2040–2069 (Hijmans, 2003). The indication for the effect of drought on potato production and cultivation can be seen from available FAO data and recent case studies. In 2011 and 2012 drought and heat waves in the USA have resulted in damage to summer crops (including potatoes) and livestock causing losses of $40–88 in billions of dollars (NOAA, 2011, 2012). In 2010, drought affected Russia and led to production losses of around 30% on industrial potato farms and households in the Central and the Volga Valley—a federal district that traditionally produces over 60% of the Russian potato crop (GAIN, 2010; Barriopedro *et al.*, 2011). Crop models predict that potato yields may reduce by ~30% as a result of water deficit in Poland. Drought limits productivity of crop plants by affecting photosynthetic processes at the canopy, leaf or chloroplast level, either directly, or by feedback inhibition if transport of photosynthate to sink organs is limited (Jones and Corlett, 1992). The response pattern of plants to drought is regulated by intensity, duration and rate of progression of imposed drought (Pinheiro and Chaves, 2011). The effect of different levels of drought and the response triggered under these levels. Under mild to moderate conditions, stomatal characteristics are affected which result in biomass loss while under severe conditions non-stomatal factors can become dominant (Liu *et al.*, 2010) constraining photochemical efficiency and Rubisco activity and thus affecting the biochemical and physiological metabolisms (Xu *et al.*, 2010). Light signal transduction pathway of guard cells remains the primary mechanism regulating stomatal opening (Lee, 2010), while mechanism of stomatal behavior is influenced by ABA in the root-to-shoot signaling under stress (Jia and Zhang, 2008). Plants grown under drought conditions tend to have lower stomatal conductance, thus helping to conserve water and maintain an adequate leaf water status but at the same time reducing leaf internal CO_2 concentration and photosynthesis (Chaves *et al.*, 2002). Nevertheless, the precise relationship is also dependent on other factors, for example genotype, influence of drought history, and environmental conditions (Schulze and Hall, 1982; Tardieu and Simonneau, 1998) (Figure 8.2).

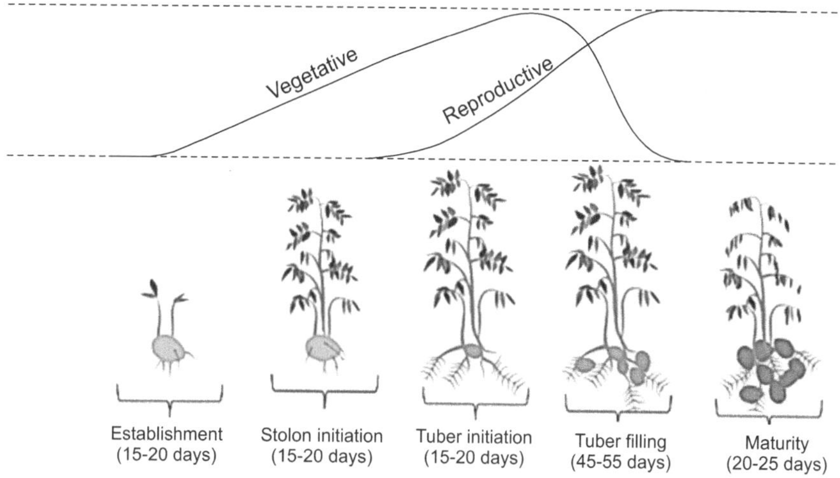

Impact of water deficit	Delayed emergence Restrict root establishment restrict plant development presence of fewer stalks/stem	Restrict plant development limited stolon initiation limited number of stolon Restrict root growth restricts uptake and response to nutrients	Limited foliage and plant development limited tuber initiation Limited number of tubers	Limited plant and tuber development restricts tuber size promotes distorted tuber shape faster senescence	Limited relative tuber limited tuber size

Fig. 8.2: Effects of water at different growth satges of potato

(**Source:** Review Literature)

It has been shown that long term exposure of leaf or canopy to low vapor pressure deficit generates a sort of "memory" in guard cells that results in loss of closing stimuli of stomatal responses (Nejad and Van Meeteren, 2007; Fanourakis *et al.*, 2011). Thus, when studying drought response, differentiation is needed between terminal or intermittent drought and its interaction with environment. In the case of terminal drought the availability of soil water decreases progressively leading to premature plant death while intermittent drought comprises finite periods of inadequate water occurring at one or more intervals during the growing season (Neumann, 2008). The timing of intermittent drought during growth may have much larger impact on biomass and yield than intensity of drought and may also depend on stress duration and phenological stage (Pinheiro and Chaves, 2011). Yield losses depend on plant growth phase affected by drought (vegetative and reproductive) (Serraj *et al.*, 2004), which indirectly reduces the photosynthetic rate, CO_2 fixation and finally resulting in less assimilate product (Mafakheri *et al.*, 2010). Different growth stages in potato and how water limited environment can influence plant growth and development and eventually yield even if the lack of water is transient. In potato, tuber yield is correlated with both harvest index (HI) and dry matter and therefore for breeding, it is critical to understand the genotypic variation dependence on assimilate distribution and the dry matter production (Jefferies and Mackerron, 1987, 1993; Mackerron and Jefferies, 1988; Gregory and Simmonds, 1992; Jefferies, 1993a; Tourneux *et al.*, 2003b). Little information is available on the effects of prolonged long term water shortage regimes but studies have widely examined short term lack of water consequences suggesting that soil moisture should not drop below 50% of crop available water in the soil for maximum yield (Mackerron and Jefferies, 1986). Drought in potato not only reduces yield, in that the crop may extract less of the available water from the soil in comparison with other crops (Weisz *et al.*, 1994), but it can also harm product quality, for example by increasing common scab incidence (Mane *et al.*, 2008). Physiological responses are variety dependant and vary with source of the seed or physiological age of the tubers (Steckel and Gray, 1979). The differences in source may influence patterns of foliage growth and yield as well as the number of root primordia and the eventual size of root system (Wurr, 1978). As might be expected, physiological responses to drought are often more closely associated with "predawn" water potential than with daytime water potentials (Jones, 2007). Physiological response strategies include drought sensitive stomata which result in low transpiration rates and relatively increased intrinsic WUE regardless of radiation level and thus promote growth in areas with limited water availability (Coleman, 2008). Transpiration is affected by leaf area, root to leaf ratio, leaf orientation, leaf shape, leaf surface characteristics (pubescence), leaf thickness, and distribution of stomata.Plants under water stress show a decrease in leaf conductance (g_1) which largely declines in parallel with leaf water potential (ψ_1) with efficient water conservative strategy dependant on the characteristics of canopy architecture such as canopy area, open/close canopy, leaf orientation, and cuticular transpiration rates. Potatoes exhibit isohydric characteristic with soil water potential (ψ_{soil}) and stomatal conductance (g_s) decreasing under water stress while maintaining ψ_1 similar to values obtained from non stressed conditions (Liu *et al.*, 2005) suggesting delay in onset of stress.Stress responsive expression is thought to be an important mechanism of adaptation as it plays an important role in tolerance. Several studies have cataloged a large number of genes showing differential expression during stress treatment both in cereals and model crops. Although this list can be differentiated into WUE, avoidance and escape and finally tolerance based on traits associated, this paragraph compiles them under one heading as these mechanisms are interactive and response of one pathway affects the other. Studies have shown that glycolysis gene transcription and amino-acid degradation are more strongly repressed in drought tolerant cultivars when compared to drought susceptible ones (Evers *et al.*, 2010). Drought stress led to strong repression of photosynthesis-related genes in drought tolerant cultivar (Reiter and Vanzin, 2001; Evers *et al.*, 2010). Under stress recovery, genes associated with PSII showed that genotype specific activation responses increased sucrose accumulation and cell wall biosynthesis (Mane *et al.*, 2008). There is evidence of high mitochondrial metabolic activity in a drought resistant cultivar (Vasquez-Robinet *et al.*, 2008) while a susceptible cultivar was characterized with higher levels of proline, trehalose, and GABA (ã-aminobutyric acid) (Vasquez-Robinet *et al.*, 2008). Several genes associated with mitochondrial function were more negatively affected in drought susceptible genotypes. Dihydrolipoamide dehydrogenase and ADP-sugar biphosphatase were activated in drought resistant clones but repressed in drought susceptible clones. Chloroplast-localized antioxidant and chaperone genes were more highly expressed in drought resistant cultivars whereas ABA-responsive transcriptional factors (TFs) were more highly expressed in drought susceptible ones (Vasquez-Robinet *et al.*, 2008). Evaluation under *in vitro*control and water-stressed conditions identified putative candidate genes for drought tolerance as transcription factors and signaling molecules, such as protein kinases and ERF1 (Ethylene Response factor 1) (Anithakumari *et al.*, 2011, 2012). Silencing of a CBP80 (nuclear cap-binding protein) gene in the cultivar *Desiree* increases water deficit tolerance through initiating Cap-Binding Complex (CBC) that recognizes and binds to the cap structure of RNA polymerase II transcripts in the nucleus (Papp *et al.*, 2004; Kierzkowski *et al.*, 2009; Pieczynski *et al.*, 2013). The drought tolerant plant silenced for the *CBP80*gene exhibited an ABA-hypersensitive stomatal closing response (Pieczynski *et al.*, 2013). Products of *miR159, MYB33,* and/or *MYB101* genes that act downstream of *CBP80* have been shown to be involved in the ABA- mediated regulation of potato responses to drought and similar studies have also identified and characterized microRNA families for drought stress response and their putative target genes including miR171 (stu-miRNA171a, b, and c), miR159, miR164, miR166, miR390, miR395, miR397, miR398, miR408, and miR482 (Hwang *et al.*, 2011a,b; Pieczynski *et al.*, 2013; Zhang *et al.*, 2013). Most of the genes identified in the above studies showing differential down regulation were involved in photosynthesis and carbohydrate metabolism, including chlorophyll a-b binding proteins, fructose-1, 6-bisphosphatase trehalose-6-phosphate synthase while sucrose synthase was up-regulated (Hwang *et al.*, 2011a,b; Kondrak *et al.*, 2012).

What are the Polyamines and Its Role in Potato

Polyamines (PAs) are low molecular weight polycations found in all living organisms (Cohen, 1998). They are known to be essential for growth and development in prokaryotes and eukaryotes (Tabor and Tabor, 1984; Tiburcio *et al.*, 1990). In plant cells, the diamine putrescine (Put), triamine spermidine (Spd) and tetramine spermine (Spm) constitute the major PAs. They occur in the free form or as conjugates bound to phenolic acids and other low molecular weight compounds or to macromolecules such as proteins and nucleic acids. As such, they stimulate DNA replication, transcription and translation. They have been implicated in a wide range of biological processes in plant growth and development, including senescence, environmental stress and infection by fungi and viruses. Their biological activity is attributed to their cationic nature. These findings have been discussed in several recent review articles (Tiburcio *et al.*, 1993; Galston *et al.*,1997; Bais and Ravishankar 2002). The use of PA biosynthesis inhibitors has shown a causal relationship between changes in endogenous PA levels and growth responses in plants. These observations led to further studies into undestanding the mode of PA action. Some of the important observations suggest that PAs can act by stabilizing membranes, scavenging free radicals, affecting nucleic acids and protein synthesis, RNAse, protease and other enzyme activities, and interacting with hormones, phytochrome, and ethylene biosynthesis (reviewed in Slocum *et al.*, 1984; Galston and Tiburcio, 1991). Because of these numerous biological interactions of PAs in plant systems, it has been difficult to determine their precise role in plant growth and development. In recent years, however, investigations into molecular genetics of plant PAs have led to isolation of a number of genes encoding PA biosynthetic enzymes and development of antibodies to some of the genes. Furthermore mutants and transgenic plants with altered PA metabolism have also been developed. Genomic and proteomic approaches are being used to further gain an understanding into the role of PAs in plant developmental processes. These findings will hopefully lead to a better understanding of their specific functions in plants. Several useful reviews on these aspects have been published (Galston *et al.*, 1997; Walden *et al.*, 1997; Malmberg *et al.*, 1998; Martin-Tanguy, 2001; Bais and Ravishankar, 2002).

Biosynthesis of Polyamine in Plant Parts

The PA biosynthetic pathway in plants has been thoroughly investigated and reviewed in detail (Evans and Malmberg, 1989; Tiburcio *et al.*, 1990; Slocum, 1991a; Martin-Tanguy, 2001). Briefly, PAs are synthesized from arginine and ornithine by arginine decarboxylase (ADC) and ornithine decarboxylase (ODC). The intermediate agmatine, synthesized from arginine, is converted to Put, which is further transformed to Spd and Spm by successive transfers of aminopropyl groups from decarboxylated S-adenosylmethionine (dSAM) catalysed by specific Spd and Spm synthases. The aminopropyl groups are derived from methionine, which is first converted to S-adenosylmethionine (SAM), and then decarboxylated in a reaction catalyzed by SAM decarboxylase (SAMDC). The resulting decarboxylated SAM is utilized as an aminopropyl donor. SAM is a common precursor for both PAs and ethylene, and SAMDC regulates both biosynthetic pathways as illustrated in figure 3. A number of investigators have used PA inhibitors to modulate the cellular PA titer in order to determine their role in various plant processes. Four commonly used inhibitors of PA synthesis are: 1. Difluoromethylornithine (DFMO), an irreversible inhibitor of ODC (reviewed in Bey *et al.*, 1987); 2. Difluoromethylarginine (DFMA), an irreversible inhibitor of ADC (Bitonti *et al.*, 1987); 3. Methylglyoxyl-bis guanylhydrazone (MGBG), a competitive inhibitor of S-adenosyl-methionine decarboxylase (SAMDC) (Williams-Ashman and Schenone, 1972); and 4. Cyclohexylamine (CHA), a competitive inhibitor of spermidine synthase (Hibasami *et al.*, 1980). Common oxidases are diamine oxidase and polyamine oxidase (PAO), as reviewed by Smith and Marshall (1988). Each PA has been found to be catabolized by a specific oxidase. Several investigations have dealt with localization of PAs and their biosynthetic enzymes in plants (reviewed by Slocum, 1991b). However, paucity of information regarding the exact cellular and subcellular localization of these entities remains one of the obstacles in understanding their biological role. Recent studies have shown that PAs are present in the cell wall fractions, vacuole, mitochondria and chloroplasts (Torrigiani *et al.*, 1986; Slocum, 1991b; Tiburcio *et al.*, 1997). The biosynthetic enzymes, ODC, SAMDC, and Spd synthase have been reported to be localized in the cytoplasm, whereas ADC is localized in the thylakoid membrane of chloroplast (Borrell *et al.*, 1996; Tiburcio *et al.*, 1997)

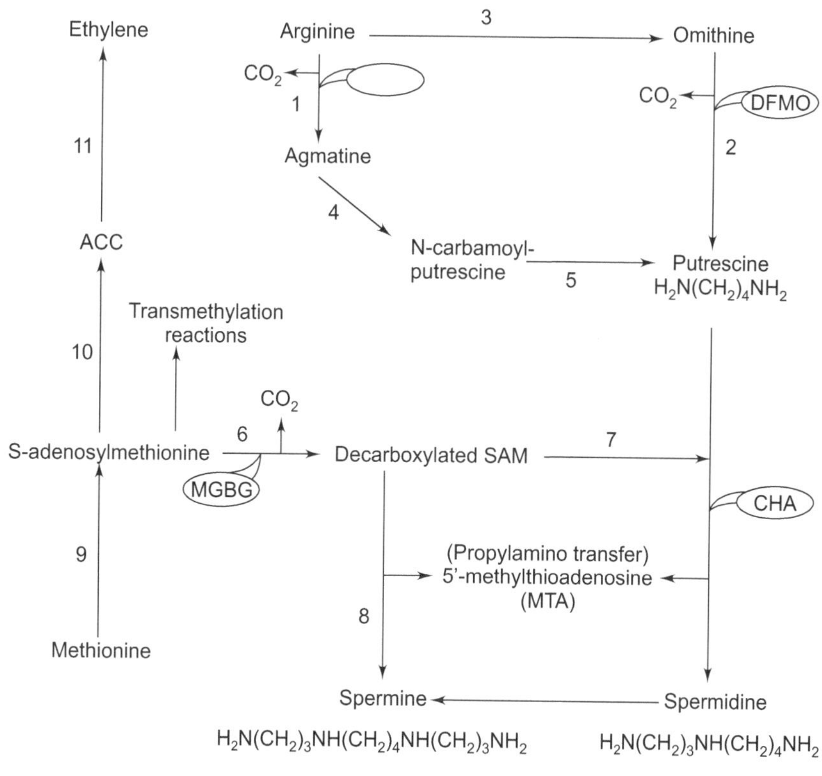

Fig. 8.3: Schematic diagram of polyamines biosynthesis

(**Source:** Based on Review and Literature)

and PAO in the cell wall (Kaur-Sawhney *et al.*, 1981). ODC activity has also been observed in the nucleus (Slocum, 1991b). However, these findings have to be interpreted with caution because various procedural problems can mask the results. Despite these advances in understanding the metabolic processes involving PAs and their localization in plant cells, the precise role of PAs in plant morphogenesis remains elusive (Figure 8.3).

Role of Polyamines in Plant Growth and Development

The availability of specific inhibitors of PA biosynthesis has helped in investigating the mechanisms involved in PA interactions to some extent, providing a partial understanding of their physiological role in plant growth and development. Clearly, PAs are involved in many plant developmental processes, including cell division, embryogenesis, reproductive organ development, root growth, tuberization, floral initiation and development, fruit development and ripening as well as leaf senescence and abiotic stresses (reviewed by Evans and Malmberg, 1989; Galston *et al.*, 1997; Bais and Ravishankar, 2002; Tiburcio *et al.*, 2002). Changes in free and conjugated PAs and their biosynthetic enzymes, namely ADC, ODC, and SAMDC have been found to occur during these developmental processes. Earlier experiments had shown that increases in PAs and their biosynthetic enzymes are associated with rapid cell division in many plant systems e.g., carrot embryogenesis (Montague and Koppenbrink, 1978; Feirer *et al.*, 1984), tomato ovaries (Heimer and Mizrahi, 1982), tobacco ovaries (Slocum and Galston, 1985), and fruit development (reviewed in Kakkar and Rai, 1993). Similar results have been reported for many other plant species (reviewed in Bais and Ravishankar, 2002). In contrast, several other studies have suggested that correlations between PAs and their biosynthetic enzymes and plant growth processes, especially somatic embryogenesis, are not universal and may be species specific (reviewed in Evans and Malmberg, 1989; Galston *et al.*, 1997; Bais and Ravishankar, 2002).

What is Mycorrhiza?

The term mycorrhiza is rooted from two Greek words myco meaning fungi and Rrhiza meaning root and its' meaning in reality means symbiosis between a fungus and root. Mycorrhiza is described as a mutual sharing of life; whereby the fungal is the major partner of the plant has the duty to supply food, growth hormones and protection of plants' root from pathogens and a fine plant will offer high energetic material to the fungus (Alizadeh, 2011). Arbuscular mycorrhizal fungi (AMF) play an important role in vegetation restoration because of symbiosis with plant root; they can facilitate mineral absorption by the host plant, stabilize and improve soil structure, affect the population structure and preserve species diversity (Bothe *et al.*, 2010). They are key components of the soil biota and account for about 25% of agricultural soil microbial biomass. The major types of mycorrhizae are ecto and endo mycorrhizae. The ecto mycorrhizae are characterized by an extra cellular fungal growth in the root cortex. The endo mycorrhizae are characterized by inter and intra cellular fungal growth in the root cortex. The largest group of endo mycorrhizae is vesicular arbuscular mycorrhizae. Now, it is called arbuscular mycorrhiza (AM). AM fungi exist in soil as chlamydospores or as vegetative propagules in roots that germinate in rhizosphere. Their hyphae penetrate the root cortex, ramifying intracellularly from the point of penetration. The fungus forms haustoria like structure called arbuscule within cortex cells, where the metabolites exchange between the fungus and the host plant takes place. The other structures are vesicles that are lipid storage and reproductive structures present in the intra cellular spaces. AM fungi transport water and mineral nutrients from the soil to the plant while the fungus is benefiting from the C compounds provided by the host.Among the mycorrhizal associations, vesicular arbuscular mycorrhizae (VAM) are most widespread in their distribution both geographically and among plant species. The Glomeromycota consists of fungi that are generally considered to be obligately symbiotic. Although probably correct, this is an assumption based on analogy with the species for which the biology is known. Such species have been shown either (in one instance) to have a Nostoc (Cyanobacteria) species as a symbiont (Schüßler, 2002), or (in all other known instances) to form an intimate symbiosis, generally known as an arbuscular mycorrhiza (AM), with embryophytes (land plants) (Figure 8.4).

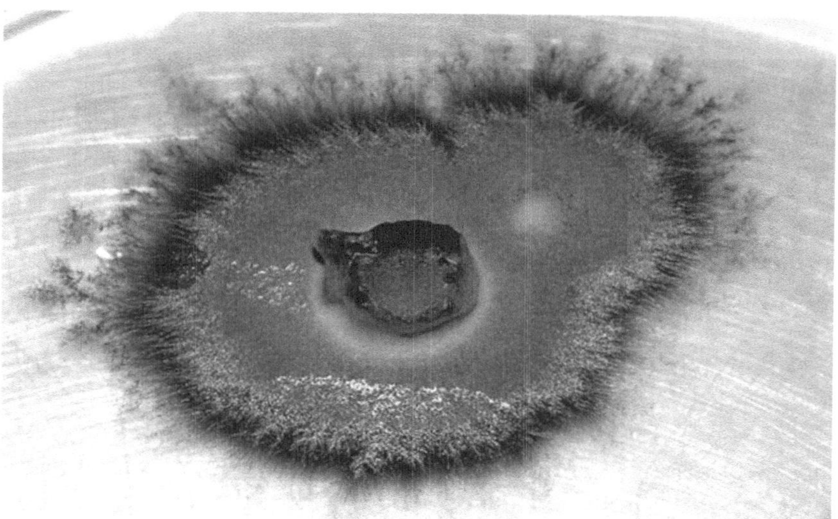

Fig. 8.4: Diagram of Ericoid Mycorrhiza

(**Source:** Review Literature)

Vasicular land plants, hornworts (Schüßler, 2000) and liverworts (Fonseca and Berbera, 2008) may also form AM. Many glomeromycotan species are known to form AM, but many others have been described from field collected specimens for which the nutritional state of the fungus is unknown (Table 8.1).

Table 8.1: Diversity of Mycorrhiza

Mycorrhizal Type	Fungal Taxa	Plant Taxa	Intracellular Colonization	Fungal Sheath	Vesicle
Arbuscular	Glomeromycota	Bryophyta Pteridophyta Gymnosperms Angiosperms	Present	Absent	Present or Absent
Ecto	Basidiomycota Ascomycota Zygomycota	Gymnosperms Angiosperms	Absent	Present	Absent
Ectendo	Basidiomycota Ascomycota	Gymnosperms Angiosperms	Present	Present or Absent	Absent
Arbutoid	Basidiomycota	Ericales	Present	Present or Absent	Absent
Monotropoid	Basidiomycota	Monotropoideae	Present	Present	Absent
Ericoid	Ascomycota	Ericales Gymnosperms	Present	Absent	Absent
Orchidaceous	Basidiomycota	Orchids	Present	Absent	Absent

(**Source:** Review Literature)

Physiology of Plants Under Drought

The effect of drought in plants is complex and plant respond with many protective adaptations. During drought the plant suffers from dehydration of its cell and tissues as well as from a considerable increase in the temperature of its body i.e. from over heating. Thus the lack of water caused by drought is usually accompanied by high body temperatures. Hence drought resistance of the plant includes the ability to withstand dehydration and secondly the ability to withstand overheating (heat resistance). High heat resistance is not always linked with high drought–resistance. It is necessary to note that drought not only effects plant in different ways but that various ecological groups or even individual species have different types of responses. In other wordsthere is no universal mechanism of adaptation of plant to drought. There are however certain types of adaptations against drought within each ecological–physiological group. According to many authors drought–resistance is a property which is formed and developed in the process of ontogenesis and is based on the whole preceding phylogeny of the plant. Hence it is clear that this property is not unchangeable but is markedly affected by the individual development of the plant. Considering drought resistance as a peculiar process means a new approach to the problem enabling plant breeders not only to establish the fact of higher or lower drought resistance but to look for and to find ways for drought hardening. The above statement bring us to following definition of drought resistance. Drought resistant plants are those which in the process of ontogenesis are able to adapt to the effect of drought and which can normally grow, develop and reproduce under drought condition because of a number of properties acquired in the process of evolution.

Hormonal Regulation of Drought In Plants

Major phytohormones, such as abscisic acid (ABA), cytokinin (CK), gibberellic acid (GA), auxin and ethylene, regulate diverse processes which enable plant adaptation to drought stress. Upon exposure of plants to drought stress, ABA is the major hormone synthesized in roots and translocated to leaves to initiate adaptation of plants to drought stress through stomatal closure and reduced plant growth. However, modulating the ABA-induced drought adaptation of plants for better yield remains a greater challenge because of the potential inadvertent reduction in carbon gain upon stomatal closure and ABA-induced senescence, especially if the drought occurs at the reproductive stage. There are ABA signaling genes, such as *OsNAP*, *OsNAC5*, and *DSM2*, which promote improved yield under reproductive drought. These ABA-induced non-stomatal adaptations of plants under drought stress can be exploited to improve grain yield under reproductive drought.

Transpiration and Stomatal Conductance

The immediate response of plants on being exposed to drought stress is stomatal closure. However, stomatal closure not only diminishes water loss through transpiration but also reduces CO_2 and nutrient uptake, and hence alters metabolic pathways such as photosynthesis. Plants growing in dry areas have developed xeromorphic traits to reduce transpiration under drought stress. Reduction in transpiration under drought stress conditions can also be achieved through leaf shedding (i.e. deciduous species in drought) as well as decrease in leaf number, leaf size, and branching. Another adaptation to counter drought stress is sclerophylly, where plants form hard leaves that will not suffer permanent damage due to wilting and can be restored to full functionality when normal conditions resume. Recent research has shown that decreased stomatal conductance in response to drought stress is related not only to reduced expression of aquaporin genes but also to anatomical traits leading to reduction of chloroplast surface area exposed to intercellular space per unit leaf area . Several other factors, including leaf developmental stage and light availability, are also known to interact with drought in modulating mesophyll and chloroplast differentiation, ultimately affecting conductance and photosynthetic capacity. Reduction in stomatal size and number on exposure to drought is another adaptation for survival under drought conditions. Previous studies have shown that while there is an increase in stomatal density under mild drought stress, there is a decrease during severe drought. Thus, all these adaptations in plants reduce the negative impacts of drought stress on photosynthesis and thereby have a positive effect on water use efficiency (WUE), which in turn will result in high yield potential and high yield.

Morphology of Roots of Potato

In many agriculturally important crops, drought stress is perceived first by the root system, which continues to grow underneath the soil even though shoot growth is inhibited under these conditions. Although the growth of the primary root is not affected by drought stress, the growth of lateral roots is significantly reduced, mainly by suppression of the activation of the lateral root meristems. The Arabidopsis R2R3-type MYB TF *MYB96* has been shown to regulate activation of lateral root meristem through an ABA signaling cascade, with an activation-tagged mutant showing enhanced DR with reduced lateral root formation. The plant microRNA miR393 has also been shown to play a role in root-mediated adaptation to drought stress response through attenuation of auxin signaling. In addition to the lateral roots, the presence of small roots is also considered as an adaptive strategy to increase water uptake by providing more absorptive surface. Presence of specialized tissues like rhizodermis, with a thickened outer cell wall or suberized exodermis, or reduction in the number of cortical layers are considered an adaptive advantage for drought stress survival. Hydrotropism is another adaptive measure taken by plants to counter stress, where studies have shown that degradation of amyloplasts in the columella cells of plant roots on exposure to drought stress increases hydrotropism. Hormonal cross-talk mediated by auxin, CK, GA, and ABA has been implicated as a potential chemical signal in response to water stress to modulate root system architecture.

Osmotic Adjustment During the Drought

Osmotic adjustment (OA) is defined as a process of solute accumulation in dividing cells when the water potential is reduced, and thereby helps in maintaining the turgor. Cell enlargement and growth in plants is highly dependent on water availability and helps in maintaining the turgor. Turgor measurement in growing regions of plants, especially the leaves and stems, shows little or no reduction, though cell enlargement is inhibited during drought stress and is believed to be due to OA. Under conditions of drought stress, OA has been implicated in maintaining stomatal conductance, photosynthesis, leaf water volume, and growth. At times of drought stress, in addition to the reduction in water content, there are also other associated changes, such as increases in salt concentration and mechanical impedance. Inorganic cations, organic acids, carbohydrates, and free amino acids are the known predominant solutes that accumulate in response to water stress. Previous studies have shown that drought-resistant wheat varieties, with yield stability under drought stress, have a greater capacity for osmoregulation than less resistant varieties . The accumulation of compatible solutes such as proline and glycine betaine help in protecting the plants from detrimental effects of drought stress not only by OA but also by detoxification of ROS, protection of membrane integrity, and stabilization of enzymes or proteins . Enzymes such as betaine aldehyde dehydrogenase (BADH), pyrroline-5-carboxylate reductase (P5CR), and ornithine γ-aminotransferase (OAT) have been shown to play major roles in OA.

Role on Mycorrhiza in Mitigation of Drought in Plant

Plants are frequently subjected to different abiotic environmental stresses that determine geographic distribution and adversely affect growth, development, and agronomic yield. Drought is one of the major constraints on plant productivity worldwide and is expected to increase with climatic changes (IPCC 2007 and EEA 2011). The symbiotic relationship between arbuscular mycorrhizal (AM) fungi and the roots of higher plants is widespread in nature, and several ecophysiological studies have demonstrated that AM symbiosis is a key component in helping plants to cope with water stress and in increasing drought resistance, as demonstrated in a number of host plant and fungal species. The alleviating effect of AM symbiosis in response to drought generally relies on the positive effects of AM fungi on the uptake and transport of water and on an improved uptake of nutrients, especially of available soil phosphorus (P) and other immobile mineral nutrients, resulting in the hydration of plant tissues, a sustainable physiology and a clear promotion of growth AM (Figure 8.5).

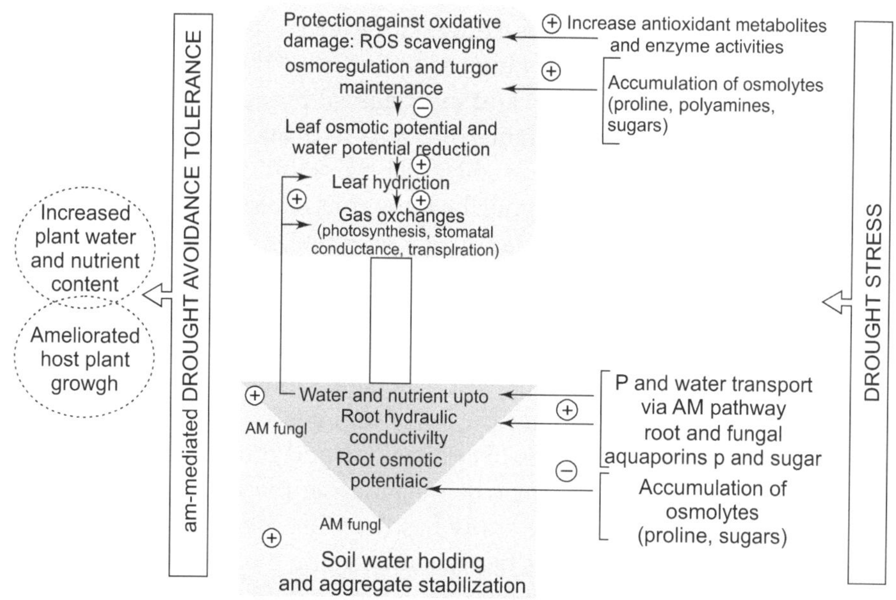

Fig. 8.5: Mycorrhiza and its importance in growth and developemmnt of plant

(**Source:** Based on review of literature)

Arbuscularmycorrhizal (AM) symbiosis can help plants to cope with the detrimental effects of soil water deficit acting, directly or indirectly, on plant functionality both above- and belowground. At the levels of both leaves and roots, the osmotic stress usually caused by drought is counteracted by mycorrhizal plants through biochemical changes that mostly include increased biosynthesis of metabolites (mainly proline and sugars) that act as osmolytes. These compounds contribute to the lowering of the osmotic potential, and in turn, of the leaf water potential. These lower potentials allow the plants to maintain high organ hydration and turgor that sustain overall cell physiological activity, mainly related to the photosynthetic machinery. AM plants withstand drought-induced oxidative stress by the increased production of antioxidant compounds that scavenge ROS and enhance the activities of antioxidant enzymes. AM root colonization can enhance root growth, architecture, and hydraulic properties and can thus induce the formation of a highly functional root system for nutrient/water uptake. At the same time, AM fungal hyphae in the soil provide an efficient pathway for nutrient/water uptake and transport, allowing a more efficient exploitation of the water and nutrient reservoirs in the soil where only fungal hyphae can grow, thereby bypassing the zones of water and nutrient depletion around the roots. Molecular mechanisms activated by AM symbiosis to counteract drought include gene activation of functional proteins, such as the membrane transporter aquaporins and, potentially, ion and sugar transporters, in both roots and fungi. Improved nutrient/water uptake and transport in roots translates into enhanced hydration of the aboveground organs that in turn affects physiological and biochemical processes. In addition, AM symbiosis can increase the resistance of plants to drought through secondary actions such as the improvement of soil structural stability that in turn increases the retention of soil water.In addition, the numerous confounding influences and system feedbacks inherent to the nature of AM symbiosis must be differentiated when describing the effects of AM on water balance. The AM-mediated response of many physiological and biochemical traits to changes in water availability may be confounded by concurrent changes in plant growth and nutrient availability (Smith and Read 2008) and can cause some drawbacks that limit our ability to clearly understand how AM fungi enable drought resistance in plants. The comparison of plants of similar size and nutritional status is thus recognized as a fair requirement when evaluating the function of AM fungi during drought stress. Extensive study has demonstrated AM-mediated plant resistance to drought conditions, but the underlying mechanisms have not yet been clearly elucidated. Our incomplete understanding of how AM symbiosis affects the ability of plants to withstand conditions of limited water represents an important challenge to meeting the goal of improved plant productivity under the projected critical global scenarios.

Role of Polyamines in the Mitigation of Drought in Plant

Elevation of endogenous PA levels is one of the metabolic hallmarks of plants exposed to abiotic stresses (Kusano *et al.*, 2008), implying that they are important for protecting plants against harsh environmental conditions. Nevertheless, in spite of many observations of changes in PA levels under stresses, the precise physiological and molecular mechanisms by which they confer protection remain elusive (Marco *et al.*, 2011). The biological function of the polycationic PAs were initially associated with their capacity to bind anionic macromolecules, such as nucleic acids and proteins, a characteristic that allows PAs to play a role in the regulation of transcription and translation (Bachrach, 2010; Gill and Tuteja, 2010; Igarashi and Kashiwagi, 2010; Tiburcio *et al.*, 2014). They have also been suggested to function in maintaining membrane stability under adverse conditions (Liu *et al.*, 2007; Tiburcio *et al.*, 2014); however, besides other than these mechanisms, there is increasing evidence that their role in stress tolerance is associated with modulating antioxidant systems.Reactive oxygen species are produced under normal growth conditions, but their homeostasis is a highly coordinated balance between generation and detoxification. Under abiotic stresses, ROS production is elevated, causing excessive ROS accumulation and oxidative stress, which is toxic to living cells due to lipid peroxidation and membrane damage, and can finally result in cell death (Biswas and Mano, 2015). PAs are thought to play a role in modulating ROS homeostasis in two ways. Firstly, they may inhibit the auto-oxidation of metals, which in turn impairs the supply of electrons for the generation of ROS (Shi *et al.*, 2010). They may also directly act as antioxidants and scavenge ROS, although there is no evidence for this mechanism at present. Secondly, PAs may affect antioxidant systems, and a number of studies have demonstrated that priming of plants with polyamines led to increases in endogenous PA contents and concomitant enhanced tolerance to abiotic stresses, such as drought, heat, and cold. The elevation of stress tolerance is concurrent with the activation of antioxidant enzymes. For example, exogenous application of Spm to *P. trifoliata* led to an elevation of POD, SOD and CAT activities, accompanied by a remarkable decrease in ROS levels under dehydration (Shi *et al.*, 2010). Exogenous supply of Spd to rice seedlings mitigated heat-induced damages, and increased activities of antioxidant enzymes and levels of antioxidant, accompanied by reduced accumulation of H_2O_2 (Mostofa *et al.*, 2014). Similar findings have been observed using other plants, such as tobacco, soybean, cucumber, and pistachio (Xu *et al.*, 2011; Radhakrishnan and Lee, 2013; Shu *et al.*, 2013; Kamiab *et al.*, 2014). On the other hand, genetic manipulation of PA biosynthetic genes has been demonstrated to promote stress tolerance via modulation of antioxidant machineries. Overexpression of *MdSPDS1* in European pear (*Pyrus communis*) resulted in an enhanced tolerance to heavy metals, which was largely ascribed to the activation of antioxidant enzymes (Wen *et al.*, 2009). Ectopic expression

physical environment that has made Earth habitable for humans. As humans, we are part of a delicate and integrated natural life system on which we depend for our existence. Biodiversity is important to human being for their sustenance, health, well-being and recreation. For example, humanity derives all of its food, medical and industrial products from the components of biological diversity. As recognized in the MDGs, human health is dependent on biodiversity and on the natural functioning of healthy ecosystems. The earth provides so many "ecosystem services" or elements of the natural world that sustain our lives: filtering toxic substances from the air, water, and soil; protecting against flooding, storm surges, and erosion; helping maintain the water cycle and stabilize local climates; and much, much more. These "services" that our earth provides for us are not only critical for our fundamental biological needs, but also for our social and economic well-being. The benefits of biodiversity conservation can be grouped into three broad categories: ecosystem services (conservation of water resources, soil conservation, nutrient storage and cycling, maintenance of ecosystems, pollution breakdown and absorption, contribution to climate stability, and recovery from unpredictable events), biological resources (food, medicines, forest products, breeding stocks, population reservoirs, and future resources) and social benefits (research and education, recreation, cultural, and religious/philosophical values).

Ecosystems provide the basic necessities of life, offering protection from natural disasters and diseases, and are the foundation for human culture. Biodiversity is essential to human development because of the goods and services it provides. An estimated 40 percent of the global economy is based on biological products and processes. Biodiversity loss is rapid and ongoing. on a global scale, biodiversity is being lost at a rate many times higher than that of natural extinction. Over the last 50 years, humans have changed ecosystems faster and more extensively than in any comparable period of time in human history. Species are going extinct at rates of 1,000 times the background rates typical of Earth's past. This is caused by a number of factors, including uncon-trolled land conversion, climate change, pollution, over-exploitation, unsustainable harvesting of natural resources, habitat destruction, the introduction of invasive species and nutrient loading which show no signs of abating. So great is the con-cern over the rate of decline, and its implications for human welfare, that biodiversity was identified as one of the five priority areas for the 2002 World Summit on Sustainable Development (WSSD, 2002).

The Convention on Biological Diversity (CBD) defines biodiversity as "the variability among living organisms from all sources including, inter alia, terrestrial, marine and other aquatic ecosystems and the ecological complexes of which they are part; this includes diversity within species, between species and of ecosystems" (CBD 1992). The biodiversity hotspots are Earth's richest and most endangered terrestrial systems. They once covered more than

12 percent of Earth's land surface but have cumulatively lost nearly 90 percent of their original natural vegetation. What remains in them now accounts for only 1.4 percent of our planet's terrestrial environment, but they harbor more than 44 percent of all plants and 35 percent of mammals, birds, reptiles, and amphibians as endemics found absolutely nowhere else. Biodiversity initiatives are designed to implement the '4 R's' of biodiversity: 1. Retain what is significant; 2. Restore habitats that have been degraded; 3. Replace habitats that have been lost; and help; 4. Recover species that are at risk (Jones *et al.*, 2010).

Conservation of Biodiversity

National Parks are created to protect the ecological integrity of one or more ecosystem for present and future generations; exclude exploitation or occupation detrimental to the purposes of designation of the area; and provide a foundation for spiritual, scientific, educational, recreational, and visitor opportunities, all of which must be environmentally and culturally compatible (Chape *et al.*, 2003). National Parks comprise the highest percentage (23%) of the total area covered by protected areas worldwide. For instance, according to estimates by Colchester, Africa has more than 1,812 National Parks covering a total 3,112,027 km^2 of the continent. In Sub-Saharan Africa alone, over 1 million km2 of land out of 23 million km^2 (constituting approximately 4%) has been set aside as National Parks (Colchester, 2003). Conservation of biodiversity in National Parks is done through two main approaches: the first approach is the preservation approach, which aims at setting aside National Parks to exclude human activities except for tourism. Through this approach, direct use of natural resources in the park for commercial or subsistence purposes is prohibited. This type of approach is often referred to as the "protectionism approach" or "the fines and fences" approach (Adams, 2004). For consistency, the term "preservation approach" is used in this paper. The preservation approach aims at excluding human activities considered inimical to the objectives of conserving biodiversity in National Parks. The preservation approaches were the most dominant approach until the 1980s, but in some National Parks, it has now been substituted by the second approach called the community-based conservation approach that allows people (especially those that neighbor National Parks) to benefit socially or economically from parks (Stolton, Mansourisn and Dudley, 2010). The community-based conservation approach was proposed to address the problems associated with excluding human activities from the park (Schroeder, 1999). The community-based conservation approach involves initiatives aimed at conserving biodiversity in the park but also letting local people benefit from the park (Galvin *et al.*, 2006).

Biodiversity and Tourism

The tourism industry represents one of the main sectors in the global economy (Anderson, 2010). It constitutes about one-third of all international trade in services, and it is a major source of foreign exchange earnings and job creation. According to the World Travel and Tourism Council (WTTC, 2016), tourism employed over 107 million people, and transport nearly 700 million international travelers per year. The WTO forecasts that the number of international arrivals will reach 1.56 billion by 2020. In 2015, tourism generated 9.8 percent of global GDP and also represents one of the top five exports for 83 percent of all countries and is the main source of foreign currency for 38 percent of countries. Although domestic tourism currently accounts for approximately 80% of all tourist receipts (Neto, 2003), there is increasing interest in international tourism. It has now become the world's largest source of foreign exchange receipts and is therefore an essential part of global trade WTO, (World Tourism Organization, 2007).

Over the last decade, nature and adventure travel has emerged as one of the fastest-growing segments of the industry. Much of this growth is taking place in biodiversity hotspots, areas harboring many species unique to that region (developing countries), where tourism represents both opportunities for and threats to biodiversity conservation. Today, tourism to natural destinations comprises around 50% of all international tourism and is increasing at a rate of around 10-30% per year, much more rapidly than the industry as a whole (Ceballos-Lascurain, 2001). However, its rapid expansion has also had detrimental environmental (and socio-cultural) impact in many regions.

Developing Countries (DCs) are generally known for their abundant species richness. However, they are often faced with problems like rapid population growth, workforce-pressure, lack of capital and foreign debts, which lead to over-exploitation of wild living resources, expansion of agriculture, forestry and aquaculture, and—with mounting pressure on the remaining habitats—to loss of biodiversity (Burgess, 1993; Vorlaufer, 1996). Industrialized countries (ICs), in contrast, are characterized by high and increasing demand for nature-based vacations, with protected areas representing first-rate attractions. Tourism could therefore be a means of redistributing economic resources, mitigating the socio-economic situation both at local and national scale and contributing to biodiversity conservation through habitat protection (Al-Sayed and Al-langawi, 2003; Blangy and Mehta, 2006; Boo, 1990; Budowski, 1976; Western and Henry, 1979; WWF, 1995). There is a broad consensus that such tourism should be fully compatible with conservation goals, while at the same time posing the minimum threat to the continuation of local culture and society. Moreover, it should contribute by means of income and education to the conservation of ecosystems. Meeting these requirements would qualify the process as ecotourism (Goodwin, 1996; Brown *et al.*, 1997).

However, it is only recently that the tourism industry has begun to acknowledge its own environmental impacts, including those on biodiversity; and hence to appreciate importance of environmental planning and management (Buckley, 1999). By linking tourism with biodiversity conservation and the well-being of local communities and understanding how and where they overlap, we can develop strategies that both conserve Earth's most endangered ecosystems and make a significant contribution to alleviating poverty at the same time. One strategy that has been embraced as an ideal mechanism for attaining both economic and ecological success is ecotourism. To succeed on both of these levels, an appreciable amount of revenue must return to local communities to foster stewardship and to change local practices so that biologically valuable habitats, populations, and ecological processes are conserved.

Andersson 2010, stated that given the complexity of its impacts, to learn how tourism can support, not degrade, biodiversity, it is essential to get a handle on the state of biodiversity itself and where it is heading. The challenge is therefore to ensure that tourism is developed in harmony with environmental considerations. Sustainable tourism can generate employment and income, thus providing a strong incentive for conservation. It can also raise public awareness of the many goods and services provided by biological diversity, and of the needs to respect traditional knowledge and practices. Sustainable tourism has the potential to reconcile economic and environmental concerns and give a practical meaning to sustainable development.

Ecotourism as a Tool for Conservation

"Ecotourism and biodiversity are mutually dependent. Biodiversity is a key tourism asset and fundamental to its sustained growth. Intact and healthy ecosystems form the cornerstone of thousands of tourist enterprises and products worldwide, attracting hundreds of millions of tourists each year. As a leading economic activity, ecotourism tourism has an important role and responsibility in managing and conserving biological natural resources. As a key source of income and employment, tourism often provides strong incentives to protect biodiversity. Sustainable tourism can furthermore generate significant revenues for conservation and community development and help to raise awareness of biodiversity issues. According to the International Ecotourism Society (TIES) (1990) ecotourism is defined as "responsible travel that conserve natural environment which benefits the socioeconomic condition of the local inhabitants and at the same time promote tourism and protect the environment". Ecotourism has often been used for biodiversity management with economic incentives to promote conservation and Sustainable development, particularly in developing countries. (Chetttri, 2000).

The role of ecotourism is an effective method of conservation that promotes biodiversity preservation through habitat protection while contributing to the socio-economic development of a highly diverse landscape (Bookbinder, *et al.*, 1998; Burger, 2000; Gössling, 1999; Ross and Wall, 1999; van der Duim and Caalders, 2002). Through ecotourism practices, the goal to maintain and protect biodiversity is possible. Ecotourism offers the opportunity to enhance protection and conservation practices in an area by contributing to the economic base of regions, while tourists influence the protection of land and biodiversity on a landscape scale (Burger, 2000). Ecotourism also facilitates outside awareness to an area's biodiversity while promoting education and conservation (Ross & Wall, 1999). Ecotourism has the potential to contribute to the conservation of biodiversity and education of all humans living within an ecosystem. Al-Sayed and Al-langawi (2003) affirm successful tourism objectives combined with ecologically derived management techniques, such as ecosystems identification, wildlife resources identification, geological aspects of land use, and environmental feasibility of conservation and rehabilitation, prevent the continual deterioration of areas where biodiversity is most prominent.

Ecotourism goes with nature tourism, which contributes to promoting efforts to conserve and maintain biodiversity, and conserve the living environment for communities in a sustainable way. Ecotourism helps human beings come closer to nature, know more about the essence of nature, and understand the rich diversity of habitats, as well as the interrelationships between habitats and living environments. Ecotourism has become a part of ecological, environmental science, being implemented in different ecological systems, and different representative territories. So, ecotourism always goes with maintaining and protecting the living resources of the Earth. Environmental conservation and balancing natural and human eco-systems is also necessary (Huynh, 1998).

Karnataka

Karnataka, one of the Southern States of India having a recorded 3.83 Million ha of forest area which is around 20 percent of its geographical area. The State is a part of the highly biodiversity rich regions of India. The Western Ghats of Karnataka is one of the mega biodiversity of the world.

The Western Ghats of Karnataka as shown in Figure 9.1, is one of the 25 global priority hotspots for conservation and one of the two on the Indian subcontinent. Karnataka forest is endowed with rich wildlife, harbors 25 percent of the elephant population of India, 10% of the Tiger population. The state has 5 National parks and 21 sanctuaries comprising about 17.3% of total forest area as protected area for wildlife and biodiversity. The state ranks 4th among all the state and union territories in respect of area under tree cover.

Geographically the State can be divided into three major zones. With the Western Ghats (Sahyadri) forming a major water divide, there are short and swift flowing rivers in the west draining into the Arabian sea. Notable among them are Sharavati, Kali, Netravati, Bedthi/Gangavalli, Aghanashini, Varahi and Chakra. To the east of the major divide, flow the river Krishna and Cauvery. A major part of the upstream of river Krishna and its tributaries Tungabhadra, Ghataprabha, Malaprabha, Bhima and Vedavati flow through northern Karnataka, pass through Andhra Pradesh before joining the Bay of Bengal. The

Cauvery river in the south flows down the eastern slopes of the ghats, passes through Tamil Nadu before joining the Bay of Bengal. The main tributaries are Hemavathi, Kabini, Arkavati, Shimsha, Palar, Uttara and Dakshina Pinakini, Manjira and Karanja are the only tributaries of river Godavary found within the State boundary.

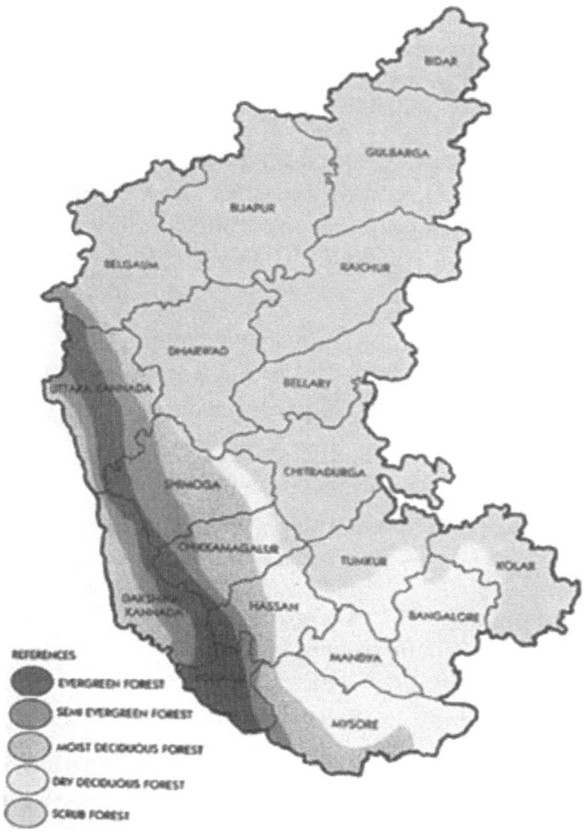

Fig. 9.1: The Western Ghats in Karnataka

Richness and Uniqueness of Western Ghats Located in Karnataka

- The Western Ghats is comprised of the mountain range that runs along the west coast of India from the VindhyaSatpura ranges in the north to the southern tip. The ecosystems of the Western Ghats include the tropical wet evergreen forests, the montane evergreen forests, moist deciduous force etc. The Shola grassland ecosystems found in the higher reaches of Western Ghats are unique to this region and harbor a number of endemic species.
- World Conservation Monitoring Centre (WCMC) has identified Western Ghats region as one of the important areas of biodiversity.

- The varied topographic, climatic and geological factors have made significant contribution to biodiversity. Almost onethird of all the flowering plant species in India are found in this region.
- The Nilgiri Biosphere Reserve spread over three states in Western Ghats was the first BR to be set up in the country.
- In the past, the forests of the Western Ghats had been selectively logged. Large tracts of forests were also converted to agricultural land for monoculture plantations of tea, coffee, rubber, oil palm teak, eucalyptus, building reservoirs, roads and railways.
- Over 20% of the original forest cover remains more or less in pristine condition and the remaining is subject to varying degrees of human pressure including large scale collection of fuel wood and NTFPs (non-timber forest products), Mass tourism, Grazing and forest fires are other concerns.
- The poverty is rife and economic development is poor in regions adjacent to forests including the PAs. The competing needs of the people residing in the forest fringes lead to frequent human wildlife conflicts.
- Of the total known fauna, 102 species fall under different categories of threat and of these, mammals (30 species, 21.9%) and amphibians (52 species; 33.3%) are the prominent groups (Prajpati, 2010).

Wildlife

The State of Karnataka located in South India has a rich diversity of flora and fauna as seen in Table 9.1. The forests support 25% of the elephant population and 10% of the tiger population of India. Many regions are yet unexplored and new species of flora and fauna are found periodically.

The Bandipur and Nagarhole National Parks were included in the reserve. In Karnataka, there are 5 National Parks and 21 Wildlife Sanctuaries and 2 Tiger Reserves, Table 9.2, and Table 9.3. The Niligiri Biosphere (Table 9.4) was established as a reserve in 1986.

Wildlife Population in Karnataka

Below is a list of the wildlife population found in Karnataka,

Table 9.1: Wildlife Population and Its Numbers Found in Karnataka

Wildlife Population	Number
Tiger	395
Elephant	6185
Panther	817

Bear	2324
Wild Bear	15760
Deer	25850
Bison	8484
Sambar	4998
Fox	957

National Parks in Karnataka

Below is a list of the National Parks in Karnataka.

Table 9.2: National Parks in Karnataka

National Parks	Area (sq.km)	Seasons to visit
Anshi National park	250	NovJun
Bandipur National Park	874.2	Junoct
Bannergatta National Park	104.27	All seasons
Kudremukha National Park	600.32	DecMay
Nagarahole National Park	643.39	Sept.Mar

Tiger Reserves Found in Karnataka

Table 9.3: Tiger Reserves in Karnataka

Name of the Tiger Reserve	Area (Sq. kms)	Year of Establishment
Bandipur	874	1973
Bhadra	492	1998

Biosphere Reserve

Table 9.4: Information on the Nilgiri Biosphere Reserve

Name of the Reserve	Area (Sq. kms)	Year of Establishment
Nilgiri	5520	1986

Recently Discovered Species

There are many areas of Karnataka, especially in the forests of Malnad region which are unexplored and new species of flora and fauna are discovered from time to time. Some of the new species of flora recently discovered in Karnataka include *Paracautleya bhatii* (a ginger) and *Isachneveldampii* (a grass), both of which were discovered near Manipal in Udupi district. Twospecies of algae, *Cosmarium bourrellyi* and *Cosmarium desikacharyi* were discovered in a paddy field in Belgaum. Other new species of flora discovered in Karnataka include *IsoetesUdupiensis* (a flowering plant) and *Pisolithus indicus* (a fungus).

Endangered Species

Karnataka is the home of few critically endangered species of flora that include evergreen trees like *Dipterocarpus bourdilloni, Hopea erosa* and *Hopea jacobi Croton lawianus* (a small tree) and *Pinnatella limbata* (a type of moss). Some of the critically/endangered species of fauna found in Karnataka include *Gyps indicus* (the Indian vulture) and two species of frogs, *Indirana gundia (found only in Gundia range, Sakleshpur) and Micrixalus Kottigeharensis* (found only near Kottigehara, Chikkamagaluru district).

Some of the endangered species of flora include evergreen trees like *Cynometra bourdillonii,Cynometra travancorica, Hopea glabra, Hopea parviflora, Hopea ponga, Hopea racophloea, Hopea wightinana, shored roxburghii and Tarenna agumbensis and flowering plants like Glochidion pauciflorum, Glochidion tomentosum, Ixora lawsoni and Syszgium stocksii.* Otherendangered trees found in Karnataka include *Isonandra stocksii, Kingiodendron Pinnatum,Maesa velutina, Myristica magnifica, Rapanea striata and xylosma latifolium.*

Endangered species of fauna found in Karnataka include the tiger, Indian Elephant, Lion tailed macaque, turtle and dhole, the Indian wild dog. Many endangered species of amphibians are found here including frogs, *Indirana brachytarsus, Microhyla sholigari,Minervarya sahyadris, Nyctibatrachus aliciae, Nyctibatrachus hussaini, Nyctibatrachus sanctipalustris, philautus charius, philautus wyaadensis, Ramanells mormorata and Rhycophorus laterals and a toad, Bufo Beddomii.* Other endangered species of fauna include *Hipposideros hypophyllus (the Kolar leafnosed bat) and Pseudomulleria dalyi (a molluse* (Prajpati, 2010)*)*.

Current Status of Biodiversity in Karnataka

The state of Karnataka is a part of the highly biodiversity rich regions of India. The state boasts of a great diversity of climate, topography, and soils. It spans the sea coast with its corals and mangrove swamps at the mouths of estuaries. It harbors verdant rain forests, paddy fields and coconut and areca nut orchards on the narrow coast flanked by the hills of the Western Ghats. It bears deciduous woods and scrub jungles, and the sugarcane, cotton, groundnut, ragi and jowar fields of the Deccan plateau. The different environmental regimes support their own characteristic set of plants and animals. The state boasts of an enormous number of species of approximately 4500 species of flowering plants, around 522 species of birds, about 158 species of mammals, roughly 158 species of reptiles (turtles, snakes, lizards and crocodiles), about 70 species of frogs, and nearly 623 species of fish. Medicinal plants are one of the most important species. There are approximately 300 species of these plants in commercial use in Karnataka today. The only reliable information on these issues, albeit limited to their own localities, resides with forest produce. The lion tailed macaque and the rackettailed Drongo are characteristic of the rain forests, the Blackbuck and the Great Indian Bustard are of the grasslands and scrub jungles of the Deccan plateau. Roughly 25% of the 17,500 species of flowering plants of India are found in Karnataka; and there are over 40% of the 1228 species of mobile birds. The fraction of smaller animals' present is likely to be closer to that for plants, since they too are not very mobile. With all the information given, Karnataka probably harbors some 22,000 known and 100,000 total species of littleknownorganisms.

There is no organized information on the status of the indigenous fish fauna of our freshwaters. The only source of information on this issue, albeit limited to their own localities, is with our native fisherfolk. There is no detailed information on the genetic diversity of cultivated plants and domesticated animals which is still being maintained under field conditions by farmers and herders. Therefore, there are many constraints to make only qualitative statements about this important sector. The development is a biomassbased progress; many people cultivate a wide range of species and varieties, consume wild fruits and fishes, use fuelwood to cook their meals and grasses to thatch their huts and cowsheds, extensively employ herbal remedies and worship peepal trees and hanuman langurs (Prajpati, 2010).

The state is rich in knowledge of uses of living resources, ranging from the classical traditions of Ayurveda, Siddha and Yunani, to folk medicinal practices and uses of vegetable perfumes, cosmetics and dyes. But Karnataka's ecological resource base is under threat, with extensive destruction of natural habitats, widespread degradation of agro ecosystems and a growing burden of pollution. Simultaneously, the knowledge base of the uses of biodiversity is also being eroded, with the younger generations becoming increasingly alienated from the natural world.

The wealth of strains of domesticated plants and animals on farms and in the camps of cowherds and shepherds also holds much promise. The hill chain of Western Ghats has a greater diversity of wild relatives of cultivated plants than any other region of comparable size in the world. Much of this diversity of domesticated organisms and their wild relatives is also being rapidly lost. Life in Karnataka's rivers, lakes, estuaries and the seas is under even greater stress than that on the land. With all attention focused on culturing of a few species of economic interest like carps and tiger prawns, there has been little thought devoted to conservation and prudent use of the state's aquatic biodiversity. Yet this loss is occurring at a time when pharmaceutical companies are focusing their attention on marine organisms as the greatest, and as yet little explored treasury of bioactive compounds on the earth. It is clear that we need to look after the ecological well-being of Karnataka's lands and waters, not only of the few remaining natural habitats, but also of farm lands and irrigation tanks, of overgrazed pastures and eroded hill slopes. Here is a need to carefully plan on conserving, sustainably using and restoring the biological diversity across the length and breadth of the state. There is also a need to conserve and benefit from the knowledge of uses and the traditions of conservation of these biological diversities.

Constraints Facing the Conservation of Biodiversity in Karnataka

Biodiversity is being eroded in all the major ecosystems of the Karnataka state, in coastal and marine tracts, in streams, rivers, lakes and reservoirs, in protected areas, as also in humid and dry forests outside protected areas, in agroecosystems, and in urban ecosystems. This erosion may be traced to four significant environmental problems, namely, (*a*) Nonsustainable harvests of living resources, (*b*) Habitat destruction and fragmentation, (*c*) Impacts of pollutants, and (*d*) Competition with colonizing, often exotic, invasive species.

Nonsustainable Harvests of Living Resources

Nonsustainable harvests have been a significant cause of depletion of biodiversity. Poaching has affected a variety of organisms, such as Turtles breeding along sea beaches including the Olive Ridley, or otters breeding along riverbanks. There have been endemic peoplewild life conflicts, especially in relation to elephants raiding crops and killing people. This has been accompanied by extensive poaching of male elephants and many other wild mammals (Prajpati, 2010).

Nonsustainable use by pharmaceutical and allied industry has led to substantial depletion of medicinal plant and other nontimber forest resources, *Rouwolfia serpentina* and *Gloriosa superba* being two wellknown examples. Wild honeybee populations have been decimated, because of the loss of nesting trees and sources of pollen and nectar and use of pesticides in orchards and plantations. This has affected the agricultural productivity.

Habitat Destruction and Fragmentation

Habitat destruction and fragmentation has plagued all of the state's ecosystems. Large tracts of forests have also been converted to monoculture plantations of teak, *Eucalyptus, Casuarinaequisetifolia* and *Acacia auriculiformis*. These processes have led to the loss of many specialhabitats such as *Myristica* swamps and high-altitude grasslands. In the dry zone, they have adversely affected several species dependent on large tracts of scrub such as the wolf and the Great Indian Bustard. The simultaneous extension of agriculture has led to a loss of grassland and scrub savanna habitats and erosion of species such as partridges and quails' dependent on them. The processes of commercialization of agriculture have prompted the liquidation of sacred groves and traditionally protected species such as banyan, peepal and other *Ficus* species, peafowl and monkeys that were a characteristic feature of the traditional agricultural landscape. Open areas in urban ecosystems are also shrinking. So are the old irrigation tanks that constitute urban wetlands. Many have been drained, others are highly polluted and eutrophicated, resulting in a loss of their biota, including indigenous fish communities and migratory waterfowl.

Impacts of Pollutants

The manifold pollution problems impacting Karnataka's biodiversity include industrial effluents that contain heavy metals like mercury, untreated sewage from towns and cities, and biomedical wastes from hospitals. Agricultural intensification has also meant high levels of use of pesticides, bioaccumulation of the pesticides and consequent erosion of biodiversity. The cotton growing tracts of Gulbarga and Raichur districts, and river command areas of Kabini, Kaveri and Ghataprabha have witnessed sharp reduction in populations of bird species, including beneficial insectivorous birds like drongos, as well as honeybees. Even the house sparrows are gone from Bangalore. Given the high levels of air pollution, only a few species of lichens persist on the tree trunks in urban areas (Prajpati, 2010).

Exotic Invasive Species

Invasive Alien Species (IAS) are species whose introductions and spread outside their natural distribution affects the ecosystem. They are generally of short life span, have high reproduction capacity, produce large quantity of seeds/ eggs and survive in hostile environment. They are easily adaptable and have no natural enemies in the new habitat. Invasive Alien Species are one of the greatest threats to biodiversity.

They have invaded every ecosystem type on earth which causes economic as well as environmental harm and adversely affect human health. Example: Lantana, Eupatorium, Parthenium, Coffee stem borer, Carnivorous Cat fish, Gambusia etc.

Globalization has resulted in greater trade, transport, travel and tourism, all of which have facilitated the introduction and spread of species that are not native to an area, reproduce and spread if the new habitat is similar to its native habitat.

The damage is further aggravated by climate change, pollution, fragmentation and loss of habitat. The convention on Biological diversity and its members (191 parties) recognize that there is an urgent need to address the adverse impacts of Invasive Alien Species, the convention expects that each contracting party shall, as far as possible and as appropriate, prevent the introduction, control and eradicate those alien species which threaten ecosystems, habitat and other species."

Steps Taken to Conserve Biodiversity

After CBD, the Government of India had enacted Biodiversity Act 2002 subsequently Karnataka State has framed Biodiversity Rule 2005 and established the State Biodiversity Board. The above are instrumental in protection of Biodiversity. The main objectives of the Act and Rules are:

1. Conservation of Biodiversity,
2. Sustainable utilization of Biodiversity,
3. Equitable sharing of benefits arising out of the commercial use of Biodiversity.

The efforts are going on in this direction at various levels. Further the goals have been fixed and the same has to be achieved by 2010 by various departments involved in resource management and Biodiversity management (Prajpati, 2010).

BANDIPUR NATIONAL PARK

History

The Park was established by the Maharaja of Mysore in 1931 with an area of 90 sq. km. It was later expanded to 800 sq. km and was named the Venugopala Wildlife Park. The place Venugopala is named after the deity of the local shrine located at Gopalswamy Betta (Hill). The sanctuary is located on the highest point about 16km on the *Gopalaswamy Betta* (Hill) from Gundlupet. It is at a height of 4,770 ft. above the seal level. It is described as Dakshina Govardhanagiri, and the hill is also called as the *Himavad Gopalaswamy Betta* as the hill appears to be covered by clouds and mist. There is old fort built by the Palegars of Terakanambi during 13th century and the Gopalaswamy temple is found within the fort. In

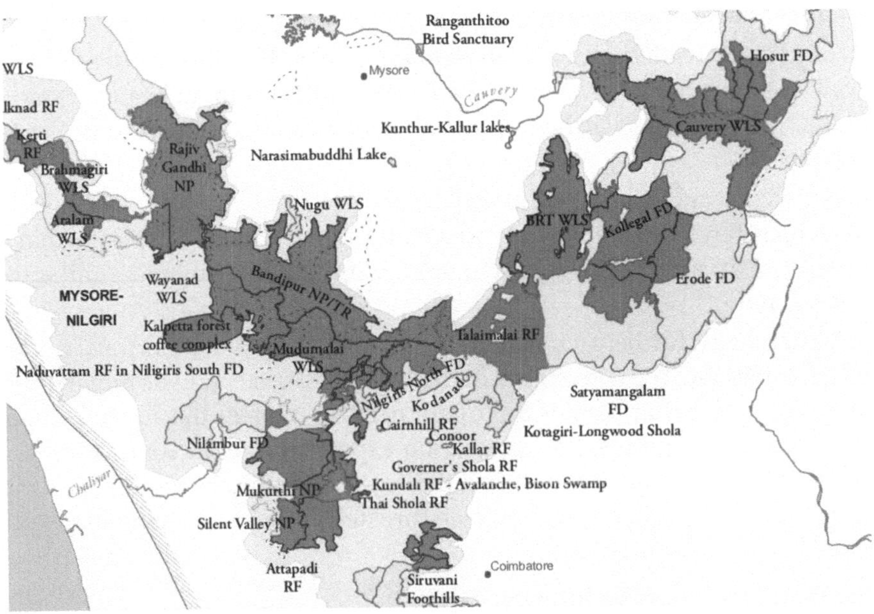

Fig. 9.2: Map showing the location of Bandipur National Park/Tiger Reserve (connecting link) within the Nilgiri Biosphere Reserve.

1941, Venugopala Wildlife Park was expanded to cover an area of 874 sq.km (337 sq. miles) and is known as the 'connecting link'. This link joined the Madumalai Wildlife Sanctuary of Tamil Nadu in the South, the Wayanad Sanctuary of Kerala in the Southwest and the Nagarhole National Park in the North to create India's biggest biosphere reserve popularly known as the 'Nilgiri Biosphere Reserve' (Figure 9.2). In 1973, the Park was re-named to Bandipur Wildlife Sanctuary when the Government of India took ownership of the property. The Park was declared as one of the 9 tiger reserves under the project 'Project Tiger'. In 1974, under the Wildlife Protection Act, the Park achieved the status of a National Park and occupies a special place in India's efforts towards Eco-conservation.

Location of Bandipur National Park

Bandipur National Park is situated in Mysore (Nanjungud and H. D. Kote taluks) and Chamarajanagar (Gundlupet taluk) districts of Karnataka state and lies in the Deccan Plateau between the North Latitudes of 110 35′ 34″ and 110 55′ 02″ and between the East Longitudes of 760 12′ 17″ and 760 51′ 32″ (Figure 9.3). Bandipur National Park lies between 680-1454 meters above sea level and is located south of the Kabini River in the foothills of the Western Ghats. The main perennial rivers of the Reserve are Nugu, Kabini and Moyar. The Nugu river flows in the middle of the Reserve. Whereas, the Moyar river forms the southern boundary between this reserve and Madhumalai Wildlife Sanctuary. The Kabini river, across which a major irrigation dam has been built at Beechanahalli, forms the boundary between this Reserve and Nagarhole National Park. The Kabini reservoir provides water facility and the grazing ground on the foreshore, for

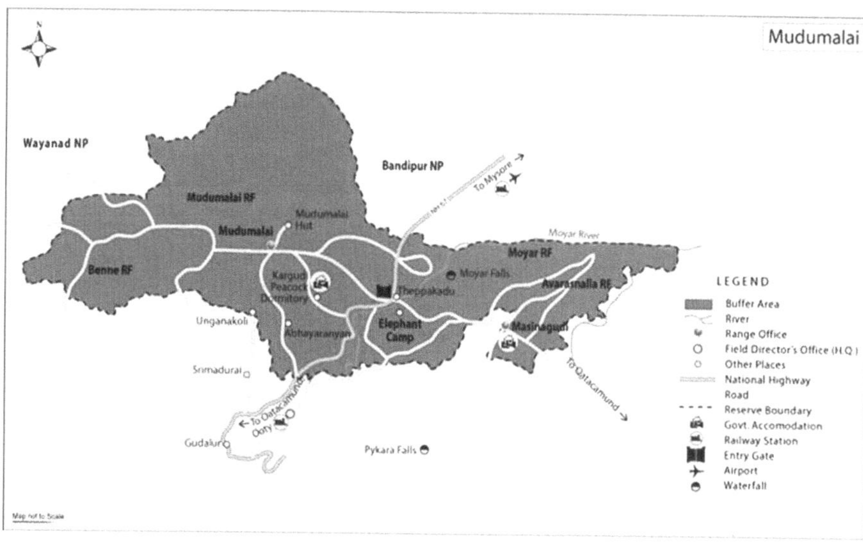

Fig. 9.3: Map showing the location of Bandipur National Park

hundreds of elephants during severe and prolonged pinch period. Seasonal streams like Wadli, Chammanahalla, Aidasanahattihalla, Hebballa, Warranchi, Chippanahalla and Mavinahalla are also present. There are a few natural and artificial saltlicks available in the Reserve which are being regularly used by the wild animals.

Climate in Bandipur National Park

The Park is endowed with a moderate climate having 28°C at its coolest and diverse geographical features, supporting a wide variety of flora and fauna. The vegetation in the park represents a wide variety of ranges from dry deciduous, evergreen forests, the scrub jungles and open grassy woodlands. Two of the most valuable timber trees of India-the rosewood and teak-grow abundantly in the park.

Flora in Bandipur National Park

Bandipur National Park consists of stunted trees, intermixed with bushes and open grassy belts. The eastern part of the Park contains scrub jungles, consisting of stunted trees, bushes and grassy patches. As we move to the northwestern fringes of the Park, there is a gradual shift in the vegetation from open dry deciduous forests to tropical mixed deciduous forests. At the northwestern fringes, there is a bit-by-bit shift in the plant life, from open dry deciduous jungles to tropical mixed deciduous jungles. These diverse habitats of plant life cover a huge variety of animal life. With the onset of monsoons, the whole area becomes lively and lush green. The meadows bloom with sprouting grass, attracting large herds of Elephants and Gaurs. The floral diversity of the Bandipur National Park supports an equally enormous diversity of wildlife.

Rosewood and Teak, the two most valuable timber trees of India, grow abundantly in the Park. Other commonly found trees in the Bandipur National Park are Sandalwood, Jacaranda (a hardwood timber tree with purple flowers), Mango, Jamun, Tamarind, Banyan, Pipal, Plumeria, Gulmohar, Honne, Mathi, and Bamboo among many more.

Fauna in the Bandipur National Park

The Bandipur National Park begins to blossom due to the arrival of pre-monsoon showers in April. The grasslands with developing grass are dominated by elephants and the gaur. Bandipur is a paradise between April to October, for the tourist coming to watch the larger mammals in their natural habitats. During the summer season, the backwaters of the Kabini Reservoir in the northwestern part of the park entertains huge gathering of large mammals. The Royal Bengal Tigers and Leopards are even more elusive here than elsewhere because the moister region that they inhabit falls under the protected core area where tourists are not allowed.

Endangered Species

In the park, among its array of fauna, the following animals are endangered species: Tiger, Four-Horned Antelope, Gaur, Elephant, Panther, Sloth bear, Crocodiles, Mouse deer, Python, Osprey, Pea fowl.

Method

This study involved two types of questionnaire surveys (1) survey for villagers and (2) survey for park officials. The villagers and park officials were briefed on the study objectives and purposes and those who agreed to participate in the survey, were given questionnaires. A total of 195 villagers and 140 park officials were randomly selected for the administration of the questionnaire for data collection.

RESULTS AND DISCUSSION

Table 9.1 shows the demographic characteristics of the villagers (respondents) who took part in the survey. From the table, it can be seen that 61.54% of the respondents were males while only 38.46% females were given permission by their families to take part in the survey. A majority of the respondents (73.84%) attended school or have some form of formal education. About 26.15% of the respondents did not have the opportunity to attend school due to reasons such as they had to help in farm work, fishing or their parents couldn't afford to send them to school. Looking at the education section in Table 9.1, lack of schooling scored the highest of the other educational characteristics.

About 51.79% of males have a high school education and higher whilst only 32.82% of females are high school educated or higher. This maybe because the girls are either married at young ages and are not allowed to go to school after marriage or that girls are perceived as being homemakers and thus at young ages are taken out of school or that families in India would rather spend money on their male child being educated because in the future he has to 'take-care of them' and a female child goes off to live with her in-laws and thus they received nothing from her.

Approximately, 22.56% of the respondents having completed their high school and continued their studies to earned an undergraduate degree were either tour guides, drivers or park workers. Around 26.15% of the respondents having an education, conducted agriculture (farming) for their livelihoods. A reason for this high percent could be as part of the relocation settlement for the people who were living on the park lands, the government gave small amounts of land to these people as compensation and as a means to re-start their lives outside the park. Agriculture (farming) has had a significant effect on biodiversity because of its prevalence over the landscape. These effects include habitat alteration (conversion to farmland for crops and grazing), exotic pest introductions and pollution from pesticides and fertilizers. According to

Statistics Canada, 1994 agriculture has the greatest impact on the environment of any human activity both because of the degree of habitat fragmentation and alterations that occurs and because of the widespread geographical scale of this fragmentation and alterations. Some of the impacts include: changes in natural genetic plant stocks, changes in established ecosystems, the introduction of exotic species and the increases topsoil erosion.

On the other hand, the next highest characteristics is fishing (23.15%). This maybe the close proximity of the villagers outside the park to the main rivers in the park, providing easy access for fishing in the three main perennial rivers in the park, Nugu, Kabini and Moyar, almost 16.0% of the villagers would fish as an occupation, as a means to support their families. Fishing has a substantial impact on biodiversity. Fishing can affect aquatic ecosystems through overharvesting of populations, nutrient additions (aquaculture), introduction of exotic fish and invertebrate species, habitat alterations and pollution (Thibault, 1995).

Only about, 8.92% of the villagers who have completed their high school and furthered their studies hold government positions or own their businesses (entrepreneurs).

The villagers used three different sources as meat as part of their protein requirements. Approximately 55.38% consumed livestock and have many thousands of herds of goat, sheep, chickens which put great amounts of pressure on the park. About 27.69% of the respondents reported that their diet consists of wildmeat/bushmeat they or someone else has caught and killed in the park. With so many thousands of herds of animals owned by these villagers you may think there will be a reduction in the tendency of hunting of wild animals for their protein's needs, but personal experience has shown that wild meats form part of their delicacies. Studies worldwide show that where humans depend exclusively on wildlife for meat, tropical forests cannot support much more than one person per square kilometer, even under the most productive circumstances (Gubbi, 2003). Wildlife hunting (poaching) has been a contention between the villagers and park management officials. However, some of the villagers (who don't take part in poaching) believed that it is this illegal activity had led the government to resettle them outside the park boundaries.

Table 9.1: Demographic Variables of Respondents

Demographic Variable	Frequency	Percent (%)
Gender	195	
Male	120	61.54
Female	75	38.46
Education	195	
High School Diploma	30	15.38

Pre-University	33	16.92
University	38	19.49
Vocation	43	22.05
Lack of schooling	51	26.15
Occupation	195	
Tour Guide	11	5.64
Driver	30	15.38
Farming	64	32.82
Entrepreneur	10	5.13
Civil Servant	16	8.21
Fishing	45	23.59
Park Worker	18	9.23
Source of Meat	195	
Fish	33	16.92
Livestock	108	55.38
Wild meat (bush meat)	54	27.69

The illegal activities carried out by the villagers are shown in Table 9.2. It can be seen that 82.56% of the villagers have practiced agriculture (farming) on parkland, 78.46% of the respondents carried out fishing activities, 74.36% took part in illegal livestock grazing, 73.33% collected fodders and 62.05% extracted fuelwood/firewood from the park. These results revealed that agriculture (farming) on parkland, fishing activities, illegal livestock grazing, collection of fodders and extraction fuelwood/firewood from the park are the main threats being faced by the park from the villages surrounding it. This is not surprising since most of these villagers' own livestock and the only place where vegetation exists especially during the monsoon season is the park. Also, most of them are farmers putting pressures on park land for their farming activities. Aside from these, fuelwood extraction and charcoal production are prominent activities in the study area because most of the inhabitants depend on fuelwood and charcoal as household energy sources. In addition, fishing is also a major occupation apart from farming among the people; villages along the course of the main perennial rivers Nugu, Kabini and Moyar are mostly fishermen whose daily subsistence rests on fishing activities in the rivers. Illegal settlements are on the increase in the park despite laws prohibiting it, and this is accompanied by increase in population of the settlers; putting undue pressures on the resources of the park thereby thwarting conservation efforts (Ramchurjee and Suresha, 2015).

Table 9.2: Showing Illegal Activities Carried Out by the Villagers in Bandipur National Park (n=195)

Illegal Activities	Frequency	Percent (%)
Fuelwood/firewood	121	62.05
Wildlife (bush meat) hunting	82	42.05
Logging for local use	73	37.44
Trophy hunting	55	28.21
Illegal timber logging	15	7.69
Livestock grazing	145	74.36
Fishing	153	78.46
Illegal setting of fire or bush burning	19	9.74
Fodder collection	143	73.33
Agriculture (farming)	161	82.56
Migration into the park	15	7.69
Non-timber forest products collection	90	46.15
Settlement on park land	46	23.59

Note: Respondents chose as many options applied to their situation

Table 9.3: Problems Affecting the Conserving of Biodiversity in Bandipur National Park Identified by the Park Officials (n=140)

Problems affecting Biodiversity Conservation	Frequency	Percent (%)	Rank
Poaching	121	86.43	4
Deforestation and habitat loss	28	20.00	9
Pollution	24	17.14	10
Increase in the population of the villages surrounding the park	135	96.43	1
Logging	35	25.00	8
Fuelwood/firewood extraction	101	72.14	5
Illegal fishing	85	60.71	6
Livestock grazing	129	92.14	2
Uncontrolled burning	57	40.71	7
Invasive species	15	10.74	11
Collection of non-timber products	124	88.57	3

Note: Respondents chose as many options applied to their situation

Table 9.3 discusses the problems affecting the conserving of biodiversity in Bandipur National Park, from the park officials' point of views. They revealed that many problems are there, but the tables identify the main threats. In order to realize the consequences of these threats, they were ranked according to their severity to show the effects they have on biodiversity within the Park from the consideration of the management. The top ranked problem faced by park officials is from an increase in the population of the villages surrounding the park with 96.43%. When the Park was expanded to protect and preserve the wildlife, many changes occurred. The first major change was resettling the people who lived on the expanded parkland outside this boundary. This major disruption in uprooting the livelihoods of the people was such a shock because now they could not rely on the Park to sustain their lives for food, fodder and fuelwood/firewood. So, with the relocation, the people had to begin to fend for themselves and become self-reliant.

Continuous overgrazing and deforestation have deprived most of the reserves in India of their natural flora. With the growth in livestock and human population, overgrazing (2nd – 92.14%) and an increase in non-timber product collection (3rd – 88.57%) would be expected. According to Salami, 1979 the degradation caused by illegal grazing has caused some animals to migrate to the neighboring states, thus the development of the Nilgiri Biosphere Reserve between Karnataka, Kerala and Tamil Nadu. Moreover, poaching activities (4th – 8643%) in and around the park, as well as the consistent collection of fuelwood/firewood (5th – 72.14%) have been major problems facing the park that have led to the extinction of some fauna and flora species. Local traditional hunting has pushed extinction of some species of wildlife and led numerous others to critical levels (Gubbi, 2003). According to WWF (2007), putting representative protected area networks in place and managing them requires money. Developed countries have managed to outline and establish ways to provide long-term sustainable financing, however, less developed countries cannot support such long-term funding. This funding gap is particularly critical in developing countries. Annual expenditure of protected areas in many developing countries is tremendously low (James *et al.,* 1999) and protected areas in tropical regions are under-funded. More so, they require resources for annual operating budgets, capital investment, staff training, community development and public awareness among a wide range of other activities (James, Green and Paine, 1999).

Table 9.4: Management Problems Disturbing Biodiversity Conservation in Bandipur National Park as Identified by Park Officials (n=140)

Management Problems distributing the Biodiversity Conservation	Frequency	Percent (%)	Rank
Inadequate park staff	140	100	1
Lack of educational awareness/materials for tourists	140	100	1
Lack of vehicles	140	100	1
Tourists/visitors disobeying park rules	99	70.71	9

Lack of equipment	130	92.86	8
Insufficient funding	140	100	1
Utilities such as electricity, waste disposal	92	65.71	10
Relocation of locals/tribal	61	43.57	12
Poor salary for park officials	140	100	1
Low levels of communication between park workers and surrounding villagers	89	63.57	11
Low park charges	140	100	1
Commercial ventures such as ranch/lodge/resorts	135	96.43	7

Note: Respondents chose as many options applied to their situation

Table 9.4 reveals the management problems faced in the aim of preserving biodiversity. Many issues are identified by the park officials as deterring them from doing their jobs, but some of these issues have been discussed in Table 9.2 and Table 9.3. In this table, there are many issues ranking number 1 listed below:

- Inadequate park staffs
- Insufficient funding
- Poor salary for park officials
- Lack of vehicles
- Low park charges
- Lack of educational awareness/materials for tourists

Inadequate park staffs, insufficient funding, poor salary for park officials and lack of vehicles are major hinderance for staffs to feel overworked and underpaid. The park has 900 sq. km of boundary line and it is very difficult for limited protection staff to 'manned' the boundaries both day and night to prevent poaching, livestock grazing, collection of fuelwood/firewood and non-timber products. Ogunjinmi *et al* (in press) reported low pay as one the variables hindering rangers (park officials). Lack of educational awareness/materials for tourists and park charges are the other problems ranking #1. When you arrive at BNP, there are no materials to enlighten tourists/visitors of the dos and don'ts about the park and so these tourists/visitors take advantages and disobey park rules sometimes even putting themselves in danger. Park fees are low and the yearly collection does not compensate for even half of the park expenses thus depending heavily on government.

CONCLUSION

Since the government is the managing and regulating agency of the Bandipur National Park, it is in-charge of implementing severe measures to prohibit illegal activities affecting conservation of biodiversity. The study found that biodiversity conservation is affected by various factors associated with the creation and management of the park, the location, and the local population surrounding the park, the national policy governing the park, and the financial funding of the park. These factors are socioeconomic and cultural in nature involving the management of local communities neighboring the National Park as much as the resources in park. Conservation awareness aimed at changing the local peoples' attitudes, and improving their living conditions is essential. With these factors, there can be positive long-term sustainable interactions that can lead to the conservation of biodiversity.

REFERENCES

Adams, W. (2004): Against Extinction: The Story of Conservation, Earthscan, London, UK.

Al-Sayed, M. and Al-langawi, A. (2003): Biological Resources Conservation Through Ecotourism.

Development, Journal of Arid Environments, 54(1): 225-236.

Anderson, W. (2010): Marketing of Domestic Tourism in Tanzania, Dar es Salaam, Dar es Salaam University Press.

Blangy, S. and Mehta, H. (2006): Ecotourism and Ecological Restoration, Journal for Nature Conservation, 14(3-4): 233-236.

Boo, E. (1990): Ecotourism: The Potentials and Pitfalls, vol. 1 and 2. WWF, Washington, DC.

Bookbinder, M. P. Dinerstein, E. Rijal, A. Cauley, H. and Rajouria A. (1998): Ecotourism's Support of Biodiversity Conservation, Conservation Biology, 12(6): 1399-1404.

Brown, K. Turner, R. K. Hameed, H. and Bateman, I. (1997): Environmental Carrying Capacity and Tourism Development in the Maldives and Nepal. Environ. Conserv. 24 (4): 316–325.

Budowski, G. (1976): Tourism and Environmental Conservation: Conflict, Coexistence or Symbiosis? Environ. Conserv. 3 (1): 27–31.

Burger, J. (2000): Landscapes, Tourism and Conservation, The Science of the Total Environment, 249(1-3): 39-49.

Burgess, J. C. (1993): Timber Production, Timber Trade and Tropical Deforestation. Ambio 22 (2–3): 136–143.

Ceballos-Lascurain, H. (2001): Integrating Biodiversity into the Tourism Sector: Best Practice and Country Case Studies. Nairobi, Kenya: Study for the United Nations Environment Programme (UNEP/UNDP/GEF/BPSP).

Chape, S. Blyth, S. Fish, L. Fox, P. and Spalding, M. (2003): The 2003 United Nations List of Protected Areas, IUCN and UNEPWCMC, Cambridge, UK.

Chettri, N. (2000): Impact of Tourism on Biodiversity, A Case Study from the Sikkim Himalaya, India, Eastern Himalayan Programme, Bhujiapani, Badogra, West Bengal, India.

Colchester, M. (2003): Salvaging Nature: Indigenous Peoples, Protected Areas and Biodiversity Conservation," in *World Rainforest Movement*, International Secretariat, Maldonado, Uruguay, 2nd Edition.

Convention on Biological Diversity (CBD), (1992): https://www.cbd.int/doc/legal/cbd-en.pdf

Galvin, K. A. Thornton, P. K. de Pinho, J. R. Sunderland, R. and Boone, R. B. (2006): Integrated Modeling and Its Potential for Resolving Conflicts Between Conservation and People in the Rangelands of East Africa," *Human Ecology*, vol. 34(2), 155–183.

Goodwin, H. (1996): In Pursuit of Ecotourism. Biodiversity Conserv. 5: 277–291.

Gössling, S. (1999): Ecotourism: A Means to Safeguard Biodiversity and Ecosystem Functions? Ecological Economics, 29(2): 303-320.

Gubbi, S., (2003). Wildlife on the run. www.wildlifefirst.info/images/wordfiles/ontherun.doc

Huynh, D. H. (1998): The Role of "Biodiversity" in the Development of Ecotourism in Vietnam, Institute for Ecological and Biological Resources, National Centre for Natural Science and Technology.

International Ecotourism Society (TIES) (1990): http://www.ecotourism.org/book/ecotourism-Definition.

James, A. N. Green, M. J. B. and Paine, J. R. (1999): A Global Review of Protected Area Budgets and Staffing, WCMC-World Conservation Press, UK: vi+46.

Neto, F. (2003): A New Approach to Sustainable Tourism Development: Moving Beyond Environmental Protection, ST/ESA/2003/DP/29 DESA Discussion Paper No. 29, Twelfth ACUNS/ASIL Workshop on International Organization Studies held in Windhoek, Namibia and Johannesburg, South Africa.

Ogunjinmi, A. A. Umunna, M. O. and Ogunjinmi, K. O. (2008): Factors Affecting Job Satisfaction of Rangers in Yankari Game Reserve, Bauchi, Nigeria, Journal of Agriculture and Social Research (JASR).

Prajpati, R. C. (2010): "Biodiversity of Karnataka" at a glance, Karnataka Biodiversity Board (Forest, Ecology and Environment Department) www.kbb.kar.nic.in

Ramchurjee, N. A, Suresha, S. (2015): Biodiversity Conservation Problems and Their Consequences on Sustainable Ecotourism: A Case Study of Bandipur National Park, Karnataka, India, JSSCWM QUEST Journal 3(1): 36-41

Ross, S. and Wall, G. (1999): Ecotourism: Towards Congruence Between Theory and Practice, Tourism Management, 20(1): 123-132.

Schroeder, R. A. (1999): Geographies of Environmental Intervention in Africa, *Progress in Human Geography*, Vol. 23, No. 3: 359–378.

Statistics Canada. (1994): *Human Activity and the Environment.* Cat. No. 11-509E. Minister of Industry, Science and Technology, Ottawa, ON: 300.

Stolton, S. Mansourian, S. and Dudley, N. (2010): Valuing Protected Areas, The International Bank for Reconstruction and Development, Washington, DC, USA.

Thibault, M. H. (1995): *Le Québec statistique - 1995*. Bureau de la Statistique du Québec, Publications du Québec, 60th ed. Ste-Foy, QC: 820.

van der Duim, R. and Caalders, J. (2002): Biodiversity and Tourism: Impacts and Interventions, Annals of Tourism Research, 29(3): 743-761.

Vorlaufer, K. (1996): Tourismus in Entwicklungsla¨nder. Wissenschaftliche Buchgesellschaft, Darmstadt, Germany.

Western, D. and Henry, W. (1979): Economics and conservation in Third World national parks. BioScience 29 (7): 414–418.

World Summit on Sustainable Development (WSSD), (2002): http://www.earthsummit2002.org/Es2002.pdf

World Tourism Organization (WTO), (2007): https://www.wto.org/english/res_e/booksp_e/anrep_e/world_trade_report07_e.pdf

World Travel and Tourism Council (WTTC), (2016): https://www.wttc.org/-/media/files/reports / economic%20impact%20research/regions%202016/world2016.pdf

World Wildlife Fund (WWF) (1995): Ecotourism: Conservation Tool or Threat? Conserv. 2 (3): 1–10.

Plant Response to Environmental Stress **Page: 168-184**
Edited by: Dr. Alka Chauhan; Dr. Pawan Kumar 'Bharti' and Dr. Avnish Chauhan
ISBN: 978-93-86841-58-2
Edition: 2018
Published by: Discovery Publishing House Pvt. Ltd., New Delhi (India)

10

Role of Polyamines and Mycorrhiza for the Mitigation of Cadmium Toxicity in Pea

Prasann Kumar[1] and Nada Jyoti

ABSTRACT

Pisum sativum also known as the Garden pea belongs to the family Fabaceae. Pea is an annual herbaceous plant with a life cycle of one year. It is believed to have originated from the Mediterrean region, Central and Western Asia and Ethopia. It is the cool season crop which is cultivated throughout the world. Pea is a rich source of protein, fibre, carbohydrate, minerals like iron, magnesium, phosphorus, zinc and vitamin like A and C, etc.There are generally 3 types of pea that are commonly eaten. They are Garden pea or green pea-*Pisum sativum*, snow pea- *Pisumsativum var. macrocarpon*, snap pea-*Pisum sativum var. macrocarpon ser cv*. These peas have rounded pods that are usually slightly curved in shape with a smooth texture and vibrant green colour. Several peas are enclosed inside the pods. Usually snow peas are used as a vegetable in their immature stage. They have tender pods and are consumed fresh, frozen or canned whereas field pea are generally grown to produce dry pea like the split pea shelled from the mature pods. *Pisum sativum* cultivars are either low growing or vining type. The vining type of cultivar grows tendrils that coils around any available support and can climb upto 1-2 m. Pea like many other legumes contains symbiotic bacteria called Rhizobia within their root nodules. These bacteria help in fixing the atmospheric nitrogen. Using the symbiotically fixed nitrogen instead of using chemical nitrogen fertilizer will help in the development of sustainable agriculture and also increase the yield production.

Keywords: Agriculture, Cadmium, Density, Pea, Rhizobium.

INTRODUCTION

Heavy metals are the naturally occurring elements with high relative density, atomic mass and atomic weight. Cadmium is one of those heavy metals that is lustrous, silver white, ductile and very malleable metal which is of considerable

[1]Department of Agronomy, School of Agriculture, Lovely Professional University, Jalandhar, Punjab, 144411

environmental and occupational concern and has a detrimental effect on anenvironment and humans. It is widely distributed in the earth's crust at an average concentration of 0.1-0.5 mg/kg. It always occurs in the combination with zinc. The highest level of cadmium compounds in the environment is accumulated in the marine phosphate and sedimentary rocks which are about 15mg cadmium/kg. They are considered as trace elements because of their presence in trace concentration i.e, less than 10 ppm [Paul B tchounwou]. Cadmium in industries are produced as an inevitable byproducts of Zinc, Lead, Copper extraction. They are used for the production of alloys, pigments

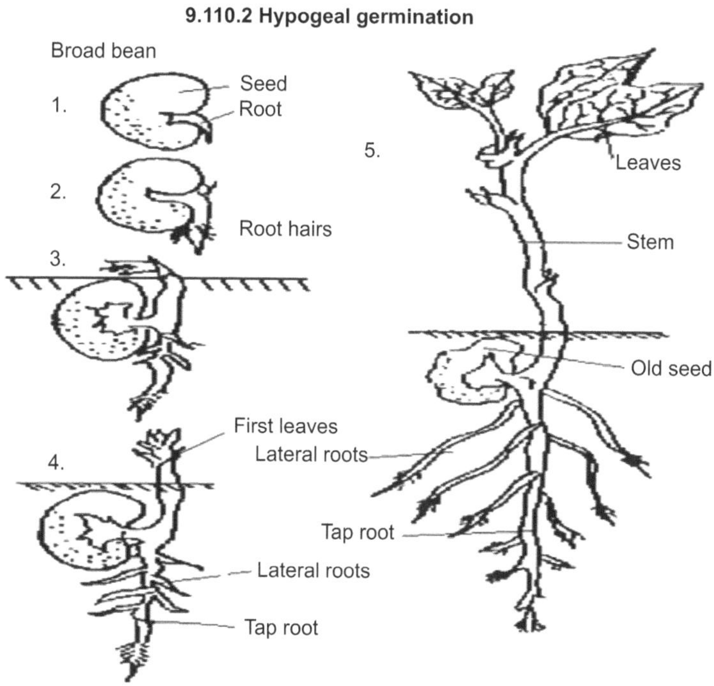

Fig. 10.1: Pea plant and its parts

(**Source:** Review of Literature)

and batteries and as stabilizers in plastics. Cadmium is used particularly to electroplate steel where a thin film provide complete protection against the sea. After being applied, they enter into the environment mainly through the ground as it is found in manure and pesticides. Cadmium toxicity in agricultural field also increases due to the continuous application of phosphorus. Cadmium is also present in trace amounts in certain food such as a leafy vegetable, potatoes, grains, seeds etc. Cadmium and its compound are classified as Group 1 carcinogens for humans by the International Agency for Research on Cancer [Henson and Chedrese, 2004]. Heavy metals like cadmium do not degrade naturally and retain in the soil for a very long period. Cadmium and its compounds are highly water soluble compared to other metals, thus their bioavailability is very high and hence it tends to be bioaccumulated by the plants. Tobacco is the main source of cadmium uptake in smokers as tobacco plants, like other plants can accumulate cadmium from the soil. They remain in the soil for a very long period, they either leach into the ground water or are uptake by the plants which then migrate into the food crops which are then consumed by the humans. Thus, having detrimental effects on the environment as well as to the human body. Exposure to cadmium causes many health problems like kidney disorder, lungs problem, hypertension, fever, DNA damages in living cells, gastrointestinal irritant, pulmonary or renal injury and comatose etc (Figure 10.1).

What is Polyamines?

A polyamine is an organic compound having two or more primary amino groups-NH2. They are also known as a group of natural compounds with an aliphatic nitrogen structure present in almost all living organisms. It plays an important role in many physiological processes such as cell growth and development. Polyamines which are commonly found are putrescine. Spermidine, spermine etc. the diamine putrescine, the triamine spermidine and the tetramine spermine are ubiquitously found in plant cells while other polyamines are of more limited occurrence. In animals, their levels are maintained from both the diet and denovo synthesis. Polyamine metabolism is regulated by the activity of the enzyme ornithine decarboxylase. Polyamine can also be synthesized from the aminoacid arginine and methionine. The first step in the pathway is the production of ornithine from arginine by the mitochondrial enzyme arginase. Ornithine is then decarboxylated by ornithine decarboxylase to produce putrescine. Polyamine is found in high concentration in the mammalian brain. The polyamines declines with the ages in the organism. For instance, Nishimura *et al.* measured polyamine levels in 14 different tissues in 3, 10 and 26 weeks old female mice and found that spermidine levels decreased in 11 out of 14 tissues while spermine decreased only in skin, heart and muscles. Putrescine level was very low in all tissues at all ages. Some other researches like Serafini-Fracassini *et al.* showed that spermine treatment delayed senescene in excised flowers of Nicotiana tabacum. After 48 hours, 70% of the flowers were still at the stage at which they had been cut, whereas in the controls, 50% were at an early senescene stage and the other 50% at senescent.Many organisms are regularly exposed to stress and the ability to resist stress is a part of survival strategy. Polyamines plays an important role in relation to stress resistance. Polyamines are particularly important for adaptation and resistance to cold stress. Polyamine levels increase in plants during abiotic stress conditions such as salinity, extreme temperature or in the presence of heavy metals. This regulation of polyamines under stress is achieved by differential expression of polyamine biosynthesis enzymes such as arginine decarboxylase, spermidine and spermine synthase. Also the exogenous application of polyamine have proved to preserve membrane integrity and lower growth inhibitory during stress conditions and also has increased the activity of antioxidant enzymes such as catalase. In contrast, polyamine synthesis inhibitors triggered decreased stress resistance. Mohapatra *et al.* studied aluminium stress in interaction with calcium in poplar cell cultures with normal or high level of putrescine. Reducing or increasing the amount of calcium had no effect on growth in the control cells except when drastically reduced, but decreased and increased respectively in cell growth with high level of putrescine. The addition of aluminium with normal or low calcium again had no effect in the control cells but the cells with high putrescine content exhibited better growth. Wang *et al.* cloned the arginine decarboxylase gene from trifoliate orange and carried out its functional studyin transgenic Arabidopsis. The transgenic plants had higher levels of putrescine but not of spermidine and spermine. They displayed a lower stomatal density, longer roots, larger cell size and higher relative water content than the controls both in normal conditions and have germinated better under osmotic stress. During dehydration, the transgenic plants lost less water, had a better electrolyte leakage and leaf turgor. The transgenic plants were also more resistant to cold (Figure 10.2).

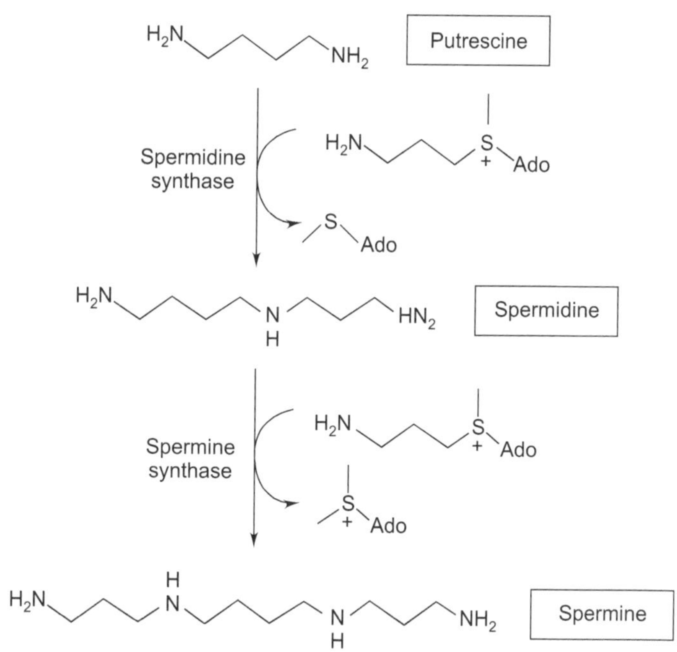

Fig. 10.2: Biosynthesis of Polyamines

(**Source:** Review of Literature)

Mycorrhiza

Mycorrhiza is a fungus having a symbiotic or mutualistic relationship with the rhizosphere or roots of the plants. They share a mutualistic relationship in which the mycorrhiza forms a network of filaments that associates with the plant roots which helps them in uptaking the mineral nutrients or water while the mycorrhiza are benefitted by getting access to carbohydrates such as glucose and sucrose. The carbohydrates are translocated from their source to root tissues and onto the plant fungal partners. Some plant roots may be unable to uptake nutrients that are chemically or physically immobilized. For example, phosphate ions and micronutrients such as iron. One form of such immobilization occurs in soils with high clay content or soils with pHstrongly basic. The mycelium of mycorrhiza fungus can however, access many nutrient sources and make them available to the plants they colonize. Thus, many plants are able to obtain phosphate without using soil as a source. Any other form of immobilization is when nutrients are locked up in organic matter that is slow to decay. In such cases, some mycorrhizal fungus acts as a decay organisms and mobilize the nutrients. Some of the fungus has shown resistance to toxicity in plants. Those fungus is found to play protective role for plants rooted in soils with high metal concentration, such as acidic and contaminated soils. Pines trees inoculated with *Pisolithus tinctorius* planted in several contaminated sites displayed high tolerance to the prevailing contaminants. One study discovered the existence of *Suillus luteus* strains with varying tolerance of zinc. Another study discovered that zinc tolerant strains of *Suillus bovinus* conferred resistance to plants of *Pinus sylvestris*. This was probably due to binding of the metals to the extramatricial mycelium of the fungus without affecting the exchange of beneficial substance (Figure 10.3).

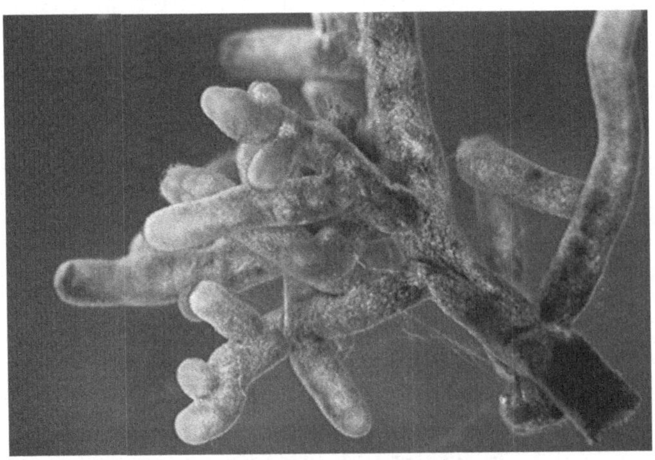

Fig. 10.3: Ectomycorrhiza

(**Source:** Review of literature)

Mechanism of Tolerance and Avoidance of Heavy Metals by Plants

Plants when exposed to stress or unfavourable condition induces some defense mechanism inorder to protect themselves from those harsh conditions. Many plants have shown many different kinds defense mechanism. Heavy metal toxicity is one of the unlikely condition in plants as it has many deterioration impact on the health of the environment as well as on human beings. Due to the adversity of such stressful conditions, plants induces some defense mechanism in their system in order to cope up with such adversities.heavy metal toxicity in plants causes in the reduction of plant growth, hampers photosynthetic activities, causes leaf chlorosis, necrosis etc. Heavy metal are of two types, essential and non-essential depending upon the requirement of minerals for the proper growth and physiological activity of the plant. Some essential metals like zinc, manganese, iron, magnesium etc are required by the plant for their physiological functions while non-essential metals like cadmium, lead, chromium etc are not required by the plants but can be uptaken by them. Increase in the toxicity level of heavy metals also has multiple effects on plant growth and development including perturbation of plant water stress. Cadmium can easily be uptaken by the plant roots and can be loaded in the xylem which further gets transported to the leaves. Many studies has shown that the cadmium have demonstrated harmful effects on the plants by hampering the plant metabolism such as decreasing the uptake of nutrient elements and changing the nitrogen metabolism. For instance, Sandalia *et al.*, 2001 has shown that the presence of cadmium in the leaves of *Brassica napus* lead to a reduction of mesophyll cell size while the leaf thickness and cell size increased in *Pisum sativum* when exposed to heavy metals. For instance, Poschenrieder et al,1989, has shown that the heavy metals induced perturbation of aquaporin function which decreases both root and shoot hydraulic conductance that leads to decrease in leaf water potential and leaf turgor, which may directly close the stomata. Decrease in leaf and root water status caused by the heavy metals can enhance biosynthesis of phytohormones abscisic acid (ABA) which acts to maintain plant water status. Root ABA biosynthesis can enhance root hydraulic conductivity [Thompson *et al.* 2007] and increase root-to-shoot ABA signaling, thereby promoting stomatal closure [Davies and Zhang 1991; Dodd 2005]. It was also proposed that stomatal closure may decrease heavy metal uptake from soil,thereby decreasing metal accumulation in vivo which ultimately leads to decrease in toxic effect of the heavy metal [Pascual *et al.* 2004]. The plants also use different metabolites as their defence to Fe-deficiencies, [Rellan-Alvarez *et al.* 2010] has shown that Fe-deficiency in the root of the sugar beet induced increase in the concentration of certain amino acids like serine, lysine, citrulline and increased the production of organic acids such as citrate and malate in the shoot of the sugar beet [Lopez-Millan et al, 2001] and roots of *Capsicum annum* [Landsberg, 1981]. For instance, [Rennenberg and Lamourex 1990, Zaharieva *et al.* 2003] showed the Fe-defieciency response in plants is Gluthathione which is known to play multiple roles in cellular metabolism, including scavenging of Reactive oxygen species under Fe stress. Synthesis of gluthathione has been shown to increase under Fe deficiency in roots of barley, wheat and maize, in shoots of rice [Bashir *et al.* 2007, Nishizawa 2007]. A study done by Mohammad Anwar Hossain *et al.* reported that the toxicity of cadmium has induced inhibition of respiration in rice (*Oryza sativa*), which has decreased the activity of α-amylase, β-amylase and sucrose phosphate synthase which in response has increased the activity of starch phosphorylase, acid invertase and sucrose synthase. They also has reported that the uptake of heavy metals by plants involves root interception of heavy metal ions, entry of heavy metal ions into roots, and their translocation to the shoot. Once an HM is bioavailable to the plant, the entry of heavy metal ions inside the plant, either through the symplast (intracellular) or through the apoplast (extracellular), depends on the type of heavy metal. One of the

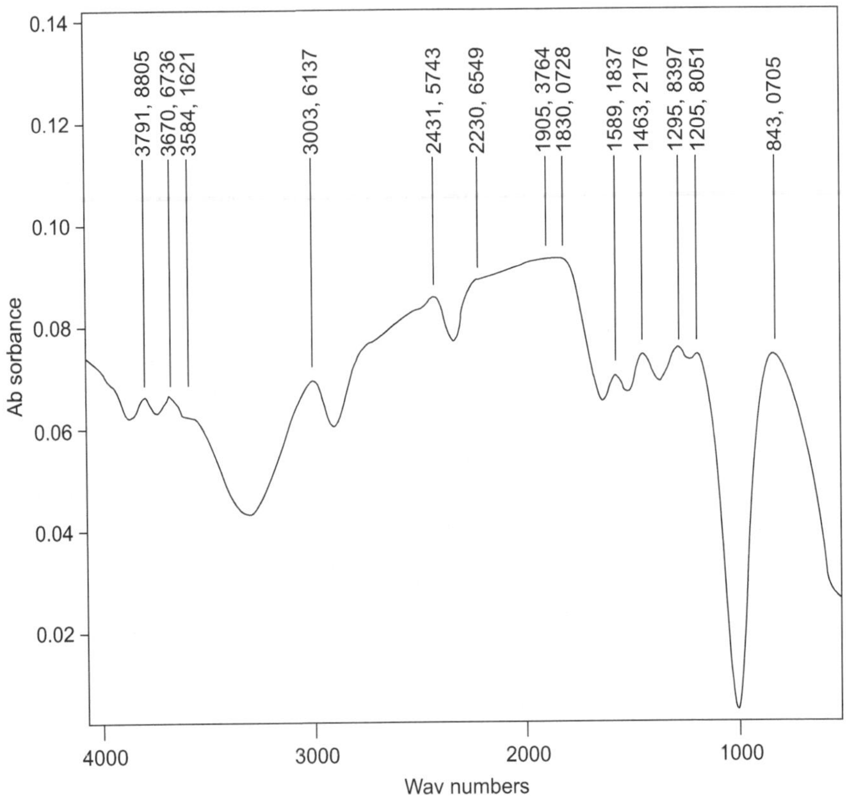

Fig. 10.4: FTIR spectra of cadmium treated plants

(**Source:** Work of authors, 2017, unpublishedmechanism of preventing or lessening the toxic effects of heavy metals is by preventing excess heavy metals entering the plant. There are two main ways in which a plant could do this, either by precipitating or by complexing heavy metals in the root environment. Plants can precipitate heavy metals by increasing the pH of the rhizosphere or by excreting anions such as phosphate. Root exudation of phosphate in maize has been detected in response to Al stress in the Al-tolerant cultivar (South American 3) with no toxicity symptoms whereas sensitive cultivars (Tuxpeno and South American 5) showed symptoms. Additionally, root exudation of malate in sorghum (*Sorghum bicolor L.)* and exudation of citrate in maize ha also been reported in response to Cadmium stress. Zhu *et al.* showed that the oxalate secreted from the root apex helps to exclude Cadmium from entering tomato (*Lycopersiconesculentum L.)* roots, thus contributing to Cadmium resistance in the Cd-resistant tomato cultivar (Micro-Tom). Their results suggest that the tolerant cultivar may have utilized exclusion of the heavy metals via precipitation as an avoidance mechanism. Al-tolerant wheat (*Triticum aestivum*) genotypes have been found to produce more malic acid than sensitive genotypes upon exposure to Aluminium. Additionally, iron plaque formation on the root surface (due to the release of O_2 and oxidants in the rhizosphere) has been suggested as a mechanism for excluding toxic heavy metal in plants and particularly in Oryza sativa.The scientist hasproposed that iron plaque adsorbs and sequesters Cadmium onto the root surface and can prevent Cd uptake by rice plants (Figure 10.4).

Heavy Metals Contamination with Specialreference to India

Cadmium is a rare element which is present in the natural environment in a very low level. It is a trace element and exposure to this element can have a very harmful impact on the human health. They are very hazardous when present above permissible levels. Cadmium contamination of the environment was established as the main cause for the endemic bone disease "itai itai" reported from Japan, due to which hundreds of the people died. Cadmium enters the environment as a contaminant from mining, zinc smelting, waste batteries, e-waste, paint sludge, incineration and fuel combustion and also through the continuously application of phosphorus. There was a study conducted over a period of two months between May-June 2015 in coimbator, Tamilnadu, 4 houses with borewells was selected as samples randomly. The size of samples, distribution, collection methods was determined using the documents issued by Central Pollution Control Board of India. The overall sample size of four samples was done for air, surface water and ground water by CPCB for its monitoring work. The samples were tested using Atomic absorption spectrophotometry using Perkin Elmer AA20 model to estimate the levels of mercury, arsenic and cadmium. All the samples collected contained metal below the detection limit of less than 0.0010 mg/lit. Only Arsenic in singanallur, Gandhipuram and Selvapuram were at alarming presence and cadmium concentration in singanallur is at alarming presence. [CPCB, 2015]. A survey was conducted on environmental pollution by cadmium in Punjab In which samples of fertilizers, water samples and common foodstuffs were tested. The study found that the wheat flour had the highest amount of cadmium content. The crops irrigated with untreated municipal waste water had two or three times higher amounts on cadmium concentration present on them. The cadmium concentration was also found to be higher in industrial areas of Jalandar and Amritsar. In the survey, it was found that the cadmium concentration in tube well irrigated areas was 6.3 ppm and 5.3 ppm, respectively whereas in sewage water irrigated were found to have 12 ppm and 12.3 ppm respectively. The cadmium content of the sea water was also estimated at ten monitoring stations located along 15 km of the madras coast over a period of one year, which showed a range of 0.001-0.047 mg/kg. In West Bengal, the sludge sample from both cola-cola and pepsi's bottling plants in the state by the West Bengal pollution Control Board discovered that the cadmium level was 50 mg/kg in jalpaiguri's Raninagar area, 76 mg/kg in Kolkata's Taratola area, 80 mg/kg at Dankuni in Hooghly and 27.12 mg/kg at Narendrapur in South 24-Parganas districts. The researcher have tested the samples of river water and have found the cadmium concentration to be 0.0001 ppm in Gomti river, Ganga river with 0.0003 ppm and Ghaghra river with 0.001 ppm [PCB,2013]. Bhatnagae *et al.* studied the effect of tannery effluent on sediments of river ganga in special reference to heavy metals at Jajmau, Kanpur and found that the heavy metals such as Arsenic, Cadmium, Copper, Iron, Chromium, Lead etc. was found in significantly higher amount. Paul and Sinha investigated the seasonal variations in the Ganga river water quality with respect to the heavy metals (Zn, Pb, Cd, Cr) contamination in the West Bengal and observed that the concentration of these heavy metals were much higher than the maximum permissible limits. In a study by, Bhagure GR *et al.* ground water samples from highly industrialized areas of Thane, Maharashtra were analysed and found to contain high amounts of Mercury, Arsenic, Cadmium and Nickel. Another study in Assam found varying high levels of Arsenic and Cadmium in Dhemaji District of Assam. The pollution in Assam was probably due to the rain water washing away, the airborne and soil borne pollutants contaminating the ground water and the aquifers.A study in the southeast coast of India by Thiyagarajan *et al.* (2012) showed that themetal concentrations (cadmium, chromium, iron, lead, copper, manganese, zinc and mercury) in the muscle of five fish species (Epinephelus chlorostigma, Lutjanus russelli, Terapon jarbua, Cynoglossus arel and Lagocephalus lunaris) from the six fish landing centres along southeast coast of India were measured. In Cuddalore and Mudasalodai, the level of toxic metals cadmium, chromium and manganese were well above the permissible limits. Concentrations of cadmium, chromium, manganese and mercury in Cuddalore were above the permissible limit and it is consistent with their habitat and diet (Figure 10.5). The results showed a relationship between metal concentrations and pollution status of the areas. Some studies have also shown the cadmium concentration in the surrounding air depends on the population and urbanization of the region. Cadmium concentration have been generally recorded as extreme low in urban areas which ranges from 0.1 to 5.0 ng/m^3, whereas in urban areas, it has shown bit higher than the rural areas ranging from 2.0 to 15 ng/m^3 and industrial areas was recorded highest with cadmium concentration ranging from 15.0 to 150.0 ng/m^3 [WHO 1992, OECD 1994]. In urban and industrial areas the concentration was probably higher due to smelting, mining, combustion activities etc.

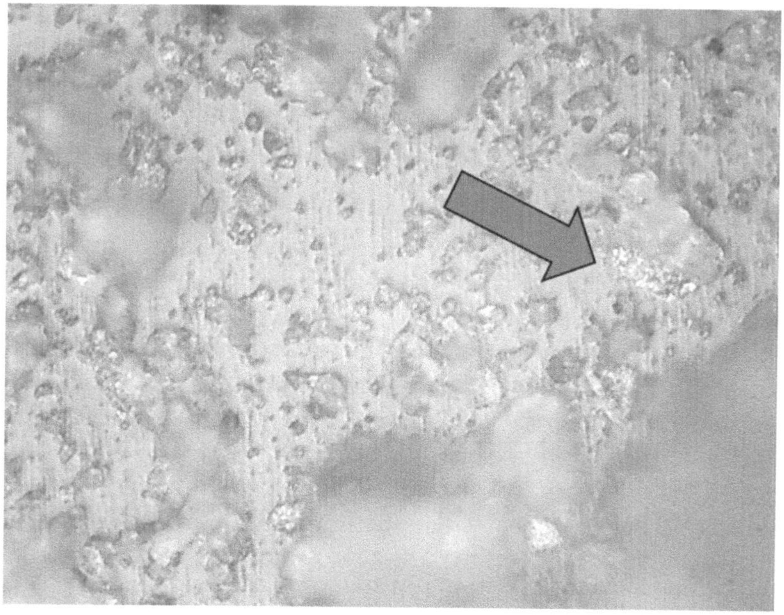

Fig. 10.5: Cadmium crystal in contaminated cadmium contaminated plant sample

(**Source:** Based on author's research work)

Phytoremediation of Heavy Metals

Heavy metal is a naturally occurring element which has a huge deterioration effect on the health of the environment and it does not degrade naturally and heavy metals cannot be destroyed biologically, they can only be transformed from one oxidation state or organic compound to another. Remediation of soil contaminated with heavy metals is more difficult than the remediation of other contaminants [De Jing *et al.* 2007]. Phytoremediation is a method in which living green plants are used in situ for the removal of contaminants in soil such as sludges, sediments, surface water and ground water. Depending on the nature of the biological processes used in the environmental treatment the following types of phytoremediation may be distinguished: phytoextraction, rhizodegradation, phytostabilisation, phytodegradation, rhizofiltration and phytoevaporation are usually used for treatment of soil contaminated with heavy metals.

Rhizofiltration

It is a type of phytoremediation that uses plant roots to absorb, concentrate and precipitate contaminants present in the soil through the plant root system into the harvestable parts of the roots and aboveground shoots (Verma *et al.* 2006, Lee *et al.* 2010). The plants are raised hydroponically and transplanted into metal-polluted water where they absorb and concentrate the metals in their roots and shoots. Root exudates and changes in rhizosphere pH may also cause metals to precipitate onto root surfaces. Roots or whole plants are harvested for disposal after they become saturated with the metal contaminants (Padmavathiamma and Li 2007). This method is mainly used to remove such heavy metals as lead, cadmium, zinc and uranium isotopes from contaminated groundwater.

Phytoextraction

Phytoextraction, also called phytoaccumulation, refers to the uptake and translocation of metal contaminants in the soil by plant roots into aboveground components of the plants. Plants that usually absorb unusual large amounts of metals compared to other plants and the ambient metals concentration are called hyperaccumulator. Natural metal hyperaccumulators are plants that can accumulate and tolerate greater metal concentrations in shoots than those usually found in non-accumulators, without visible symptoms. (Padmavathiamma and Li 2007). The success of phytoextraction depends primarily on the choice of the plant, which should have a high tolerance to high concentrations of heavy metals and a substantial degree of heavy metal accumulation, as well as a high degree of movement of metals from roots to parts exposed to air. A very important feature of a plant used for phytoextraction is the abundant production of biomass and a high cut top for easy harvesting. Phytoextraction efficiency is measured by the accumulation of the metal per unit of mass, thus plants that produce a large amount of biomass, such as crop plants (e.g. *Brassica juncea(L.) Czern.*) may be an alternative to a hyper-accumulators (Kumar *et al.* 1995, Bricker *et al.* 2001, Lasat 2002, Tomoviæ *et al.* 2013).

Phytostabilisation

The phytostabilisation uses the abilities of exudates of some plant roots for a reduction in the bio-availability of toxic substances (Cheraghi *et al.* 2011) as the primary purpose of phytoremediation is to prevent the migration of metals in the environment. Root exudates may act in two ways: toxic metal ions precipitate as insoluble salts (e.g. lead in the form of lead phosphate) or reduce the harmful ions (such as CrO_4^{2-} and CrO_7^{2-} to Cr^{3+}) by changing the soil redox (reduction-oxidation) potential. Plants used in phytostabilisation should have an extensive root system and a low degree of metal translocation from roots to shoots (for example the grass studied by a group of British researchers (Wong and Bradshaw 2002) – Agrostis teniuis sp. Goginan and Parys and Festuca rubra sp. Merlin).

Phytoevaporation

Phytoevaporation is the process in which the contaminants are assimilated and transpired by a plant and are further release into the atmosphere in the same or modified form. Mostly soils and water contaminated with inorganic compounds such as arsenic, mercury, selenium and their volatile derivatives (Zayed *et al.* 1998) are treated by this method of remediation. The best-known example of phytoevaporation is remediation of soil and groundwater contaminated with selenium. Selenium is taken up by plants in the form of soluble ions SeO_4^{2-} and SeO_3^{2-} and secreted in the form of dimethyl selenide (de Souza *et al.* 1999).

Rhizodegradation

It is also known as phyto-stimulation. It helps in degrading the contaminants in the rhizosphere by the means of microbial activity which the presence of the plant's roots. Microorganisms such as yeast, fungi or bacteria consume these contaminants as their source of energy and nutrition. In this process of biodegradation, certain microorganisms are capable of breaking down hazardous pollutants such as fuels or solvent into nontoxic and harmless product. Biodegradation is aided by plants. Plants released natural carbon containing substances such as sugar, alcohols and acid and, thereby, providing the microorganisms with additional nutrients which stimulate their activity.

Phytodegradation

Phytodegradation is also known as phyto-transformation is the breakdown of contaminants taken up by plants through metabolic processes within the plant, or the breakdown of contaminants surrounding the plant through the effect of enzymes produced by the plants. Plants are able to produce enzymes that catalyze and accelerate degradation. Hence, organic pollutants are broken down into simpler molecular forms and are incorporated into plant tissues to aid plant growth (Figure 10.6 and 10.7).

It is found that heavy metals are one of the major concern as it is one the reason for environmental pollution having a hazardous effect on the environment as well as on human beings. Heavy metal toxicity is found to have a detrimental effect on the physiological function of the plant. Some plant has the bio-availability to accumulate heavy metals in their system, which can be loaded into the xylem vessel which further gets transported to the grains. Consumption of foodstuff with heavy metals present on them gets in the human body which causes many health problems like kidney disorder, liver problems, lungs problem etc. Many studies have found that the toxicity of heavy metals are increasing rapidly and have caused many environmental issues like contamination of heavy metals like Cadmium, Arsenic, Lead, Chromium etc in

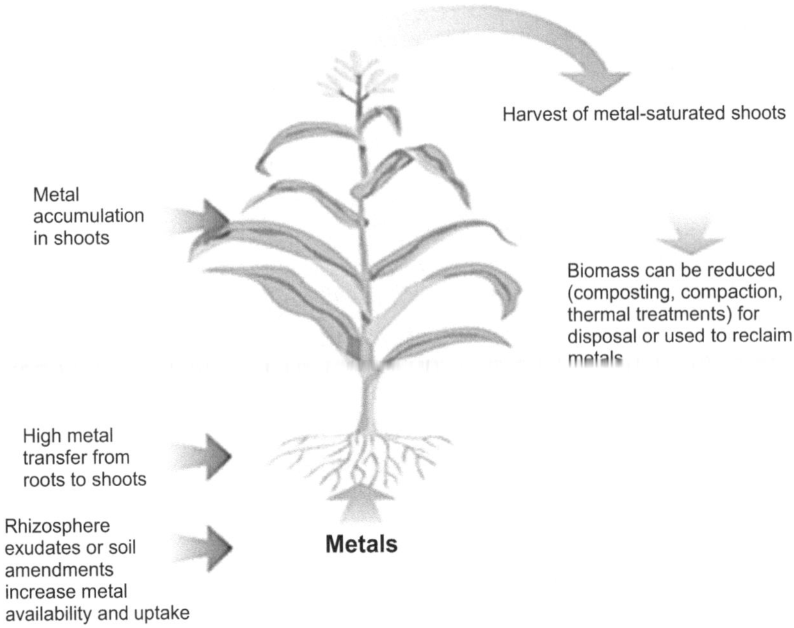

Fig. 10.6: Process ofphytoextraction

(**Source:** Review of Literature)

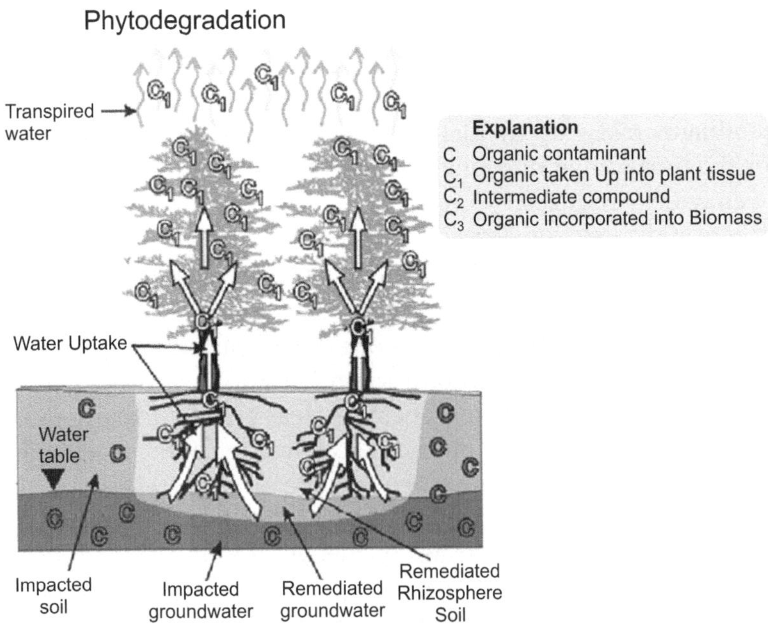

Fig. 10.7: Process of phytodegradation

(**Source:** Review of Literature)

the river water of Ganga, Yamuna etc. The water pollution caused by these heavy metals had caused many health hazards as some fishes consumes these heavy metals which then enters the foodchain after being consumed by the humans and other larger aquatic organisms. Many studies also found that many areas are prevailing concentration of heavy metal toxicity more than its permissible limit.

CONCLUSION

Cadmium is one of the trace elements that occur naturally in the earth's crust. Cadmium, like anyother heavy metals does not degrade naturally, they remain in the soil for a very long period. Heavy metal with high concentration is very toxic and it cannot destroy, they can either be reduced biologically or can be transformed from one oxidation state to another. The studies have shown that the toxicity of heavy metals like Arsenic, Cadmium, Lead, Copper, Chromium etc has contaminated the soil, Such contaminations can be checked by biological organisms like mycorrhiza, by using of polyamines like putrescine, spermine, spemidine etc. some plants to induce defense mechanism when exposed to certain unfavourable conditions, some plants have the ability to accumulate the heavy metals in their system. These remediation is helpful in reducing the amount of heavy metal toxicity of the soil. Heavy metal toxicity can be balanced with the environment by using phytoremediations like phytodegradation, phytostabilization, etc.

REFERENCES

A.Lehman, E.F.Leifheit, M.C.Rillig (2017). Mycorrhizal Mediation of Soil, Fertility, Structure and Carbon Storage, *Elsevier* – page 241-262.

A.W. Galston, R.k Sawhney (1990). Polyamines in Plant Physiology, *American Society of Plant Biologist* – 94(2): 406-410.

Abolghassem Emamverdian, Yulong Ding, Farzad Mokhberdoran and Yinfeng Xie (2015). Heavy Metal Stress and Some Mechanisms of Plant Defense Response, *The Scientific World Journal* –Article ID 756120, 18 pages.

An Environmental Toxicant March 2007 http://cpcb.nic.in/upload/Newsletters/ Newsletters_ 61_CADMIUM.An%20 Environment Toxicant-March-2007.pdf

Andrey A. Belimov, Ian C Dodd, Vera I. Safronova, Nikita V. Malkov, WilliamJ. Davies and Igor A. Tikhonovich (2015). The Cadmium-tolerant Pea *(Pisum sativum L.)* Mutant SGEdt is More Sensitive to Mercury: Assessing Plant Water Relations, *Journal of Experimental Botany* – 66(8): 2359- 2369.

Anna Malachowska Jutsz and Anna Gnida (2015). Mechanisms of Stress Avoidance and Tolerance of Plants Used in Phytoremediation of Heavy Metals, *Archives of Environmental Pollution* – 41(4): 104-114.

Arleta Malecka, Aneta Piechalak, Barbara Zielinska, Agnieszka Kutrowska and Barbara Tomaszweka (2014). Response of the Pea Roots Defense System to the Two-element Combinations of Metals (Cu, Zn, Cd, Pb), *ACTA ABP Biochimicapolonica* -61(1): 23-28.

Chahal Vanita, Chand Piar, Nagpal Avinash, Katnoria Jatinder Kaur and Pakade Yogesh B. (2014). Evaluation of Heavy Metals Contamination and Its Genotoxicity in Agricultural

Soil of Amritsar, Punjab, India, International Journal of *Research in Chemistry and Environment* -4(4): 20-28.

Dipak Paul (2017). Research on Heavy Metal Pollution of River Ganga: A Review, *Annals of Agrarian Science* – 15(2): 278-286.

Ehsanul Kabir, Sharmilla Ray, Ki-Hyun Kim, Hye-On Yoon, Eui-Chan Jeon, Yoon Shim Kim, Yong-Sung Cho, Seong-Taek Yun and Richard J.C. Brown (2012). Current Status of Trace Metal Polltution in Soils Affected by Industrial Activities, *The Scientific World Journal*-2012; 916705.

Garden Pea (Pisumsativum) http://eol.org/pages/703192/details.

Groundwater Arsenic Contamination in West Bengal-India http://www.rediff.com/money/2003/aug/08cola3.htm.

Hazardous Metals and Minerals Pollution in India https://insaindia.res.in/pdf/Hazardous_Metals.pdf.

http://archive.bio.ed.ac.uk/jdeacon/microbes/mycorrh.htm

http://mycorrhizae.com/

http://www.lenntech.com/periodic/elements/cd.htm

http://www.mykepro.com/mycorrhizae-benefits-application-and-research.aspx

http://www.rediff.com/money/2003/aug/08cola3.htm

https://en.wikipedia.org/wiki/Cadmium

https://en.wikipedia.org/wiki/Heavy_metals.

https://en.wikipedia.org/wiki/Mycorrhiza

https://en.wikipedia.org/wiki/Pea

https://en.wikipedia.org/wiki/Polyamine

https://en.wikipedia.org/wiki/Polyamine#Putrescine

https://gobotany.newenglandwild.org/species/pisum/sativum/

https://knowhowtogmo.wordpress.com/2011/01/31/phytodegradation/

Irena Januskaitiene, (2012).The Effects of Cadmium on Several Photosynthetic Parameters of Pea *(Pisum sativum L.)* at Two Growth Stages, *Zemdirbyste*-99(1): 71-76.

K. Mohankumar, V. Hariharan and N.PrasadaRao (2016). Heavy Metal Contamination in Groundwater Around Industrial Estate vs Residential Areas in Coimbator, India, *Journal of Clinical and Diagnostic Research* -10(4): BC05-BC07.

Kabir AH, Paltridge NG, Roessner U and Stanqoulis JC (2012). Mechanisms Associated with Fe-deficiency Tolerance and Signaling in Shoots of *Pisumsativum*-147(3): 385-95.

Lauro Bucker-Neto, Ana Luiza Sobral Paiva, Ronei Dorneles Machoda, Rafael Augusto Arenhart and Marcia Margis-Pinheiro (2017), Interaction between Plant Hormones and Heavy Metals Responses, *Genetics and Molecular Biology*-40(1): 373-386

Mazid M, Khan TA, Mohammad F (2011). Role of Secondary Metabolites In Defense Mechanisms in Plants, *Biology and Medicine* – 3(2): 232-249.

Mohammad Anwar Hossain, Pukclai Piyatida, Jaime A. Texiera da Silva and Masayuki Fujita (2012). Molecular Mechanisms of Heavy Metal Toxicity and Tolerance in Plants: Central Role of Gluthathione in Detoxification of Reactive Oxygen Species and Methylglyoxal and in Heavy Metal Chelation, *Journal of Botany* – Article ID-872875, pages 37.

Monisha Jaishankar, Tenzin Tseten, Naresh Anbalagan, Blessy B. Methew and Krishnamurthy N. Beeregowda (2014). Toxicity, Mechanism an Health Effects of Some Heavy Metals, *Interdisciplinary Toxicology* – 7(2): 60-72.

Nancy Collins Johnson, Catherine Gehring and Jan Jansa (2016). Mycorrhizal Mediation of Soil. Fertility, Structure and Carbon Storage, *Elsevier-* pages 526-494.

NedegeMinois, Didac Carmona-Gutierrez and Frank Madeo (2011). Polyamines in Aging and Disease, *Impact Journals Aging*-3(8): 716-732.

Paul B Tchounwon, Clement G Yedjou, Anita K Patlolla.(2014). Heavy Metal Toxicity and the Environment, *HHS Public Access-101: 133-164.*

Rahmi Verma and Pratima Dwivedi (2013). *Heavy Metal Water Pollution-A Case Study, Research in Science and Technology -5(5): 98-99.*

Sarvajeet Singh Gill and Narendra Tuteja (2010). *Polyamines and Abiotic Stress Tolerance in Plants, Plant Signaling and Behavior – 5(1): 26-33.*

Status of Trace and Toxic Metals in Indian Rivers http://www.cwc.nic.in/main/downloads/Trace%20&%20Toxic%20Report%2025%20June%202014.pdf.

Thiyagarajan D *et al.* (2012). *Metals in Fish Aslong the Southeast Coast of India, Bull Environ Contamtoxicol-88(4): 582-8.*

Index